Albert Stratford G. Canning

British Rule and modern Politics

A historical Study

Albert Stratford G. Canning

British Rule and modern Politics
A historical Study

ISBN/EAN: 9783743332270

Manufactured in Europe, USA, Canada, Australia, Japa

Cover: Foto ©ninafisch / pixelio.de

Manufactured and distributed by brebook publishing software (www.brebook.com)

Albert Stratford G. Canning

British Rule and modern Politics

BRITISH RULE

AND

MODERN POLITICS

A HISTORICAL STUDY

BY THE

HON. ALBERT S. G. CANNING

AUTHOR OF

'THE DIVIDED IRISH' 'HISTORY IN FACT AND FICTION' ETC.

'This precious stone set in the silver sea,
This blessed plot, this earth, this realm, this England,
Dear for her reputation through the world'

SHAKSPERE

LONDON

SMITH, ELDER, & CO., 15 WATERLOO PLACE

1899

[All rights reserved]

IN this work I endeavour to examine the results of British power and thought in promoting civilisation, and allude to English literature, believing that it specially illustrates the tendency and value of the national influence.

A. S. G. CANNING.

CONTENTS

CHAPTER I
INTRODUCTORY
                                                                       PAGE

Greece, Judea, and Rome the chief sources of European civilisation 1

CHAPTER II

Success of the Romans in ruling foreign subjects—Among modern nations, the British and the Russians most resemble them in this respect 15

CHAPTER III

Religious divisions in Christian Europe—Political influence of the Papacy throughout the Christian world—Passive attitude of the Greek Church in political affairs . . 25

CHAPTER IV

Position of France among European nations—Its triumphs under Napoleon throughout Europe—Alliance of the chief European powers against him—His final defeat and banishment 34

CHAPTER V

British supremacy in India—Its gradual consolidation—Improvement effected by British rule in that country—Failure of Spain and Portugal in retaining their American colonies 44

CHAPTER VI

Rule of the Turks in south-eastern Europe—Revolt of the Greeks against them in 1824—British sympathy with the Greeks partly owing to classical associations—Their emancipation effected by the aid of Britain, France, and Russia 54

CHAPTER VII

Change in the French monarchy after the fall of Napoleon—Its replacement by a republic in 1848—Revolts in Italy and Hungary against Austria—Accession of Napoleon III. to the throne of France—Expedition of the French against Rome 62

CHAPTER VIII

Alliance of Napoleon III. with Britain in the Crimean war against Russia—Establishment of the Italian kingdom—Civil war in the United States of America . 75

CHAPTER IX

Russian progress in Asia—Louis Napoleon's early ambition—Secular spirit of modern European policy—Conquests and supremacy of Europeans in Africa . 86

CHAPTER X

Increasing success of British rule in foreign colonies and dominions—Historical enmity of Ireland to British authority—Eloquence of Irish revolutionists—Comparative absence of eloquence during British revolutions . 97

CHAPTER XI

England's historical relations with Scotland and with Ireland—Religious intolerance in these countries during the time of Cromwell—Disputes among rival Protestant sects, who all oppose Roman Catholicism . . 107

CHAPTER XII

Religious differences in Britain and Ireland after the restoration of the British monarchy—Northern Europe, except Russia, which adhered to the Greek Church, became Protestant, while its southern countries except Greece remained Roman Catholic . . . 118

CHAPTER XIII

The Jacobite revolts in Scotland arouse no Irish sympathy—The rebellion of 1798 in Ireland unlike all other revolts in that country—Increase of British influence in Europe after the fall of Napoleon 129

CHAPTER XIV

Influence of literature in celebrating British civil wars and revolutions—Shakespeare and Milton on British history, in historic plays and political essays . . . 140

CHAPTER XV

Sir Walter Scott and Thomas Moore on Scottish and Irish history—Shakespeare's caution in describing historical personages of his own time—His impartiality in historical allusions 150

CHAPTER XVI

Instructive nature of Shakespeare's historical plays—Their monarchical tendency—Loyalty of London people to the monarchy—Beneficial influence of Scott's historical novels 168

CHAPTER XVII

Differing views of London expressed by Johnson, Cowper, Scott, and Dickens—Scottish and Irish rebellions differently treated by their respective historians—Unfairness in blaming men of former times for enforcing laws still unrepealed 174

CHAPTER XVIII

The cordiality between England and Scotland increased by Scott's writings—Reception of George IV. in Scotland—Contrast between Scott's and Macaulay's opinions of Scottish Highlanders—British parties united during the wars of Napoleon I. 183

CHAPTER XIX

Great change in European policy towards the Turks since the Greek revolution of 1824—Britain and France unite in favour of the Turks against the Russians in the Crimean war of 1854—Extension of British and Russian influence in Asia 190

CONTENTS xi

CHAPTER XX

PAGE

Increasing loyalty of Mohammedans and other non-Christians to Great Britain, France, and Russia—Friendship of these three powers for the Turks—They discourage the Greeks in warring against Turkey—Indignation of Mr. Gladstone at this policy . . . 198

CHAPTER XXI

Continued decline in Mohammedan political power, despite the firm retention of that faith under Christian rule—Danger from political conspiracies in Europe—Revival of the warlike spirit in European countries . 207

CHAPTER XXII

Spread of secret societies for political assassination in Europe—Value and efficiency of the detective force more developed—Increasing popularity of the military profession among influential classes, especially on the Continent 215

CHAPTER XXIII

Loyalty of non-Christian subjects to Christian rulers specially displayed in recent years—Discouragement of the Christian subjects in Turkey by the European powers in their aspirations for independence . . 222

CHAPTER XXIV

Increasing secularisation of politics—Reliance of European rulers on non-Christian subjects—Disavowal of Atheism by all Governments—Different opinions among the modern Jews about their national destination . . 229

CHAPTER XXV

Danger to monarchs, statesmen, and influential persons from political assassination in civilised European countries—Efforts and efficiency of the detective force—Difference between political assassins and other criminals 239

CHAPTER XXVI

Scott and Dickens on religious fanaticism and on religious hypocrisy—Dickens generally avoids historical allusions—Lever and Lover rather avoid Irish politics . . 244

CHAPTER XXVII

Contrast between Macaulay's and Bulwer Lytton's love of classic literature and Thackeray's dislike or indifference to it—Macaulay's power of making history attractive—Different influences of these writers on the British reading public 253

CHAPTER XXVIII

Literary pursuits of Messrs. Gladstone and Disraeli—The former's denunciation of the Turks and partiality for the Greeks—Remarkable views of Disraeli respecting the modern Jews 261

CHAPTER XXIX

The literary efforts of Dickens and Thackeray chiefly devoted to describing modern London and modern English character—Their works, while delighting and enlightening the British public, had comparatively little effect in Ireland 271

CONTENTS xiii

CHAPTER XXX

PAGE

Difficulties of British statesmen in dealing with Ireland—
Its exceptional position amid European changes and
enlightenment 285

CHAPTER XXXI

Enduring power of clerical influence in Ireland—Its
diminution on the Continent in political questions—
O'Connell's popularity in Ireland compared with that of
Mr. Parnell 294

CHAPTER XXXII

Failure of Protestant political leaders in Ireland—Final
success of the priesthood in opposing Mr. Parnell
—They still politically represent the Irish majority . 302

CHAPTER XXXIII

Friendly feelings between opposing political parties in
Britain—In Ireland party spirit retains its former
bitterness 311

CHAPTER XXXIV

Consolidation of British and of Russian power over
colonies and non-Christian nations—China gradually
attracts more European interference — Increasing
importance of the colonies publicly acknowledged by
British statesmen 320

CHAPTER XXXV

European supremacy apparently firm and permanent over foreign conquests and colonies—Continued danger to European rulers from assassination—Efficiency of modern police in protecting life and property . . 880

WORKS REFERRED TO

Alison, Sir Archibald: History of Europe.
Asiatic Quarterly Review, October 1897 and January 1898.
Balfour, Right Hon. Arthur: Speech in Dumfries, August 1897.
Blackstone's Commentaries.
Buckle: History of Civilisation.
Byron, Lord: The Giaour, Childe Harold.
Caldecott's Civilisation.
Carlyle, Thomas: Heroes and Hero-worship.
Chamberlain, Right Hon. Joseph: Speech in Glasgow, November 1897.
Civilisation of our Day, The.
Cowper, William: The Task.
Dante: Inferno. Cary's translation.
Dickens, Charles: Reprinted Pieces, American Notes, Pictures from Italy, Dombey and Son.
Disraeli, Right Hon. Benjamin: Life of Lord George Bentinck.
Döllinger, Dr.: Studies in European History.
Dryden: The Hind and the Panther.
Farini: History of Rome.
Fénelon, Archbishop: Adventures of Telemachus.
Friedländer: The Jewish Religion.
Gibbon: Decline and Fall of the Roman Empire.
Gladstone, Right Hon. W. E.: Letters in the 'Times' during 1897.
Green: History of the English People.
Hallam: Constitutional History of England.

Hegel: Philosophy of History.
Homer: Iliad. Pope's translation.
Humboldt's Cosmos.
Hume: History of England.
Japanese Editor's Opinion on British Power.
Jewish Quarterly Review, October 1897.
Johnson, Dr.: Lives of the Poets.
Kidd, Benjamin: Social Evolution.
Lecky, W. E. H.: Democracy and Liberty, History of Ireland, European Morals, Political Value of History.
Lytton, Lord: Last Days of Pompeii, Caxtoniana.
Lytton, Lord: Life of, by his Son.
Macaulay, Lord: Essays, History of England, Lays of Ancient Rome.
Martin, Sir Theodore: Life of the Prince Consort.
Milman, Dean: History of Christianity.
Milton: Paradise Regained, Prose Works.
Müller, Max: Chips from a German Workshop, India, What can it Teach Us?
Renan, Ernest: The Anti-Christ, Future of Science.
Ruskin: Modern Painters.
Scott, Sir Walter: Waverley Novels.
Shakespeare: King John, Henry VI., Henry VIII., Macbeth.
Sloane: Life of Napoleon.
Spenser, Edmund: View of Ireland.
Stowe, Mrs. H. B.: Uncle Tom's Cabin.
Thackeray, W. M.: Journey from Cornhill to Cairo, Vanity Fair, Roundabout Papers.
Tynan: The Irish Invincibles.
Virgil: Æneid. Dryden's translation.
Zenker: Anarchism.

BRITISH RULE AND MODERN POLITICS

CHAPTER I

INTRODUCTORY

Greece, Judea, and Rome the chief sources of European civilisation

IN examining historical events it is remarkable how some nations succeed in conquering or in ruling, yet these separate capacities do not always belong to the same nation. The French, for instance, made vast conquests, but retain few of them, while some powerful nations neither conquer nor rule others, but remain independent, preserving their religion and laws from external control. The position of those nations who both conquer and rule is exceptionally important, even glorious, and comprises a double success, since the mere subjugation of hostile races is often caused by unfair means, preponderance of numbers, intrigue, or unscrupulous alliances for effecting a joint conquest. The greatest triumph that men can obtain over others is to rule them successfully after conquest, thus proving that their subjects are better and happier than when they were under rulers of their own nation. Until recent years no people equalled the Romans in accomplishing this grand result of combined wisdom and valour, and fortunately for subsequent nations, the literary genius of the Romans transmitted their ideas, laws, and political success to posterity in literature of imperishable value.[1]

The famous emperors, Julius Cæsar in his Commentaries and Justinian in legal codes, proclaimed to future ages those deeds and thoughts which at their time were only known to few. This transmission the greatest of English poets notices in recording the united martial and intellectual glories of Julius Cæsar.

> That Julius Cæsar was a famous man,
> With what his valour did enrich his wit,
> His wit set down to make his valour live.
> Death makes no conquest of this conqueror,
> For now he lives in fame, though not in life.
>
> *Richard III.*

Among modern nations probably none has so much studied and profited by classic history as the British. The result is that to the present time in legislative rule throughout distant colonies, the British Empire resembles the Roman more than any other.

It may be truly said that modern Britain owes

---

[1] 'Civilisation followed in the train of Roman conquest; the ferocity of her martial temperament seemed to have spent itself in the civil wars, and wherever it had spread, a rich and luxuriant vegetation broke forth.'—Milman's *History of Christianity*, vol. i.

little to ancient Britain.[1] Its habits, customs, and ideas, like its religion, almost vanished, while Judea, Greece, and Italy were the countries whose varied influences combined to form the civilisation of Europe. Egypt, Assyria, and other ancient lands are in this century through European research revealing more of their former history than ever; but owing to want of literature, their influence on modern civilisation amounts to little. The early education of enlightened Europeans depends mainly on Greek, Roman, and Jewish histories. From these sources, not only religious faith, but legislative and political principles are almost exclusively derived by the modern world. The exploits, habits, and thoughts of heathen ancestry have almost completely vanished from the knowledge of northern and western Europe. They not only lost hold on the credulity, but even on the interest or curiosity of their Christian descendants. Among the British and Germans especially, esteem for the classical literature of Greece and Rome became greater or more profound than among modern Greeks and Italians.[2]

[1] 'Nothing in the early existence of Britain indicated the greatness she was destined to attain. She was subjugated by the Roman arms, but she received only a faint tincture of Roman arts and letters. Of the western provinces which obeyed the Cæsars, she was the last that was conquered, and the first that was flung away.'—Macaulay's *History of England*, vol. i.

[2] Macaulay enthusiastically writes: 'All the triumphs of truth and genius over prejudice and power in every country and in every age have been the triumphs of Athens. Wherever literature consoles sorrow or assuages pain, there is exhibited in its noblest form the immortal influence of Athens.'—Essay on Mitford's *Greece*.

The latter in mediæval and recent times hardly displayed the learned enthusiastic admiration for their remote ancestry evinced by British, German, and French scholars.

> From sunrise until sunset,
> All earth shall hear thy fame;
> A glorious city thou shalt build
> And name it by thy name.
> Where fur-clad hunters wander
> Amidst the northern ice,
> Where through the sand of morning land
> The camel bears the spice,
> Where Atlas flings his shadow
> Far o'er the Western foam,
> Shall be great fear on all who hear
> The mighty name of Rome.
> Macaulay's *Lays of Ancient Rome.*

This difference was greatly due to the mediæval history of Greece and Italy, for evidently no lovers of classic lore equal the British and Germans, who, comparatively neglecting traditions of their own ancestry, studied those of Greeks and Romans with profound attention. Yet no nation in western Europe has conquered the classic lands. The invading and colonising energies of Britain were less displayed in Europe than in other quarters of the world. While European scholars or literary men devoted themselves to the classic works of Greece or Italy, their rulers and soldiers were attending to other countries. The vast colonisations effected by Spain and Portugal in America finally resulted in the successful revolts of their colonies, while the British retain nearly all theirs, except the United

States, whose inhabitants are chiefly of their own race. The French in their brilliant career of conquest under Napoleon were compared to a consuming fire, ending in its own extinction, without increasing their power or territory. It was indeed an extraordinary strife that France waged against most other civilised nations, apparently for no very definite purpose. Unlike former wars no religious enthusiasm or temptation inspired the French nation. The vast ambition and wonderful genius of a man ruling them with almost superhuman knowledge of their national character were the chief if not the sole causes of his extraordinary career. Since the fall of Napoleon, the French have conquered Algiers, with parts of Cochin China and Madagascar, whereas their great general had preferred to see them triumph in Europe rather than in Asia and Africa. Since his time, the only power rivalling Britain in foreign conquest and subsequent annexation is Russia.

The Russian conquests, unlike those of Spain and Portugal, were singularly permanent. No country conquered by that nation regains independence. Unlike other European nations, the Russians made their conquests by land alone. No free countries interpose between their dominions from the Swedish frontier to the north of China. Russian conquests, like those of the Romans and the British, usually, if not always, end in firm retention of territorial acquisition. Yet Russian power over foreign lands is of comparatively recent growth. After the fall of the Roman Empire and its gradual replacement by Christian kingdoms throughout Europe, the most important or rather extensive foreign conquests were made by the maritime nations—Britain, Spain, and Portugal. The French, the Italians, and those nations of central Europe now mostly comprised in the German and Austrian empires remained comparatively stationary, while British, Spaniards, and Portuguese severally made not only conquests in Asia and Africa, but gradually subjugated the whole continent of America and its islands, called the West Indies. All these conquests, mostly followed by colonisation, were effected chiefly by the British in Asia, and by Spaniards and Portuguese in America. The French and the Dutch in Canada and south America occupied some territory, but of a trifling extent compared to the vast conquests made by Spain and Portugal, while the British in north America made conquests of less territory, but perhaps of more political or social importance. In these exploits the aborigines in America were quite overcome, and some nearly exterminated, while all had to submit more or less to European invaders.

Unlike Europe, Asia, and Africa, the new quarter of the world had no political or religious history which could oppose or dispute the introduction and spread of Christianity. In Africa, Egypt chiefly claimed a remarkable classic and religious interest from its peculiar association with the Jewish Old Testament. The history of northern Africa bordering on the Mediterranean was also involved with subsequent Roman history. But Egypt, like Assyria, though almost devoid of a connected literature, still affords extraordinary revelations of a most remote past.[1] Its pyramids and the Assyrian monuments with brief inscriptions are perhaps more interesting than wholly gratifying. As far as such limited revelations can be understood, the Scriptural references to these ancient lands seem to some extent confirmed. Yet hitherto they encourage and instruct rather than fully satisfy learned antiquaries. Some of these marvellous relics during many centuries remained the wonder of all who saw them, as unlike those of Greece and Rome they were comparatively little explained by history, tradition, or poetry. Their further discovery and increasing elucidation are alike due to European scholars, following closely in the track of European power and influence. Neither the Jews, who in the time of their independence were absorbed in their national history, nor subsequent ruling Mohammedans deserve much credit for making historic revelations. They are almost the exclusive achievements of European intellectual energy, guided by educational knowledge.[2]

[1] 'The empire of the solitary Nile is only present beneath the ground in its speechless dead, ever and anon stolen away to all quarters of the globe, and in their majestic habitations, for what remains above ground is nothing else but such splendid tombs.'—Hegel's *Philosophy of History*, section i.

[2] 'In the more remote ages of antiquity the world was unequally divided. The East was in the immemorial possession of arts and luxury, while the West was inhabited by rude and warlike barbarians. Under the protection of an established government the productions of happier climates and the industry of more civilised nations were gradually introduced into the western countries of Europe.'—Gibbon's *Decline and Fall*, chap. ii.

To Europeans the revelations of the Old World seem nearly as due as the discovery and colonisation of the New throughout America and Australasia.

Even in political history these countries seem to record few if any ancient heroes or venerated traditions. Little if anything remains of their unknown past to encourage or promote patriotic recollections among subdued native races. European religion, language, laws, and habits soon appeared in these new countries, which unlike the classic lands offered no intellectual protest or complaint against their complete subjugation by invading conquerors. The additions to the natural history of the Old World from these regions, however, were extensive and valuable. New plants, birds, and animals were not only discovered, but many introduced and acclimatised throughout Europe. It was in the intellectual departments of religion, literature, art, and science that the Old World received little benefit from the New. During this century especially the grandeur and importance of the most ancient lands in Europe, Asia, and Africa have been more elucidated and made known among the civilised cities of western Europe than ever before. This result of combined conquest, exploration, and classic learning has been the almost exclusive triumph of European nations. Except Turkey they are all Christians of differing denominations, and their religious and political education, training, habits, and principles on the whole show a consistent resemblance to each other. Their earliest studies are chiefly devoted to, or founded on, the political and intellectual achievements of the Greeks and Romans, and on the Jewish version of religious history. These first two nations were historically separated for centuries from each other. The Romans admired and studied the early wisdom of the Greeks long after the latter had ceased to distinguish themselves, while the Jews, successively ruled by both, are to this day united with them in European estimation as the three chief models for study, imitation, or religious belief. The British, French, Germans, and Russians, now forming the strongest nations in the world, agree with Italian and Spanish scholars in a common esteem for these three celebrated nations. From them indeed nearly all ancient and mediæval history is derived. Whatever knowledge may proceed from other ancient lands, it is of slight importance compared to the religious, intellectual, and political instruction transmitted to the modern world by the Greeks, Jews, and Romans of antiquity.[1]

As an instance of the deep impression made by the histories of these three nations upon learned Europeans, Milton's 'Paradise Regained' may be cited. Believing the Scriptural tradition of the temptation of Jesus by the enemy of man trying to arouse worldly ambition, Athens and Rome at once

[1] 'When I seriously compute the lapse of ages, the waste of ignorance, and the calamities of war, our treasures rather than our losses are the object of my surprise. The mischances of time and accident have spared the classic works to which the suffrage of antiquity had adjudged the first place of genius and glory.'—*Decline and Fall*, chap. li.

occur to Milton's classic mind as possessing the chief interest for human thought. The vague if not fabulous histories of other ancient countries, Milton scarcely notices. But the intellectual supremacy of Athens and the martial glory of Rome impress the great English poet as the greatest worldly temptations indicated rather than expressed by the language of Scripture. The Greeks and Romans surpassing every nation in European estimation, Milton, like other learned men of his time, selected them specially for intellectual and political superiority, while the Jews were viewed as sole possessors of religious truth, almost the only subject about which the Greeks and Romans were supposed to be in a state of inevitable ignorance.

> Our Hebrew songs and harps, in Babylon
> That pleased our victor's ear, declare
> That rather Greece from us these arts derived,
> Ill imitated while they loudest sing
> The vices of their deities and their own.
> *Paradise Regained*, book iv.

Thus Milton ascribes to the Christian prophet a patriotic preference for the Jews and a condemnation of paganism scarcely founded on Scriptural evidence. These views expressed the religious philosophy of Milton's own times, rather than the utter antinational impartiality which Jesus always evinced. The sympathetic national pride, Milton imagines, seems little consistent with the calm cosmopolitan views of Jesus and His first apostles—in fact of all under His personal influence. But among European

Christian nations, the patriotic or exclusively national sentiment which often tempted and induced Christian rulers to violate the precepts of their Faith, evidently inspires Milton. The popularity of this dominant feeling therefore induces him to attribute it to the Christian Founder whose few words, but general conduct, would seem to disapprove of it. He seldom mentions the Jews, calling themselves His fellow-countrymen oppressed by the Romans, without censure, and seldom if ever recalls their national glories. To invest Him, therefore, with national preferences, or partialities for the Jewish race, is a mere poetical fancy. In no respect did He identify Himself with their peculiar likes and dislikes, but on the contrary intimated a political or national impartiality more practically expressed by Roman rule over foreign nations than by any record of Jewish legislation or sentiment. With religious faith, intellectual taste, and legislative principles founded on the teaching of Jews, Greeks, and Romans, modern Europe now possesses supreme power or indirect influence over nearly all the world. The difference between the religious systems of Jewish Deism and the classic paganism of Greece and Rome needs careful examination to explain the total extinction of the latter, and the retention, if not revival, of the former during mediæval and recent history. The numerous pagan deities, though superior to mankind in power and intellect, yet shared many if not most human feelings, passions, and weaknesses. Of this sympathy between the heathen deities and men, Homer and Virgil describe remarkable instances.

In the famous immortal poem celebrating the siege of Troy by the Greeks, Homer, apparently inspired by the national belief of his fellow countrymen, describes their gods taking active yet opposite sides in the contest.[1]

He imagines the King of the Sea rushing over his subjected element to the aid of the Greeks, while the supreme Jupiter rather favours the Trojans.

> At Jove incens'd, with grief and fury stung,
> Prone down the rocky steep he rushed along;
> He mounts the car, the golden scourge applies,
> He sits superior and the chariot flies;
> The sea subsiding spreads a level plain,
> Exults and owns the monarch of the main;
> The parting waves before his coursers fly;
> The wondering waters leave his axle dry.
>   *Iliad*, book xiii.

In the Latin poet's account of the Trojan fugitives, ancestors of the future Romans, settling in Italy after a perilous voyage, a rather similar interference of the goddess Juno is described. She thus addresses the King of the Winds:

> A race of wand'ring slaves, abhorred by me,
> With prosperous passage cut the Tuscan sea.
> Raise all thy winds, with night involve the skies,
> Sink or disperse my fatal enemies.
> Twice sev'n the charming daughters of the main
> Around my person wait and bear my train,
> The fairest, Deiopeia, shall be thine.—*Æneid*, book i.

---

[1] 'I believe the true mind of a nation at any period is always best ascertainable by examining that of its greatest men. And without doubt, in his influence over future mankind, Homer is

In each instance the pagan deities share the spirit of thoroughly human though supremely powerful allies or foes rather than that of a Divinity above earthly passions, yet possessing irresistible power. Many centuries elapsed between the appearance of these wonderful poems, the Iliad and the Æneid, which to a great extent represented the religious ideas of Greeks and Romans.[1] While their political divinities gratified the fancy and to some extent ruled the conduct of their intellectual votaries, the ancient faith of Odin in northern Europe was little known and has apparently left hardly any poetic description of its nature. Carlyle says that no document of it remains, that it is only known to descendants of believers through vague traditions.[2] Gibbon, however, briefly mentions Odin as a reality, 'the Mahomet of the North,' who instituted a religion adapted to the climate and to the people.[3]

eminently the Greek of Greeks.'—Ruskin's *Modern Painters*, vol. iii.

[1] 'The deities of Olympus, as they are painted by the immortal Homer, imprint themselves on the minds which are the least addicted to superstitious credulity. Our familiar knowledge of their names and characters, their forms and attributes, seems to bestow on those airy beings a real and substantial existence, and the pleasing enchantment produces an imperfect and momentary assent to those fables which are the most repugnant to our reason and experience.'—*Decline and Fall*, chap. xxiii.

[2] *Heroes and Hero Worship*.

[3] 'Numerous tribes on either side of the Baltic were subdued by the invincible valour of Odin, by his persuasive eloquence, and by the fame which he acquired of a most skilful magician. In a solemn assembly of the Swedes and Goths he wounded himself in nine mortal places, hastening away, as he asserted, to prepare the feast of heroes in the palace of the God of War.'—*Decline and Fall*, chap. x.

The four religions of the classic paganism, of Odin, Judaism, and Christianity, were gradually made known to the natives of Britain. They evidently preferred the faith of Odin to that of Jupiter, but finally yielded to the higher claims of Christianity which replaced European paganisms, while declaring itself the true continuation of Judaism despite the incredulous opposition of the Jewish race. Yet the progress of time never affected the religious faith of the Jews, whose Old Testament remains the acknowledged foundation of Christian Gospel and of Mohammedan Koran.[1]

[1] 'The experience of ages had betrayed the weakness as well as the folly of Paganism, the light of reason and of faith had already exposed to the greater part of mankind the vanity of idols.'—*Decline and Fall*, chap. xxviii.

CHAPTER II

Success of the Romans in ruling foreign subjects—Among modern nations the British and the Russians most resemble them in this respect.

THE Roman Empire, comprising under its mighty sway the richest countries in Europe, Asia, and Africa, seems the connecting link between ancient and mediæval times.[1] The Romans were peculiarly fitted to study, appreciate, and transmit Greek literature to posterity, while adding to its imperishable excellence their own valuable contributions to the legal, military, and political knowledge of modern Europe. Some of their emperors apparently showed an observant world almost every grand and noble quality of which mankind is capable, while others again seemed as samples of everything odious and dangerous. The poetical fancy of the ablest poets and novelists could hardly describe more astonishing contrasts in human nature than were displayed by these imperial masters of the ancient civilised world. Between the two Cæsars, Julius and Augustus, and their unworthy

[1] 'This empire exhibited mankind in all the various gradations from civilisation to barbarism, and in the possession of ancient knowledge and long practised arts, no less than in the imperfectly lighted dawn of intellectual awakening.'—Humboldt's *Cosmos*, vol. ii.

successors, Tiberius Cæsar and Nero, there seems as complete a difference in character as if they had not belonged to the same race. Yet their vast empire, whether under good or evil rulers, was during a great part of its existence the chief model for subsequent foreign and colonial government.[1]

Even when Rome itself was the scene of cruel public games, stern despotism, or disgraceful licence, Roman rule over distant provinces was usually the standard of comparative good order. During the rise and early progress of Christianity, Rome was fated to obey some of her worst emperors, who succeeded the illustrious and beneficent Julius and Augustus Cæsar.[2] Their conquests and subsequent beneficence to subjected millions remain the admiration of civilised posterity; but they vanished, and in their stead reigned the artful Tiberius, and some time after the relentless Nero. While possibly the former may have heard some account of Christianity or its Founder from his viceroy Pontius Pilate, he may never have known a Christian;

[1] 'The firm edifice of Roman power was raised and preserved by the wisdom of ages. The obedient provinces were united by laws and adorned by arts. They enjoyed the religion of their ancestors, whilst in civil honours and advantages they were exalted by just degrees to an equality with their conquerors. The tranquil and prosperous state of the Empire was warmly felt and honestly confessed by the provinces as well as by the Romans.'—*Decline and Fall*, chap. ii.

[2] 'In the conduct of those monarchs we may trace the utmost lines of vice and virtue, the most exalted perfection and the meanest degeneracy of our species. It is almost superfluous to enumerate the unworthy successors of Augustus. Their unparalleled vices and the splendid theatre on which they were acted have saved them from oblivion.'—*Decline and Fall*, chap. iii.

but Nero was said to have seen or heard of the great Christian saints, Peter and Paul, both of whom were supposed to have perished in his reign, though no precise account of their fate was ever known. Some idea of Christianity was probably revealed to Nero, through pagan informants doubtless hostile to it, partly from political motives; while a sovereign more incapable of appreciating the Faith could hardly be imagined. His terrible career and character have been and still remain the types of all the evil that united power and wickedness could perpetrate upon this earth. The name of 'Anti-Christ' was often bestowed on him as being the utmost imaginable contrast to Jesus, while ruling the largest empire in the world, including the land of the Christian prophet's nativity. Nearly all the civilisation of the ancient world was comprised in his dominions, as those lands in eastern Asia whose remote history is to some extent elucidated in this century were then almost unknown or unexplored.[1]

Within the European, Asiatic, and African limits of the Roman Empire were contained during the rise and early progress of Christianity all countries which time had rendered famous, or whose ancient histories were known. The chief intellectual glories of Greece and Rome were now vanished, and over each reigned a prince apparently the incarnation of every evil quality usually ascribed by mankind

[1] 'Among the numerous productions of Arabic and Persian literature our interpreters have selected the imperfect sketches of a more recent age. The art and genius of history have ever been unknown to the Asiatics.'—*Decline and Fall*, chap. li.

to the eternal foe of their benevolent Creator. The name of Nero has therefore ever since been the sign of relentless tyranny united in his terrible instance with supreme power over the most civilised nations of his period. The real character of this extraordinary sovereign has been more carefully examined or elucidated of late years than ever before.

The vast discoveries in historical literature of different countries, owing to the increase of international intercourse, present to scholars of this century an unprecedented amount of varied information. Accordingly this infamous emperor, an evil spirit as it were in human form, is now revealed to posterity as he probably was in reality. He seems a combination of cruelty, vanity, and intellectual taste, very different from the coarse, ignorant ruffians of ordinary life, or the partly attractive, partly repulsive villains of the sensational poet or novelist. Nero was a man of education, even refinement, musical, poetical, imaginative, yet perhaps of all men the most insensible to the claims of mercy or generosity ever recorded in human history.[1] Neither the noble verses of Homer, which he well knew, nor the best music of his

---

[1] 'There was at the same time something frightful and grotesque, grand and absurd, about him. His madness was chiefly literary. He was a conscientious romancer, an emperor of the opera, a music-madman, trembling before the pit and making it tremble. Nero proclaimed daily that Art alone should be held as a serious matter. The dilettante threatened the people with the torture if they did not admire his verses. A monomaniac drunk with literary glory—that is the master to whom the empire is subjected. Nothing equal in extravagance has ever been seen.'—Renan's *Antichrist*, chap. vi.

time, of course at his command, had the least elevating or softening effect on this most cruel of sovereigns. Though professing the religion of Jupiter to the last, his odious character made his advocacy of little avail to the declining paganism. His hatred or fear of Christianity may perhaps have aided rather than checked its wonderful progress through his empire, as despite his relentless persecution the new Faith steadily advanced during and since his time throughout the Roman dominions. The ancient paganism was, however, for some time advocated both by unpopular despots or virtuous believers like Marcus Aurelius and Julian, while the pagan clergy showed little ability or even energy in its defence. Of the various subjects of the Romans, none defied them in so peculiar and successful a manner as the Jews. In almost every respect this wonderful nation was a complete contrast to its martial conquerors. Though politically subjected, the Jews evidently never recognised any intellectual superiority in their rulers, who controlled them by main force. These two extraordinary nations were singularly opposed in character, genius, and aspiration, though sharing some of the highest qualities of human nature. Each strangely undervalued the other, from their first acquaintance till the fall of the Empire.[1]

[1] 'The moderation or the contempt of the Romans gave a legal sanction to the form of ecclesiastical police which was instituted by the vanquished sect. Such gentle treatment insensibly assuaged the stern temper of the Jews. Awakened from their dream of prophecy and conquest, they assumed the

While the sacred history of the Jews was either never read or never trusted by the Romans, the grandeur of Roman history and literature, even the beneficence of Roman laws, were never acknowledged by the Jews. These great nations, in fact, never appreciated, understood, or admitted the merits of each other, of which it may be supposed they were wilfully ignorant. It was reserved for a long subsequent period, when paganism was completely replaced by Christianity, to examine both Jewish and Roman history with scholastic and comparatively impartial interest. The final result was the intellectual formation of Christian Europe on classic models, while ancient Jewish history till the time of Christ was believed as firmly by Christians as by the Jews themselves. But the political and legislative principles of the Romans became the chief examples of succeeding Christian nations, who utterly repudiated what they thought their fantastic paganism. When the Roman Empire disappeared and was replaced throughout Europe by different Christian states, Roman history, and, in many respects, legislative system, were not only studied and admired, but practically imitated by the most civilised of its Christian replacers. Thus the political system or ruling policy of pagan Romans formed to a great extent the foundations of succeeding Christian

behaviour of peaceable and industrious subjects. They embraced every opportunity of overreaching the idolaters in trade, and they pronounced secret and ambiguous imprecations against the haughty kingdom of Edom.'—*Decline and Fall*, chap. xvi.

governments in ruling various races and religions. Like the Romans, some European powers were destined to govern a great variety of nations, countries, and religions. In this grand and noble task the Romans among ancient races were the chief if not the only examples for subsequent Christian political rule.[1] The indiscriminate national enmity towards other races, shown in Jewish history, was almost incompatible with the duties of foreign or colonial rule or of friendly alliance with other nations. While, therefore, the theological history of the Jews was long believed by Christians the sole depository of religious truth till their rejection of Christ, their sentiments about other nations were altogether repudiated.

The policy of the Romans was gradually recognised by Christian nations as their proper guide, in great measure, in dealing with subjected races. Foremost among these modern nations whose conquests like those of the Romans appear to be permanent are the British and the Russians, while the Spaniards and Portuguese, though effecting larger colonisations, have seen their yoke thrown off by

[1] 'The obedience of the Roman world was uniform, voluntary, and permanent. The vanquished nations, blended into one great people, resigned the hope, nay, even the wish, of resuming their independence, and scarcely considered their existence as distinct from the existence of Rome. The established authority of the emperors pervaded without an effort the wide extent of their dominions, and was exercised with the same facility on the banks of the Thames or of the Nile as on those of the Tiber. In this state of general security, the leisure as well as opulence both of the prince and people were devoted to improve and to adorn the Roman Empire.'—*Decline and Fall*, chap. ii.

most of their colonial subjects. The short-lived, though extensive, triumphs of these two nations were chiefly achieved in a new world. The vast continent and islands of America were discovered and mostly colonised by the southern nations, who were never permanently successful in Europe. The Portuguese still retain the small settlement of Goa in India, while the reign of the Spaniards over the Netherlands reflected no credit on their capacity as wise or humane rulers. But throughout the New World the invading colonising enterprises of these nations were eminently successful, yet without strengthening their political position in Europe. After overcoming all native opposition in America, Spain and Portugal found themselves opposed by their own colonists, who obtained and retain complete freedom from their control. After the successful revolt of their American colonists, these two European powers shrank back as it were to their former dimensions, independent of other European nations, yet with little influence among them. Their emancipated colonists have hardly assisted them at any time, and the Spaniards, once a danger even to the British, have again retired to their original dominions, but apparently neither they nor the Portuguese have the desire or capacity for further conquest. The British and Russians in different directions and by rather different systems have extended their conquests with more permanent success than any other nation except the Roman has ever achieved. The political supremacy of Christianity in Europe was for a time rather diminished by the Mohammedan invasions of the Moors in Spain and of the Turks in the south-east of Europe. In the last case Mohammedanism was permanently established as a ruling power by the Turks, who have showed not only great political vitality, but a capacity for ruling hostile or varied subjects which no other Mohammedan race has equalled. Except the Persians, still ruling some Armenian and Nestorian Christians, no Mohammedans have possessed much authority over Christian subjects. The Moors in Spain, who evidently showed more cultivation when there than in their own country, were finally expelled by the Spaniards, and returning to Morocco never regained power in Europe.

Meantime, Europe remained divided entirely among Christian states, with the sole exception of Turkey. Its Christian lands, except republican Switzerland, obeyed kings or emperors professing Christianity in the differing forms into which the Faith became divided. The Russians alone vindicated and politically represented the Greek Church, which the subjected Greeks always steadily retained under Turkish rule. The other European countries, though divided by the Protestant Reformation, never abandoned their common Christianity, except France, or rather Paris and other French towns which for a brief time openly renounced all religious belief. They, however, never influenced the French majority, which soon re-established the Romish form of Christianity. Throughout Europe the two ancient faiths of Jupiter and of Odin utterly vanished, being replaced by Christianity in every country.[1]

While the religion of Odin lost interest with its moral influence, that of Jupiter after its political and doctrinal downfall retained, and perhaps always will retain, its peculiar charm, independent of either trust or confidence, in civilised lands. The political wisdom and legislative superiority of its votaries, proved in the permanent extensive and glorious rule of the Romans, became valuable examples to succeeding nations. Their subjects, whether in southern Europe, western Asia, or northern Africa, alike felt the good effects of what Gibbon terms their 'mild and beneficent' sway. Yet towards resisting foes the Romans were sometimes very cruel, though seldom more so than Christians and Mohammedans often proved to be. It was said indeed that the Romans conquered like savages, but ruled like philosophic statesmen. Towards peaceable, obedient subjects, of whatever creed, their rule generally deserved the high encomium of a learned English historian when noticing that illustrious nation.[2] Their example in this respect has been followed and latterly, it may be hoped, improved upon by modern Europeans and especially by the British.

[1] 'So rapid yet so gentle was the fall of paganism.'—*Decline and Fall*, chap. xxviii.

[2] 'It is probable that in no other period of the history of the world was speculative freedom so perfect as in the Roman Empire. The fearless scrutiny of all notions of popular belief did not excite an effort of repression.'—Lecky's *European Morals*, chap. iii.

CHAPTER III

Religious divisions in Christian Europe—Political influence of the Papacy throughout the Christian world—Passive attitude of the Greek Church in political affairs.

THOUGH Christian nations became gradually separated in Europe by three chief divisions of the Faith, the most numerous was the Roman Catholic. The Russians alone represented the Greek Church in political power, while Protestantism was established in Great Britain, north-western Europe, and in central Germany. But Christianity itself was never repudiated by any Christian nation except in parts of France for a short time. The subjected Jews scattered among Christian states preserved their hereditary and national unbelief, which they never ventured to vindicate by argument. Their views on Christianity were privately transmitted among successive generations in their own families, but were seldom if ever revealed to the Christian world around them. With modern sceptics or atheists who arose among Christians, they could have nothing in common, as the former rejected the Old Testament as well as the New. The Jews, who gradually passed almost entirely under either Christian or Mohammedan rule, preserved ancestral faith as firmly and as little affected by disastrous political

history as when it was the established religion of
their native king and country.

Although religious interests or prejudices long
influenced British history, that of the Continent
was apparently more actuated by political motives.
The joint seizure and permanent partition of Poland,
a Catholic kingdom, by Russians, Prussians, and
Austrians, proved decisively that they were quite
agreed in political sentiment when acquiring territory without religious design. This extraordinary
triumph of might over national right was thus shown
to be the joint work of the three chief Christian
divisions of Europe.

Since its accomplishment the subjected Poles
have occasionally revolted against their conquerors,
but inevitably failed, as the three powers, despite
wars between themselves, always united in retaining
their common prey, thus acknowledging each other's
right to the territorial plunder. Of the three
powers, Russia, Prussia, and Austria, the first alone
has wonderfully succeeded in ruling millions of foreign
subjects. In this respect the other two have hitherto
not much distinguished themselves, though both
remain military powers of great strength and influence. Recently, indeed, Prussia, now styled the
German Empire, rivals the Italians and Portuguese
in their invasions of Africa, but France, Russia, and
Britain, the last two especially, are the chief
countries now claiming the allegiance of subjected
nations. It was the fate of the warlike French,
the chief heroes in former crusades, instead of taking

the lead in promoting European triumph in Asia and Africa, to wage desolating warfare with the civilised countries of Europe. To this destructive purpose the genius and ambition of Napoleon had devoted the French, who obeyed him with the most docile yet heroic enthusiasm. It was fortunate, however, for Europe that while its chief nations were waging war with each other, the outside world of independent Mohammedans and other non-Christians took no advantage of this Christian strife. The days of their warlike glory had evidently departed, and while they remained in subjection or friendly peace, the chief Christian powers in Europe ravaged each other's countries and destroyed each other's armies without interference from any other part of the world. Yet when the terrible contest was over, they soon resumed foreign enterprises, extending their influence more and more over races which had clearly lost the power of opposing them. The European powers who chiefly waged war with the French under Napoleon were the British, Prussians, Russians, and Austrians. Spain and Italy could no longer take that leading part in European warfare or politics which ancient and mediæval times had enabled them to do in different ways. The position of modern Italy, once among the most interesting of European lands from its martial prowess and mediæval artistic splendour, was changed in a remarkable manner. It became the spiritual instead of the political ruler of nearly all Europe. Unlike Greece, whose noble literature might have been lost but for its preservation in western Europe, Italy was able to cherish her intellectual glories during the terrible trials of the Middle Ages. Her great poet, Dante, full of admiration for his pagan predecessor, Virgil, wrote his extraordinary poem on Paradise, Purgatory, and Hell, when the Romish form of Christianity was paramount in civilised Europe. He was 'the authorised topographer of the mediæval Hell,' and his poetical ideas, even according to Protestant critics, represented ' what all men believed, feared, and hoped.'[1]

This comprehensiveness, however, only meant the Christian world, then a comparatively small minority of men. Historical students of Dante may form a tolerably correct idea of the exclusive, bigoted, and gloomy view of religion which in his time prevailed throughout Europe.[2] The mild merciful faith of Jesus and of those Apostles who knew Him personally was in Dante's work, as in Christian legislation of his time, associated with a bigoted cruelty, which for centuries disgraced Christian nations, both Roman Catholic and Protestant. Error, or supposed error, in religious belief was thought, irrespective of conduct, to be punished in the next world by torments inflicted on human bodies, revived after death for the sake of suffering them.

[1] Milman's *Latin Christianity*.
[2] 'I marvel at the acceptance of the system (as stated in its fulness by Dante) which condemned guiltless persons to the loss of heaven, because they had lived before Christ, and which made the obtaining Paradise turn frequently on a passing thought or a momentary invocation. That in this faith it was possible to obtain entire peace of mind, to live calmly, and die hopefully is indisputable.'—Ruskin's *Modern Painters*, vol. v.

> Lo! how is Mohammed mangled! before me walks
> Ali weeping, from the chin his face
> Cleft to the forelock; and the others all
> Whom here thou seest while they lived did sow
> Scandal and schism, and therefore thus are rent.
> *Inferno*, canto xxviii.

Yet the Creator was still termed merciful as well as omniscient and omnipotent, ruling a world of short-lived men, most of whom were involuntarily ignorant of religious truth.

Rome, once the seat of complete political supremacy, had virtually exchanged this pre-eminence for a spiritual authority, throughout yet more extensive territories, over races and countries previously unknown. But her position was no longer politically supreme in Europe as in pagan times. It was the singular exchange of political for spiritual power that has made some writers term Roman Catholicism the Roman Empire over again, in supremacy for a long period over all civilised lands. Ancient, mediæval, and modern Italy thus held a peculiarly interesting position throughout European history, in its varied political, religious, and artistic influences. Politically divided into small states without large colonies or foreign possessions, till of recent years, and with little national influence, she yet maintained in her august capital or rather chief city the spiritual control for a long period over the Christian replacers of her pagan subjects. The cosmopolitan character or position of the Papacy during centuries of national ignorance, prejudice, and exclusiveness is noticed with some admiration by modern Protestant historians, who are evidently more inclined to write fairly on this subject than their predecessors were during the rise of the Reformation.[1]

While Christian rulers eagerly, often jealously, advocated political rights or interests at the expense of other nations, and of opponents in their own, and while some nations apparently thought that only they deserved the commonest rights of humanity, the Papacy during centuries soared above political or national exclusiveness. Christianity, in every part of the world, was under its special protection, and wherever it appeared the spiritual aid or sympathy of Rome was devoted to it, regardless of race or of nationality.[2]

This influence, so admirable when devoted to promoting universal charity, was brought to a tremendous test when some of the most civilised

[1] 'From the time when the barbarians overran the Western Empire to the time of the revival of letters, the influence of the Church of Rome had been generally favourable to science, to civilisation, and to good government. It is difficult to say whether England owes more to the Roman Catholic religion or to the Reformation. For the amalgamation of races and for the abolition of villenage, she is chiefly indebted to the influences which the priesthood in the Middle Ages exercised over the laity. For political and intellectual freedom, and for all the blessings which political and intellectual freedom have brought in their train, she is chiefly indebted to the great rebellion of the laity against the priesthood.'—Macaulay's *History of England*, chap. i.

[2] 'The spiritual supremacy arrogated by the Pope was in the dark ages productive of far more good than evil. Its effect was to unite the nations of Western Europe into one great commonwealth. Thus grew up sentiments of enlarged benevolence; races separated from each other by seas and mountains acknowledged a fraternal tie and a common code of public law.'
—Macaulay's *History of England*, vol. i.

Christian lands repudiated its authority, while others supported it with undiminished firmness and credulity. Amid the religious strife accompanying the Reformation, the Papacy preserved its authority over the greater part of central and southern Europe. The great political loss it sustained by the spiritual revolt of northern and part of central Europe evidently made it more circumspect in its policy, as no opposition between rival popes, which had aroused some scorn among sceptics, occurred since the Reformation. It was placed for the first time on its defence, no longer against pagans or infidels, but against devoted and zealous Christians.

The previous separation of the Greek Church from that of Rome had been comparatively a local or national dispute. The former was never aggressive or ardent for making converts. It remained almost entirely confined to Greeks and Russians. Neither in political contest nor in literary argument did the Greek and Latin Churches come into serious collision. But Protestants disputed with Roman Catholics alike in war, political intrigue, literary controversy, and enthusiastic preaching. The exaggerated unreasoning abhorrence with which they mutually regarded each other, almost irrespective of personal character, motive, or principle, forms perhaps one of the saddest pages in the religious history of civilised men. The result of the Reformation, however, did not materially affect the position of Italy. It remained during, and after, the great movement endowed with little political power, while the spiritual dominion of Rome, though diminished in Europe, prevailed over the greater part of America, and has survived the political changes that have since agitated the Christian world. Italy of mediæval and to some extent of modern times has, despite its political inferiority, exercised a powerful though indirect influence among civilised nations. The splendour of its fine arts, the excellence of its music, painting, and sculpture, have always delighted men of culture in every country. Political weakness, therefore, could never diminish its vast artistic rather than intellectual superiority. This pre-eminence, united with the religious supremacy it maintains over the majority of Christians, makes Italy an exceptional country and Rome an exceptional city. Italy is at once the artistic teacher, the historical referee, and the religious guide of many more powerful nations, whose armies, fleets, and extended commerce, like those of ancient Rome, seem to direct the progress of civilised enlightenment throughout the world. Italy now presents a spectacle of a comparatively uninfluential or unimportant country, containing a city which in different respects has always possessed and retains more influence over Christians than any other has aspired to hold in either ancient or modern times. Rome, once the seat of pagan, martial, and political rule, became for a period the religious arbiter of the Christian world. The long succession of popes, believed the spiritual successors of the first Apostles, had with brief interruptions reigned in Rome as rulers of the religious world in Christian lands, yet without attempting or perhaps desiring to increase the political power of the Italian nation. All Christian people in the Catholic faith, of whatever race or country, were to the Papacy alike its religious subjects. The separation of the Greek Church removed some of its votaries in eastern Europe from papal influence, but the greater part of the Christian world always remained under its authority.

The subsequent Reformation, however, repudiated Roman Catholicism in some of its most important dominions. Northern Europe, except Russia, became chiefly Protestant, while its southern countries, except Greece, remained Roman Catholic. The vast American colonies founded chiefly by Britain, Spain, and Portugal, followed the religious example of their respective countries. The large majority in the islands, the centre, and the south, being mostly descendants of Spaniards and Portuguese, retained Roman Catholicism, while British colonists in the north were chiefly Protestant. Spain, however, unlike Italy, was viewed in the Middle Ages as a strong aggressive power in Europe. The loss of the Netherlands, the destruction of the Spanish Armada, and the vast colonisation of America, alike combined to effectually lower the political power of Spain. The subsequent emancipation of her American colonies finally reduced this once arrogant and haughty power to the secondary though independent position she still maintains among the nations of Europe.

CHAPTER IV

Position of France among European nations—Its triumphs under Napoleon throughout Europe—Alliance of the chief European powers against him—His final defeat and banishment.

FRANCE, perhaps the most chivalrous of Christian countries, proudly termed the eldest son of the Church by the Papacy, was for a time one of the most enthusiastic of Christian champions. In the Crusades she took a leading part; and though those strange enterprises ended in failure, she remained one of the strongest of the European nations. Yet as a ruling people the French, for a long period, were not much distinguished.

During the extensive conquests and colonisations made by Spain and Portugal in America, and the gradual subjection of India by the British, the French, despite their brave enterprising nature, effected few foreign conquests. Their national enmity to Britain continued for a long time without any religious object, being entirely caused by political rivalry or ambition; but afterwards religious interests became involved, France retaining Roman Catholicism, and Great Britain becoming one of the chief Protestant powers of Europe. At the end of the eighteenth century France became the victim of a domestic revolution of peculiar atrocity, soon followed by the most extraordinary and aggressive empire of modern times, under Napoleon the First. This wonderful general, though a Corsican by birth, and said by some to have possessed many Italian national qualities, yet evidently understood and captivated the French people with a success as complete as could be imagined by either a poet or sensational novelist. He inspired love, implicit obedience, ambition, and fear alike among his followers, who became as thoroughly the instruments of his sole will as if he had belonged to a superior race.

What would Napoleon have done with an army of reasoners?[1] an able modern French writer exclaims, doubtless after carefully studying the success with which this extraordinary man so absolutely ruled a high-spirited, warlike nation.

Napoleon had neither royal ancestry nor powerful allies to aid him. His amazing triumphs were really due to his personal gifts or merits alone. Shakespeare's words on Cardinal Wolsey's pre-eminence may apply perhaps with equal truth to the rise, power, and triumphant career of this greatest of French rulers :

> Not propp'd by ancestry, whose grace
> Chalks successors their way, nor call'd upon
> For high feats done to the Crown ; neither allied
> To eminent assistants ; but, spider-like,
> Out of his self-growing web, he gives us note,
> The force of his own merit makes his way ;
> A gift that Heaven gives.—*Henry VIII.* act i.

---

[1] Renan's *Future of Science.*

Napoleon when he first rose to power in France found it in a most distracted state. A people eminently religious in the country districts, though less so in the chief towns, were ruled by an infidel republic chiefly popular in Paris. This new government had avowedly repudiated religious worship and enacted persecuting laws against the clergy. The King and Queen had been publicly executed in the capital, and the royal family banished, but still encouraged by partisans to expect a restoration of the fallen monarchy. No form of Christianity had replaced the Roman Catholic in France, despite its condemnation by ruling republicans. Some British and foreign Protestants were alike surprised at this result. In fact, a nation always Roman Catholic was for a short time governed and oppressed by an energetic infidel minority, specially if not solely influential in the chief towns. The deposed royal family, though devotedly Catholic, was so weak or unpopular that, while representing a large French majority in religious opinion, it was unable to upset or even disturb the energetic vehement republicans who when established in Paris from thence ruled France.

Some thought that Napoleon might have followed the historical example of General Monk when restoring the British monarchy in the person of Charles II. But he attempted nothing of the kind. The position of France and Britain in the times of Cromwell and of Napoleon was strangely different, while certainly presenting some points of resemblance. Throughout Britain the monarchy was always preferred by the majority, especially in London, where the rule of the Commonwealth, and afterwards of Cromwell, was never popular. Despite his successful wisdom, his warmest admirers owned that he was the reverse of a popular ruler.[1]

The British nation in his time showed no particular desire for foreign conquest or territorial extension. The majority was well represented by Monk, who though obedient to Cromwell had no wish to obey any republican successor to that irresistible chief. Hence the joyful undisputed restoration of the British monarchy. This event, though it must have greatly interested foreign nations, provoked no interference from them. The practical indifference of Continental nations during the great British revolution was a remarkable and fortunate fact. Their political peacefulness or apathy towards Britain was the cause of Cromwell's never displaying his great military talents against any other people, save those of the British Isles, which Macaulay notices. But Napoleon, who thoroughly understood the French nation, its powers, weaknesses, and passions, resolved to turn its martial energies against the European powers by invading warfare. By this policy he succeeded in drawing almost all Frenchmen to his side.[2]

[1] 'The army and its great chief governed everything. Oliver had made his choice. He had kept the hearts of his soldiers, and had broken with almost every other class of his fellow countrymen.'—Macaulay's *History of England*, chap. i.

[2] 'He was the personification of France, as she was in his time, when he arrived by her desire and connivance at the height of his power.'—Sloane's *Life of Napoleon*, chap. xxiii.

The royal family were fugitives, while the Papacy, though silently and steadily supporting their claims, was yet acknowledged by Napoleon as entitled to a religious authority denied it by his republican predecessors. He preferred no form of Christianity to the Roman Catholic, and, while making political designs his main object, he thus indirectly confirmed its spiritual supremacy among the French. He therefore, though only to a limited extent, conciliated the French clergy, while enlisting all the energy and ambition of that fiery nation to promote his grand designs for the conquest of Europe. His wonderful career, more like a poet's or a novelist's invention than a reality, at first seemed to fulfil his hopes. The French army under him and his generals was as obedient as if he had succeeded a long line of royal ancestors, claiming hereditary allegiance, and became victorious throughout the greater part of Europe. Italy and Spain were easily overcome, but Prussia and Austria offered a stubborn resistance, yet were each defeated in successive battles of great severity.

The Russians then became the objects of Napoleon's attack, but they proved a foe of a different kind. The Prussians and Austrians had encountered the French in pitched battles. Every resource of discipline, artillery, military training, and valour, were in them put to a decisive test, and in each case the French were completely victorious. But the Russians rather avoided open contests, and, retiring farther and farther within their immense territory, were followed by the invading French to the old capital, Moscow. This city the Russians set on fire, and the French, instead of defeating them in the open field, as they had probably anticipated, found themselves in a hostile country and exposed without shelter to the dreadful rigour of a Russian winter. Then began their disastrous retreat, memorable in the annals of warfare as perhaps the most destructive to human life ever recorded even in its terrible history.

Though the French, completely victorious in central and southern Europe, were thus practically repulsed in Russia, the British, in Spain, Egypt, and Syria, steadily thwarted their progress. It was said Napoleon deeply regretted that he had not attacked Britain in the first instance, and history proves that of all his foes the British and the Russians were alone successful. After the disastrous retreat of the French from Russia, in which numbers perished more from cold, hardship, and exposure, than from actual defeat, Napoleon, after a short warfare against the allied powers, abdicated his authority and retired to the island of Elba. The European rulers whom his indiscriminate hostility had forced into alliance against France, restored the banished royal family with the cordial approval of the Pope and of the French clergy, yet, with their important exception, the French people generally remained as devoted to Napoleon in adversity as in triumph.

The restored Bourbon family was never really

popular. Its restoration seemed almost to represent the defeat and political humiliation of unwilling subjects. The restored princes were in grateful or dependent alliance with those nations most of whom the French had previously defeated. Napoleon, moreover, during his brief triumph, had conferred kingdoms, provinces, titles, and honours, derived from European conquests, among his followers, which were now repudiated and made of no effect. Only one general, Bernadotte, King of Sweden, managed to retain his new dominions, and transmit them to his descendants, who to this day rule that country in undisputed possession. In other instances Napoleon's lofty promotions ended in disavowal and failure, the allied powers considering it a duty to restore Europe, as much as possible, to its former condition before the rise of Napoleon. But the French nation, though compelled to receive back their deposed royal family, never really preferred it, though the clergy did all in their power to encourage or inspire loyalty to the restored monarchy, which had always been devoted to the cause and interests of the Papacy. The love of military glory and the bitter consciousness of national defeat, however, combined to make the vast French majority utterly hostile to the royal family. Napoleon they considered their national hero, and his sudden return to France from Elba aroused an enthusiasm for him which astonished all Europe. The man who had nearly ruined his country by destructive wars, who had drawn down upon it the vengeance and enmity of united Europe, who had, in fact, been the chief if not the sole cause of her disastrous humiliation before the civilised world, was yet welcomed back to France with the universal rejoicing due only to a national benefactor. Except at the restoration of Charles the Second, there were perhaps never seen such frantic demonstrations of loyal devotion and obedience as greeted the return of the defeated Corsican upstart, as his foes called him, to the French people.

The French King had to take a hasty departure, to the sincere regret of the clergy, and again Napoleon became the popular head of the armed French nation. Then ensued the famed hundred days (March 20 till June 29, 1815) of Napoleon's second reign. Though some thought he had become, or pretended to be, more peaceful in his views, the European powers resolved never to trust him. He had, indeed, made them feel too severely the terrible consequences of his insatiable ambition and absolute power over the French nation, to permit any confidence being placed in him again. None believed he could be trusted either as a peaceful neighbour or steady ally. Again, therefore, the European powers were united against him. All religious differences among them were disregarded in their determined union for a strictly political purpose. British and German Protestants, Austrian Roman Catholics, and Russian members of the Greek Church, were, as before, unanimously opposed to the French nation, who, under their extraordinary general, again encountered the

allied forces at the decisive battle of Waterloo. Its
result in the total defeat of the French caused the
second fall of Napoleon; but this time all chance of his
escape was carefully prevented. The remote lonely
isle of St. Helena was chosen for his future exile.
There, under the charge of the British Government,
but with the full consent and desire of the European powers, the great Napoleon passed the remainder of his life.[1]

During the middle of this century, and even later,
observant English travellers have noticed the intense
enduring love of the French for Napoleon's memory,
and their indignation against Britain as his chief
enemy at Waterloo and final custodian.[2] This
animosity, it may be reasonably hoped, is now
changed or modified. The French at this time
dislike the Germans, their latest foes, far more than
they dislike the British. Owing to the almost
universal enmity Napoleon had aroused against

---

[1] 'When chained to the rock of St. Helena, he was still an object of dread to the European powers; his name was more powerful than an army of 150,000 men. It had been truly said that his cocked hat and great-coat, if placed on a stick on the coast of Brittany, would cause Europe to run to arms, from one end to the other.'—Alison's *History of Europe*, chap. ix.

[2] 'The French pant for an opportunity of revenging their humiliation, and if a contest ending in a victory on their part should ensue, elating them in their turn, and leaving its cursed legacy of hatred and rage behind to us, there is no end to the so-called glory and shame, and to the alternative of successful and unsuccessful murder, in which two high-spirited nations might engage. Centuries hence we Frenchmen and Englishmen might be boasting and killing each other, still carrying out bravely the devil's code of honour.'—Thackeray's *Vanity Fair*, chap. xxxii.

himself, without making allies of importance, his wonderful career, despite many glorious victories, ended in making little real change in the territorial divisions of Europe. After his final exile, Europe remained in much the same state as before his time, except Sweden, which obeyed General Bernadotte as lawful king. Again the fugitive Bourbon royal family returned to France, reinstated in hereditary dominion as before by the will of the chief European powers, with the cordial approval of the Papacy and of the French clergy.

CHAPTER V

British supremacy in India—Its gradual consolidation—Improvement effected by British rule in that country—Failure of Spain and Portugal in retaining their American colonies.

OF all British conquests and permanent settlements, India is undoubtedly the largest, the most important, and the most interesting. Unlike their possessions in America, Australia, and south Africa, India presents a religious and political history of peculiar interest as well as of great antiquity.[1]

Its ancient religions of Brahminism and Buddhism were singularly involved with the newer and more proselytising faith of Mohammedanism, before the invasion of the British, who had therefore to encounter their differing votaries, but were finally successful over all. Rival Hindoos and Mohammedans alike passed under British rule, which has apparently increased in popularity over divided subjects, as the irritating remembrance of conquest was somewhat effaced through the progress and the lessons of time.

[1] 'The English are the lords of the land, for it is the necessary fate of Asiatic empires to be subjected to Europeans, and China will some day or other be obliged to submit to the same fate.'—Hegel's *Philosophy of History*, section xx.

Yet the British had to encounter different races in India and on its frontiers before acquiring the complete supremacy they still retain. The last Indian wars of much importance were the Sikh invasion in the north, and the short sanguinary mutiny among the sepoys or native troops. The Sikhs were for a long time the independent allies of the British; but after the death of their shrewd pacific ruler, Runjeet Singh, invaded the British territory. Though possessing splendid artillery, brave and well disciplined by European officers whom Runjeet had employed to train them, they were not only defeated in pitched battles by the British, but finally pursued into their own country of the Punjaub, which was then annexed to the British dominions.

The Sikhs previous to their invasion had murdered or driven away their European officers, chiefly French and Italian, and were therefore commanded by their own chiefs, and utterly unable to cope with the disciplined and well-managed British forces. Since this war, however, the Sikhs, who never had apparently much idea of patriotism in the European sense of that term, but were more like soldiers of fortune, caring for little but their pay, entered the British service and proved loyal to British rule. During the subsequent mutiny of the sepoys, the Sikhs eagerly served the British in suppressing the revolt. Thus these former foes practically assisted to defeat the revolted native soldiery, enlisted to obey the British. It was the political destiny of the latter to thus encounter and finally overcome almost every variety of native race in India.[1]

In succession, Hindoos, Mohammedans, Sikhs, and mutinous sepoys were alike defeated and without exception reduced to political obedience. In this general submission, however, the religious element was altogether absent, and neither persecutions nor favouritism were sanctioned by British laws respecting differences of faith or theological opinion.[2]

Wherever this judicious forbearance is shown, the history of most countries proves that the enmity of conquered to conquerors is far less lasting, and often yields through time to comparative loyalty and even attachment. Such apparently was and continues, on the whole, the case with India's divided population under British authority. Subjected Brahmins, Mohammedans, and others, alike treated with tolerance and justice, may well, and probably do, compare their condition with historical records or tradition of their treatment not only by each other, but by rulers of their own faith. The sec-

[1] 'No achievement of secular government since the Roman Empire can compare in its magnitude and splendour with the British Empire in India. The men who built up that gigantic empire, who have maintained for so many generations, and over so vast an area, peace, prosperity, and order, who have put a stop to so many savage wars, and eradicated so many cruel customs, are the statesmen of whom England should be most proud.'—Lecky's *Democracy and Liberty*, vol. i.

[2] 'The English Government presents a comparative continuity in policy and a power to enforce its regulations; with the growth of administrative strength and the pressure of Western ideas the policy changed to one of non-interference in religious matters, subject to the prohibition of obnoxious rites.'—*Asiatic Quarterly Review*, October 1897.

tarian aversion sometimes expressed or indicated by Mohammed towards all religions but those of 'the Book,' Judaism, Christianity, and his own, had long caused hereditary though not exterminating enmity between his followers and the Brahmins and Buddhists.[1]

The faith of Buddha, proceeding from that of the Brahmins, and an improvement upon it, according to Max Müller, still prevails in Ceylon and parts of central and eastern Asia. But in the Indian peninsula it seems to be rather superseded by its predecessor Brahminism, which the sublime teaching and virtuous example of Buddha have done much to improve. Buddha, the mild, humane, self-denying prince, who compassionated all suffering, even of birds, animals, and insects, was yet the fellow countryman and teacher of people who committed great cruelties on each other. He was evidently one of those rare extraordinary men who practically belong to no particular country, a friend not only to mankind, but to living nature. His faith and ideas, like those of the Christian prophet, were thus often nominally shared or politically established by professed believers, who had little resemblance to him. It was, indeed, well for mankind that when the rule of the British was established in India, their own previous religious dissensions at home had practically ceased. The British, whose not very

---

[1] 'After some acts of intolerant zeal, the Mohammedan conquerors of Hindustan have spared the pagodas of that devout and populous country.'—*Decline and Fall*, chap. li.

remote ancestry had cruelly oppressed each other owing to comparatively slight differences in the same faith, were at a later period called upon to deal with a subjected population of mingled Brahmins, Buddhists, Mohammedans, and Parsees, whom their Christian ancestors would have viewed with an abhorrence equally ignorant and indiscriminate. It is therefore an historical fact that the descendants of men who had cruelly yet conscientiously persecuted fellow Christians and fellow countrymen, yet showed and continue to show a justice, tolerance, and charity to millions of non-Christians among various races, rendering their rule a practical and a noble illustration of the principles of the Christian faith.[1]

Though some doctrines in Brahminism, but especially the character and teaching of Buddha, indicate virtuous thoughts and precepts, there remained some degrading superstitions among its votaries, with which the British had to deal. Evidently some of the high principles taught among the Brahmins and by Buddha were either unknown to many of their followers, or were surpassed

[1] 'England is at present the greatest Oriental empire the world has ever known. England has proved that she knows not only how to conquer, but how to rule. It is simply dazzling to think of the few thousands of Englishmen ruling the millions of human beings in India, in Africa, in America, and in Australasia. England has realised and more than realised the dream of Alexander, the marriage of the East and the West, and has drawn the principal nations of the world together more closely than they have ever been before.'—Max Müller's *Chips from a German Workshop*, vol. i.

through attraction or terror by some abject, even dangerous superstitions. The Suttee, or voluntary widow burning, the self-sacrifice before the car of the idol Juggernaut, and the sect of Thugs believing it their duty to murder without shedding blood, to propitiate their goddess, have been nearly suppressed by the vigilance of British rule. These superstitions were always confined to the Hindoo or native population in India. The Mohammedans of course regarded them with contemptuous abhorrence. Yet the vast majority even of the Brahmins apparently viewed their suppression by the British with satisfaction, though indicated more in peaceful acquiescence than by expressed approval. Among the many philanthropic deeds of the British in India was their protection of the Parsees chiefly at or near Bombay. These descendants of the ancient Persians are a race peculiarly interesting to the students of antiquity. This remarkable sect, with their prayers expressing thanks for the four elements and their apparent worship of the rising sun, as symbolic of their good deity Ormuzd, are, though few in number, among the most loyal of British subjects in India. Europeans often wonder at the cruel and idolatrous practices of many people in Burmah, China, and India, who profess to follow or to respect the great teacher Buddha or the enlightened lawgiver Confucius. Yet when Christian history is fairly examined it shows that not only sentiments but practices equally incompatible with what Christians now term their faith for a long time animated the rulers, inspired the clergy, and influenced the legislation of most Christian countries. The combined principles of charity and justice, so admired by pious Christians when they hear them enjoined in the Gospel, were equally well known to the most bigoted and relentless of their persecuting ancestors. All those religious sentiments calculated to inspire kindness, truth, and justice were equally known to cruel Christian rulers and to bigoted Christian fanatics. But they were often construed, more through fanaticism than hypocrisy, to justify or extenuate almost every crime in behalf of the political triumph of that faith whose spirit its zealous advocates were thus tempted to violate. The barbarous cruelties or immoral absurdities still prevalent among some Buddhists cannot be greater contrasts to the spirit of their Prophet than were the legalised atrocities of Christians in the Middle Ages to the precepts of Jesus. It is indeed of rather recent date that what are now termed Christian principles in dealing with unbelievers were embodied in legislative enactments and practically enforced by Christian rule.

The contrast between Christian policy towards 'infidels' before, during, and even since the Crusades, and the present time, is well worth examination. England, Italy, France, and Austria, in a common policy towards Mohammedans showed an animosity against them that prevented all chance of conciliation, and they were finally forced to abandon their crusading enterprises without retaining either Mohammedan subjects or territory. Since those disastrous wars, the result of religious enthusiasm, the change in Christian feeling, policy, and conduct towards unbelievers has had its practical reward in the acquisition not only of supreme but popular authority over millions of different non-Christians. As if to prove this fact to thoughtful men, the spectacle is now shown of British, French, and Russians governing non-Christians in India, north Africa, the Caucasus, and parts of Tartary. In these several instances Protestants, Roman Catholics, and members of the Greek Church rule with success and apparent popularity millions of people belonging to different creeds. This achievement of really superior wisdom as well as valour is new in Christian history. During the Crusades, when allied Christian nations waged war against Mohammedans in Syria, the idea of conciliating or winning the esteem of non-Christians was almost unknown, if not repudiated, and perhaps would have been thought inconsistent with either the duties or the interests of Christianity.

Throughout many centuries the Christian powers ruled few avowed unbelievers except the Jews, whom they treated, especially in Spain, with extreme and sometimes persecuting severity. At present British rule in India, Russian rule throughout northern Asia, and that of the French in Algiers may be instructively compared. These powers have hitherto been most successful in the firm consolidation as well as retention of their supremacy. The authority of these nations, representing the three chief Christian divisions, to the present date, seems permanently established, that of French and Russians over different Mohammedan nations, while the British rule a far larger variety of religions and races of men.

Mohammedans under these Christian powers now obey them not only in peaceful avocations, but as soldiers enlisted, or as officials engaged, in their service. No interference is allowed by Christian laws with the religious thoughts or observances of their various political subjects. Legal justice allied with religious tolerance is thus shown by British, French, and Russians, who resemble each other in their treatment of non-Christians. Historical students may be surprised that nations, still preserving the same faith formerly supposed to sanction persecution even of its own differing versions, now agree in observing a steady toleration of all religious opinions utterly unknown or condemned during the first years of Christian political power. Yet among European countries, Britain, Russia, and France have alone had much means of proving themselves good rulers over large or varied populations. The Portuguese in small Indian settlements, the Dutch in the Malay Archipelago, and the Spaniards in a few towns in Morocco may claim some credit in this respect, to a limited extent. But in discharging the arduous and responsible duty of governing millions of foreign subjects alien to their own religion, France, Britain, and Russia are decidedly pre-eminent. France in Algiers, besides newer settlements in Africa, Madagascar, and Cochin China, may claim to equal them in the success or justice of her colonial government, while the original conquests made by Spain and Portugal showed only the brief predominance of mere power over ignorant natives. These two powers have now lost nearly all their American possessions by the successful revolts of their own colonists, who retain the same religion with the language and most of the habits of their mother countries. With few exceptions, of which the most important is the island of Cuba, now struggling desperately against Spain, the Spanish and Portuguese colonists now compose independent republics. No monarchy, except in Brazil, which has become a republic, was ever long established throughout America by the colonists. Except Canada, Jamaica, and other West Indian islands still under Britain, and some Dutch possessions, nearly all America is under republican government, a system which in Europe has generally failed in modern times. Switzerland has certainly long preserved it, and France has lately re-established it, though rival monarchist claimants to the throne are evidently watching their opportunity. In the rest of Europe, monarchy in more or less absolute forms now prevails and apparently by the popular will. Christianity in its three chief divisions is also established in every European land except some Turkish provinces, where in the south-east of Europe Mohammedanism has long ruled a Christian population. During many years Turkish power has gradually declined, but at the close of this century it certainly seems more firm, owing evidently to the moral support it receives from the Christian powers of Europe for political reasons.

CHAPTER VI

Rule of the Turks in South-eastern Europe—Revolt of the Greeks against them in 1824—British sympathy with the Greeks partly owing to classical associations—Their emancipation effected by the aid of Britain, France, and Russia.

The genius or success of the Turks as a ruling nation has been differently viewed by opposing politicians,[1] yet it is evident that this originally Tartar tribe has hitherto ruled millions of Armenians, Greeks, and other Christians, besides Jews, without assistance from either Christian or Mohammedan governments till the singular Crimean war of 1854-5. In that peculiar contest the political views of France and England were much changed since they had aided the Greeks in their revolt against Turkey in 1824. In that short but important and interesting war the insurgent Greeks, by the active aid of

[1] 'What renders the government of the Christians, though so superior in number, by the Mohammedans more easy in Turkey is the variety of tribes and races of which the subjected population is composed, their separation from each other by mountains, seas, and entire want of roads, and the complete unity of action and identity of purpose in the dominant race. The Turks command and are alone entrusted with the military power.'—Alison's *History of Europe*, chap. xiii.

Alison omits to add that Circassian and Kurdish Mohammedans support their Turkish rulers and co-religionists in maintaining authority over the Christian population.

Russians, British, and French, had finally become free, having preserved their Christianity during centuries of Turkish rule. The loss of Greece was perhaps the first of a series of losses sustained by the Turks in Europe and Africa during the middle and end of this century. Their extraordinary empire was once said to comprise 'the finest slices' of Europe, Asia, and Africa. Though repulsed during the Middle Ages when invading central Europe, the Turks as a ruling nation have certainly succeeded far beyond other Mohammedans. The previous Saracen rule was chiefly over their co-religionists. The Persian and Moorish Mohammedans never retained power for any length of time over foreign subjects, while the Tartars of central Asia almost exclusively ruled over co-religionists. The Moors, after their singularly intellectual rule in Spain, when driven back to Morocco by the Spaniards ruled no nation but their own, while preserving their independence. It is remarkable that the Moors certainly displayed in Spain a knowledge or appreciation of civilisation about which they gave little sign in their own country, as if the air of Europe had inspired them with a refinement or intellectual power of which they gave little proof in Africa. Scarcely anything in their native African countries of Fez and Morocco displays the cultivation which had distinguished their rule in southern Spain. No palace to compare to the magnificent Alhambra was ever erected by the Moors in Africa. When finally obliged to return to Morocco, though they

lost some few towns on the coast, captured by the
Spaniards, the Moors have remained a free nation,
occasionally defeated by the French on their Algerian
frontier, but without much if any loss of territory.
They seem since their expulsion from Europe never
to have been an aggressive or a ruling people. But
the Turks have certainly governed many different
races in their varied empire with remarkable political
success during a long period. As the European
powers, however, gradually increased in strength,
enlightenment, and resources, the Turks ceased to
keep pace with them. Their Christian subjects in
Europe and Asia began to increase their intercourse
with European nations. Evidently the fame of
Greek classic literature, during centuries preserved
in western Europe chiefly in colleges, among a
learned minority, with the advancement of education,
the invention of printing, and the increasing facilities
for travelling, became far more extended and general.
The appreciation of classic literature greatly increased
European interest in modern Greece, whose preservation of Christianity under Mohammedan rule added
in Christian minds to the interest attached to classical
associations. During a long period of Turkish rule
Greece had been little noticed by western Europeans.
In the beginning of this century the increasing
weakness of the Turks became known, and no European powers as before dreaded invasion from them.
The increasing number of British travellers revealed
the state of Greece to European scholars; many, full
of admiration for Greek classics, began to explore

the ancient land of Homer, Socrates, Plato, and Aristotle, with ardent peculiar interest in its ancient achievements and compassion for its modern political and religious degradation. Indulging fancy perhaps rather than restraining it, some European travellers eagerly associated the oppressed modern Greeks with their remote ancestry, or rather with that race which thousands of years before had inhabited the same land. Among these accomplished tourists, whose classic knowledge and attractive genius made him pre-eminent, was Lord Byron.[1] He visited it during its gallant revolt against Turkish rule, and not only by his splendid verses, but by practical assistance, tried to aid the Greeks. Though so many changes had come over their famous land since classic times, the modern Greeks seemed, to many learned Europeans, to be interesting, and by their sudden bravery not altogether unworthy descendants of their heroic remote ancestors. The surprise of the Turks, at this time at peace with Europe, was doubtless great at this sympathy of European travellers with their revolting subjects. Always a military nation, the Turks, chiefly delighting in riding fine horses, cared little for any literature

---

[1] 'A nation once the first among the nations, pre-eminent in knowledge, pre-eminent in military glory, the cradle of philosophy, of eloquence, and of the fine arts, had been for ages bowed down under a cruel yoke. On a sudden this degraded people had risen on their oppressors. Byron could not but be interested in the event of this contest. To Greece he was attached by peculiar ties. Much of his splendid and popular poetry had been inspired by its scenery and by its history.'—Macaulay's Essay on Moore's *Life of Byron*.

except their own Koran. The illustrious ancestry
of rebellious Greek subjects were certainly of no
interest to them, nor were they in any way fitted or
inclined to study their immortal works. But Byron,
like many of his less gifted fellow-countrymen, in
his noble poetry evidently viewed insurgent Greece
as reviving from apparent death and aspiring to
recover ancestral fame. Hence his pathetic comparison of the suffering degraded country to perishing
human nature.

> He who hath bent him o'er the dead
> Ere the first day of death is fled,
> And mark'd the mild angelic air,
> The rapture of repose that's there,
> So fair, so calm, so softly seal'd,
> The first, last look, by death reveal'd;
> Such is the aspect of this shore;
> 'Tis Greece, but living Greece no more.
> *The Giaour.*

After this touching eloquent tribute to its vanished
intellectual glory, Byron became the enthusiastic
practical sympathiser with the Greeks of his own
period. He sees their revolt while he was in
Greece, yet almost despairs of assistance from
Europe owing to the Turks being at peace with
its countries. In some respects the poet's grand
ideas were not without practical influence, or
perhaps they expressed the feelings of many
Europeans in language which none but he could
command. It is most remarkable how much admiration as well as discovery of ancient times, countries,
and literature, distinguish this century compared

to its predecessors. Greece, which during many centuries of Christian history had remained comparatively unknown to Europe except through classic literature, understood only by a small minority of learned men, suddenly claimed political notice as a new nation full of old memories, as if awakening from a trance. Byron eagerly reminds the Greeks around him of their ancestral renown, in words as glowing and pictorial as if it were in living memory.

> O! servile offspring of the free,
> Pronounce what sea, what shore is this.
> The gulf of the rock of Salamis!
> These scenes, their story not unknown,
> Arise and make again your own,
> Snatch from the ashes of your sires
> The embers of their former fires.
> *The Giaour.*

Yet many centuries had elapsed between the days of Byron's favourite Greek heroes and their descendants, or rather successors, in the same land. The latter were now certainly bravely resisting Turkish oppression, and, like other political victims, deserved the sympathy of any Christian government or community. But their ancestral merits had long departed. No national poets or philosophers remained or arose to appreciate them like their students in western Europe.[1] The European rejoicing at the final emancipation of Greece doubtless astonished

---

[1] 'Christendom had come to the rescue. Never, surely, since the taking of Jerusalem in 1199 by the crusading warriors had so unanimous a feeling of exultation pervaded the Christian world.'—Alison's *History of Europe*, chap. xiv.

the dignified, stolid Turks, who were at peace with the Christian powers. They might have plausibly declared that their rule over the Greeks was never more unpopular than that of Russians, Prussians, and Austrians over the Poles, and that it had certainly been originally acquired in a more honourable manner. Byron died before the final success of the Greek revolt. This gallant struggle had at length elicited the active sympathy of Britain, France, and Russia in the practical form of armed intervention. The French and British fleets defeated the Turks at the naval battle of Navarino, while the Russians made war on the Turks at their northern frontier. In this naval engagement the Turks were aided by their Egyptian subjects and co-religionists summoned by the Sultan to assist him as their sovereign. After this battle, ending in the total defeat of the Turks and Egyptians, the freedom of Greece was soon established, though it must always be regretted that Byron did not live to see it. His beautiful lines, however, warning the Greeks not to trust foreigners, not even French or Russians, but to depend on themselves, were rather contradicted by real history.

> Hereditary bondsmen! know ye not
> Who would be free, themselves must strike the blow?
> By their right arms the conquest must be wrought.
> Will Gaul or Muscovite redress ye? No.
>
> *Childe Harold*, second canto.

The Greek insurgents, who were nearly crushed by the allied Turks and Egyptians before the Navarino battle, could never have obtained their freedom but for the timely aid of the Gaul, the Briton, and the Muscovite. The Turks, beset by three Christian powers aiding the revolted Greeks, had no alternative but to submit to the wishes of Britain, France, and Russia. Greece was finally made an independent kingdom under the protection of its three deliverers, with Athens for its capital and a Bavarian prince for its king. This monarch, King Otho, however, became unpopular through time, and was replaced by a Danish prince, brother to the Princess of Wales, now King of Greece (1898). The strange position of the Turkish Empire was remarkably shown soon after the Navarino battle. The Pasha of Egypt, the shrewd Mehemet Ali, whose son Ibrahim Pasha had commanded there, followed the Greek example in rebelling against the Turks, despite their common faith and recent alliance. The Egyptians accordingly invaded Syria and defeated the Turks, whose empire now seemed in imminent danger, when the European powers again interfered, but this time in favour of the Turks, compelled the Egyptians to return to their own land, maintained the Sultan's authority, and arranged a treaty between him and his mutinous viceroy. This treaty made Egypt virtually independent of the Turks, giving Mehemet Ali's family hereditary rights over Egypt, while insisting on a tribute being paid to the Sultan, whose nominal supremacy was thus acknowledged by the Egyptians. From this time the Turkish power, at least in Europe, became weaker and weaker till the Crimean war of 1854.

CHAPTER VII

Change in the French monarchy after the fall of Napoleon—Its replacement by a republic in 1848—Revolts in Italy and Hungary against Austria—Accession of Napoleon III. to the throne of France—Expedition of the French against Rome.

In 1821 Napoleon died at St. Helena, a fretful, melancholy exile, under the charge of the British Government. His remains were brought to France in 1840, and honoured with a most imposing funeral. Between these events a revolution had occurred in France in 1830. Charles the Tenth, the reigning king, and his dynasty were deposed and exiled by a domestic, even peaceful revolt, wholly unaided by foreign interference; and his cousin Louis Philippe, Duke of Orleans, assuming the more popular title of King of the French, instead of France, reigned in his stead. The new king, a prudent, pacific monarch, was always more anxious to please his subjects than the older branch of his family had shown themselves to be. Accordingly he and his numerous sons professed and perhaps may have felt a respect for Napoleon's memory rather surprising considering his usurpation of their family's royal rights.

The second funeral of Napoleon was celebrated with more than all the 'pomp and circumstance' due to a prince of the reigning house, rather than to a condemned exile who had usurped its hereditary rights. When he was no longer able to disturb France, his memory was honoured alike by the French Government and people as that of a national hero or benefactor. From the royal princes to the poorest peasants, and with the apparent sympathy even of the clergy, all classes of Frenchmen paid to Napoleon's memory the enthusiastic veneration due to an eminent patriot, champion, and martyr. One of the ablest of modern English writers, witnessing the extraordinary scene, describes it in his peculiarly graphic yet rather sarcastic style.[1]

The admiring sympathy for Napoleon's memory in other parts of Europe surprised some observant English travellers. He had been sometimes called the 'modern Attila,' the 'mighty murderer,' and 'the scourge of Europe' in Britain and probably in Germany. But in the more romantic or imaginative

[1] 'Accompanied by gun-banging, flag-waving, incense-burning, trumpets pealing, drums rolling, and at the close received by the voices of six hundred choristers, sweetly modulated to the tones of fifteen score of fiddlers. Then you saw horse and foot, jack-boots and bear-skins, cuirass and bayonet, national guard and line, marshals and generals all over gold, and high in the midst of all, riding on his golden buckler, Imperial Cæsar with his crown over his head, laurels and standards waving about his gorgeous chariot, and a million of people looking on in wonder and awe. His Majesty the Emperor and King reclined on his shield with his head a little elevated; *O vanitas vanitatum!* here is our sovereign in all his glory, and they fired a thousand guns at Cherbourg and never woke him.'—Thackeray's *Second Funeral of Napoleon.*

south of Europe all the misery his career had caused
was apparently forgotten in admiration of his many
victories and in pity for his fate, a pining exile in
charge of an English official, Sir Hudson Lowe.
This man, some said, treated the illustrious captive
with unnecessary harshness and rigour. Charles
Dickens in Genoa during 1844 saw Napoleon's last
days represented in a theatre, where, to his surprise,
general indignation was aroused against the British
and great sympathy for the French Emperor.[1] In
all his works this delightful author seldom mentions
history, and he never examines the causes of Italian
sympathy for Napoleon, which evidently astonished
him. His surprise at it after the woe he had caused
to Italy, and at the dislike shown to the English,
is expressed briefly without comment. Napoleon's
heroic and for a time victorious career had evidently
inspired an admiration among the French generally,
and among some Italians, which quite effaced dis-

[1] 'I went to see a play called *St. Helena, or, The Death of Napoleon*. Sir Yew ud se on Low (the 'ow' as in cow) was a perfect mammoth of a man compared to Napoleon, hideously ugly, with a monstrously disproportionate face and a great clump for the lower jaw to express his tyrannical obdurate nature. He began his system of persecution by calling his prisoner "General Bonaparte," to which the latter replied with the deepest tragedy, "Call me not thus! I am Napoleon, Emperor of France!" Throughout the piece Napoleon was very bitter on "these English officers" and "these English soldiers," to the great satisfaction of the audience, who were perfectly delighted to have Low bullied, and who, whenever Low said "General Bonaparte" (which he always did, always receiving the same correction), quite execrated him. It would be hard to say why, for Italians have little cause to sympathise with Napoleon, Heaven knows.'—*Pictures from Italy*.

approval of his destructive wars. Britain, however, in the estimation of the whole Continent, became far more powerful after Napoleon's final defeat. Among his many foes England had always been the most persevering and finally the most successful. As the chief, therefore, of the powers allied against him, the important though invidious responsibility of his personal custody was willingly entrusted by them to the British. Napoleon himself in his last days evidently attributed his final defeat chiefly to them; and his antipathy to his last conqueror, the Duke of Wellington, was curiously shown by leaving money to a man who had tried to shoot the Duke in Paris.[1]

The European pacification which ensued after Napoleon's fall in every way encouraged Britain and Russia to extend their foreign conquests as well as to consolidate, improve, and study those they had already made.[2]

Since Napoleon's time no dangerous foe to Britain has appeared in Europe. The Emperor Nicholas of Russia was on the defensive against the Christian powers during the Crimean war, and

[1] 'Napoleon left Cantillon a legacy of 400*l.* expressly in consequence of his having attempted to murder the Duke of Wellington.'—Alison's *History of Europe*, vol. i.
[2] 'Russian territories embrace an eighth of the habitable globe, and her influence is paramount from the Wall of China to the banks of the Rhine. Great as the acquisitions of the Muscovite power have been during the last thirty years, they have almost been rivalled by those of the British in India.'—Alison's *Europe*, vol. i.
Since Alison thus wrote about 1852, Russia, though checked in Europe by the Crimean war (1854), has extended and strengthened her power throughout eastern Asia.

British military energy was directed after the middle of this century chiefly against Asiatics and Africans. Among these the Affghans and Sikhs were more formidable than the Zulus or Kaffirs of Africa. The Sikhs were, indeed, defeated in pitched battles, while the Affghans, though always unable to face British discipline in the open field, still remain independent in their mountainous country, and of all eastern nations may be said to have resisted the British with the most success. While in India the latter were always successful in every war with its different races, the Russians were equally so against the brave Circassians in the Caucasus, and also against the Tartars of Khiva and Bokhara. All these central Asiatic tribes were less formidable foes to the Russians than the well-drilled, well-armed Sikhs were to the British, who encountered among them a certain amount of European discipline. Yet in these wars the two European powers, without sympathising with or assisting each other, were finally more or less successful; the Affghans, indeed, retained independence, but can hardly be considered an aggressive power like the Sikhs of former days. In their mountain region they remain midway to some extent between British possessions in north-western India and the Russians in southern Tartary; yet Britain and Russia, so permanently victorious in Asiatic warfare, have had, especially of late years, to turn attention to domestic foes, often among fellow countrymen, the Anarchists, Nihilists, and Dynamiters. These conspirators during Napoleon's career had made little sign and attracted little attention. After his fall France was ruled by different princes of the restored Bourbon family, professing a well-merited friendship for Britain. Prince de Joinville, however, a younger son of Louis Philippe, showed an opposite feeling. This sailor prince had indicated a dislike to England, which made him rather popular among some of the French; but his prudent, pacific father, always friendly to the European powers, steadily preserved the peace with them.

The next French conquest of importance was that of Algiers, which they completely subjected and have ever since retained, its Mohammedan population being either loyal or quite subdued.[1]

During many years a brave Arab chief, Abd-el-Kader, like Jugurtha of old against the Romans, successfully resisted the Europeans, but was at length captured. After this event the French, who had previously defeated both the Algerians and their Moorish allies, have remained in undisputed possession of their African territory, while the neighbouring state of Morocco, though nominally independent, is completely overawed by its French and Spanish neighbours. In the island of Madagascar, in Cochin China, and part of Africa, the French have recently made more settlements.

[1] 'Algiers is a valuable conquest to France, and it has proved of immense service to that country by affording a field for the exertion of its warlike qualities, and a school for the training of its officers and soldiers.'—Alison's *History of Europe*, chap. xlix.

In none of these remote countries, however, has French triumph hitherto aroused much European jealousy, whereas Napoleon's defeat had caused the recovery from French rule of every country he had conquered. The triumphant allied powers, bound together by their common success, were for some time afterwards friendly with one another. The British and Russians steadily pursued their foreign conquests with about equal success, though always without assisting, or even wishing well to, each other. The Prussians and the Austrians, after the humiliation of France, strengthened their power at home. Their discontented Polish subjects became rather more obedient, despite some occasional outbreaks, after the fall of Napoleon, from whom they had vaguely expected a national deliverance. The Prussians ruled few foreign subjects except some Poles, but the Austrians were supreme in northern Italy, where they were most unpopular with their subjects. Yet the Austrians as devoted Roman Catholics were acceptable to the Papacy and to the Italian clergy, who dreaded the republican spirit which in Italy was peculiarly hostile to Austrian rule. The reason for the almost universal dislike of the Italians to Austrian authority has been variously explained by differing politicians; but evidently, except by the Italian clergy, the Austrians were generally detested in both their Italian provinces of Lombardy and Venetia. In this national antipathy all Italy was apparently agreed, and the years '48-9 beheld the Italians in revolt against the Austrians.

At first the latter prevailed; the King of Sardinia, Charles Albert, who attempted to head the Italians, was defeated and abdicated his throne. His son and heir, Victor Emmanuel, became after a time king of United Italy, chiefly through the aid of the French, who, after a short period of republican rule, following the deposition of Louis Philippe, had made Louis Napoleon, the great Emperor's nephew, their ruler under the title of Napoleon III. The peaceful Louis Philippe was easily deposed early in 1848 by a republican revolt in Paris, almost without resistance. He was then an old man, and though surrounded by his sons in the vigour of their manhood, they were all banished from France.

At this time the two branches of the French monarchy, the eldest represented by the Duc de Bordeaux, or Comte de Chambord, and the younger by Louis Philippe and his family, were alike exiled from their country. The short rule of a weak republic, presided over by the amiable, accomplished Lamartine, followed by the brief authority of the more stern General Cavaignac, yielded eventually to the enduring popularity which the name of Napoleon maintained over the French nation. Cavaignac, though a brave distinguished officer, yet when opposed for the Presidency of the Republic by Louis Napoleon, was defeated, and again a representative of the loved name of Bonaparte amid enthusiastic applause guided the destinies of France. This prince's previous history was more like in some respects that of a fanciful or eccentric hero in romance, than of a practical ruler over thousands of warlike men.

When a young man, he had made two rash attempts to upset the rule of Louis Philippe, and when captured his life each time was spared by that monarch, who, though strangely undervalued by the French nation, was always on the side of civilisation, peace, and clemency. The way Louis Napoleon's second revolt was made, by entering Boulogne with an eagle trained to fly to the top of the great Napoleon's statue, with his eager proclamation in high-flown language recalling his uncle's career, proved how he estimated and tried to influence the ardent feelings of his excitable fellow countrymen. When captured and imprisoned, his two fantastic attempts at revolt in Strasburg and Boulogne were generally ridiculed throughout Europe. He, however, made a skilful escape from his French prison at Ham, and took refuge in London. Here he chiefly remained 'biding his time' in peace till recalled by the French people, the majority of whom, after the mild rule of Lamartine, had then used the more practical Cavaignac to control the Red or extreme republican party in Paris, and finally allowed the tried meritorious general to be defeated by the almost unknown Prince Louis Napoleon as President of their Republic. The latter was soon styled Prince-President, as a preparation for a higher title, and some time after, though not without resistance from Parisian Republicans, became sole ruler as the Emperor Napoleon III. He never showed the ambitious comprehensive designs of his uncle, and for some time seemed a calm, observant politician, always friendly to Britain.

The eventful year 1849 beheld Hungarians and the northern Italians in revolt against the Austrians. The former, however, defeated their foes in many battles, but at length the Russians interfered against them. By their assistance the Hungarian revolt was repressed and Austrian power re-established.

The Hungarians had some gallant Polish officers, Bem, Dembinski, and others, in their service, while the eloquent Louis Kossuth was their acknowledged head, though not a military man. The Russians, however, perceived in this formidable revolt a danger to themselves from its probable success in rousing their Polish subjects to rebellion. Allied thus with the Austrians by common interests and apprehensions, the Russians intervened at the very time when the Hungarians, headed by civil and military leaders of uncommon ability, were carrying all before them, finally reducing the Austrians to entreat Russian aid.[1]

In this case the interests of Russia and Austria were the same, as by suppressing the Hungarian revolt their Polish subjects were effectually deterred from following what might otherwise have formed

---

[1] 'Austria, distracted by an Italian and Hungarian revolt, was within a hair's-breadth of destruction, and the presence of 150,000 Russians on Hungarian plains alone determined the contest in favour of Austria. Immense was the addition which this decisive move made to the influence of Russia.'—Alison's *History of Europe*, vol. i.

an attractive example of revolutionary triumph. Napoleon III., as President of the French Republic, took no active part in this Hungarian war against the Austrians, but insisted on taking precedence of the latter in protecting the Pope, Pius IX., from revolutionary subjects in Rome. The French troops when before that city met with some resistance from the Italians, who with Mazzini and Garibaldi as their civil and military leaders ruled in Rome for a short time after the Pope's flight from thence to the kingdom of Naples. These two leaders were alike remarkable men, surprising contrasts to each other, yet united in wishing to effect Italian independence. Mazzini was a thorough consistent republican, of a thoughtful, intellectual, perhaps dreamy nature, while Garibaldi, though in some ideas agreeing with him, was yet personally attached to King Victor Emmanuel, whose courage in battle he could not fail to admire. While Garibaldi proclaimed Italy and Victor Emmanuel as his motto throughout Italy, Mazzini remained a confirmed republican.[1]

Amid these revolutionary perils, foreign and domestic intrigues, the mild philanthropic Pius IX. occupied an extraordinary position. His high pure

[1] ' Garibaldi, who in his countenance and bearing gave one the idea of the head of an Indian tribe, when danger was distant either reposed under his tent, or from the summit of a hill reconnoitred the ground, or went about in disguise and quite alone to explore it. When the trumpet sounded for battle he was everywhere giving orders, encouraging his men. Mazzini fancied himself the Providence of Italy; Rome was the fit atmosphere of Mazzini—to Rome he was attracted by his revolutionary mysticism.'—Farini's *History of Rome*, vols. iii. and iv.

character placed him above the power of moral or political misrepresentation. Though he preferred the Austrians to other allies as a nation of tried fidelity or devotion to the Papacy, he was at length induced to return to Rome under the guardianship of Napoleon III. The French proudly declared that their country was always the eldest son of the Church, and therefore the first who should protect its head from all foes either foreign or domestic. The Austrians, though more acceptable to the Papacy, as likely to be less troublesome protectors than the more arrogant or excitable French, had no desire to offend the latter, who therefore continued for some years to occupy Rome as the Pope's defenders against his revolutionary subjects. This apparent humiliation of the Papacy aroused alike the hopes of eager Protestants and the fears of devout Catholics. The time seemed to have come at last, so desired and so dreaded during centuries of Christian history, when Protestant enlightenment or heretical error, in the words of both partisans and opponents, would freely assail the power of the Papacy. The previous dangers to which it had been exposed in the end of the eighteenth century by the French republicans, partook largely of the nature of a foreign invasion. At that time no form of religion was proposed or encouraged by the reckless French Government. The alternative was only between Atheism, avowed or implied, and the retention of Roman Catholicism. The despotic violence of the French republicans in proscribing all religious worship under legal penalties naturally associated Catholicism in France and Italy with the free choice and will of the people, and directly republican rule ceased, Roman Catholicism was publicly restored in both countries. But after the very different revolutions of 1848 and of subsequent years, all Christian doctrines were free in Italy, while the political power of the Papacy was from this time prevented from controlling theological discussion. Thus the liberty so longed for by Protestants and apprehended by Catholics had at length arrived. Yet the result hitherto has neither gratified Protestant hopes nor justified Catholic fears. It seems proved by the religious state of France and Italy that political power is neither essential to Roman Catholicism, nor political freedom sure to promote Protestantism. Though all the former intolerant safeguards are now withdrawn from the arena of Christian discussion, the grand question between Roman Catholicism and many forms of Protestantism still divides the highest intellects throughout modern Christendom.

CHAPTER VIII

Alliance of Napoleon III. with Britain in the Crimean war against Russia—Establishment of the Italian kingdom—Civil war in the United States of America.

FRANCE, in the eventful reign of Napoleon III. as President, Prince-President, and lastly Emperor, gradually rose to almost the dignity and importance of his uncle's empire. The Emperor always maintained friendly relations with Britain despite reasons for ancestral enmity, and became its firm ally in the Crimean war. The causes of this remarkable contest at first seemed religious as well as political. The Russians, whose power everywhere had much increased since the fall of Napoleon, were always the religious champions and representatives of the subjected Greek Church. Their Emperor Nicholas I., a man of stern will and firm resolution, at first rather appealed to European powers to assist him in the dismemberment or rearrangement of the Turkish Empire, contemptuously styled by him or his followers the Sick Man, now in a hopeless state. France and Britain, however, resolved to support the Turks, who, as their endangered and therefore compliant allies, were more favourable to their interests than the arbitrary aggressive Russians were likely to prove, whose long desired conquest of Constantinople now seemed within the range of practical politics. This result may have been naturally desired by many Christian subjects of Turkey as well as by the little independent Greek kingdom. But they now beheld a complete change of policy in the western powers. France and Britain, whose allied forces had liberated Greece through destroying the Turkish fleet at Navarino some thirty years before, had since then obtained a vast accession of Mohammedan subjects, and therefore, though still allied, were rather changed in political views about Turkey. They each could boast of having more loyal Mohammedan subjects than ever, and were therefore more friendly to a Mohammedan government from which they had nothing to fear. Napoleon III. had soon the proud satisfaction of heading the French allied with the British against the Russians in the Crimea, and of effectually checking the progress of the great northern power whose stubborn resistance to his uncle had greatly aided to cause his overthrow.

This extraordinary alliance between the British and the French aroused among some of the wisest Englishmen hopes and expectations destined to be greatly falsified in subsequent history. The idea of the Crimean war being one against tyranny, in favour of European freedom, was believed by some who apparently forgot that the power and popularity of the Napoleon family were based rather on military ambition and enthusiasm than on philanthropy towards other nations.¹ The belief that the British and French in the Crimea were promoting liberty by maintaining the Turks against the Russians was certainly denied by the Christian subjects of the former. The Eastern question so strangely involved in that contest has always represented Turks and Russians as alike oppressing their respective subjects. The Poles and Circassians complain of Russian rule, while the Armenian and Greek subjects of Turkey complain with equal sincerity of Turkish oppression.

The Russians found themselves attacked, defeated, and politically thwarted by their former friends allied with the nephew and heir of their former foe. The Austrians, despite their preservation or rescue by the Russians during the Hungarian revolt in 1849, lent them no assistance. This apparent ingratitude may be partly explained, though perhaps not morally justified, by the fear they shared with other European powers of the increasing strength of their formidable neighbours.²

In this war, therefore, the Russians were left entirely alone opposed to allied British, French, and Turks. Their only friends were among the Christian subjects of Turkey in Europe and Asia, and

---

[1] 'France and England are in a state of intense progression, change, and experimental life. They are beginning to examine more distinctly than ever nations did yet the dangerous question respecting the rights of the governed, and the responsibilities of governing bodies, with the help of a good Queen and great Emperor.'—Ruskin's *Modern Painters*, chap. xviii.

[2] 'The Hungarian insurrection, by reviving the ambitious dreams of Russia, led to the invasion of Turkey and the Crimean war.'—Alison's *History of Europe*, vol. viii.

perhaps the kingdom of Greece. But these sympathisers were too weak to take part in warfare, and would have found it both impolitic and even dangerous to express their feelings.

The result of the war left the Turks in confirmed authority, the Russians being completely repulsed, their troops defeated, and their fleet in the Black Sea destroyed. The western powers naturally hoped that henceforth their influence over the Turks would be greater than ever, but in this expectation they have lately been rather disappointed by the independent bearing of the present Sultan. Since the Crimean war however, and even before it, the Turks in Europe gradually lost hold on some of their northern provinces, which have become almost independent or are under the protection of Austria. But no new European power has apparently gained strength by this gradual decline of the Mohammedans, as these provinces, chiefly inhabited by Christians of the Greek Church, or Roman Catholics, have established semi-independent governments of their own, in alliance with either Russia or Austria. The defeat of the Russians in the Crimea, however, was said to have caused or hastened the death of the Emperor Nicholas, and for a time it gave all the more strength and influence to the western powers.

It was the singular fate of Napoleon III. to make war upon the three most powerful of his uncle's enemies, the Russians, the Austrians, and the Prussians—to be successful against the first two, and to be completely vanquished by the last. Some years after his occupation of Rome in the Pope's behalf, he allied himself with Victor Emmanuel, King of Sardinia, aspiring to be King of Italy, against Austria, and defeated the Austrians in Lombardy. The Italian rulers of Naples, Tuscany, Parma, and Modena had to yield to the national desire for a united Italy, and left the kingdom. Garibaldi, though by some called a republican, was yet for a long time at least personally attached and obedient to Victor Emmanuel. In his name and cause, this singular and enterprising warrior freed Naples from its unpopular king, whose dominions, together with those of other Italian princes, were then formed into a new kingdom.

The Austrians, however, at first stubbornly resisted the allied French and Italians in Lombardy, but were at length forced in succession to give up their Italian provinces, first Lombardy, and, some time after, Venice. These finally became, like the rest of Italy, merged into one kingdom under Victor Emmanuel, and Italy still remains a free kingdom under his son King Humbert. Rome has now become the political capital of Italy, and yet the fixed residence of the Head of the Catholic Church. The King in the Quirinal Palace and the Pope in the Vatican thus co-exist as two sovereigns, spiritual and temporal, in the same most august of all cities. Neither Pius IX. nor his successor the present Pope Leo XIII. ever recognised the Italian King as lawful sovereign in Rome. Yet the latter's political supremacy there and throughout Italy remains undisputed, and Roman Catholicism continues to be the established faith, though the Papacy yet views the Italian monarchy with passive hostility.[1]

Since the fall of Napoleon I. Spain and Portugal were each agitated by civil wars between members of their own royal families, and have lost nearly all their American colonies. Neither country has, therefore, taken an active part for a long period in the affairs of Europe; but Greece and Italy, the two famed lands of ancient intellectual and martial glory, have again since Napoleon's time come to the front as independent monarchies among European nations, and the latter seems rising rapidly to the position of a strong power.

Prussia and Austria since the Crimean strife were at war with each other, in which the more modern superior artillery of the Prussians inevitably caused the utter defeat of the Austrians. After this contest, in which no other power interfered, Prussia annexed several small German countries, and the Prussian monarch assumed the title of German Emperor.

Napoleon III., whose victories over the Russians when he was allied with the British, and over the Austrians when allied with the Italians, had to

[1] 'Who can fail to be struck with the contrast between the modern Popes, who have been vainly appealing to all Catholic kings and peoples to restore Rome to their dominion, and the ancient Popes, at whose command, during nearly two centuries, the flower of martial Christendom poured into the Holy Land, and the chief sovereigns of Europe consented to subordinate all temporal objects to the recovery of Jerusalem from the infidel?'—Lecky's *Democracy and Liberty*, chap. vi.

some extent avenged his uncle's defeat, finally declared war against Prussia in 1870-1. This sanguinary though rather brief war ended in the complete defeat of the French, the surrender of Napoleon to the Prussians, and the establishment of a Republic by the French, which still remains their form of government.

All these destructive contests between Christian powers were of no avail to Mohammedan or non-Christian countries. The Moslem champions of former days no longer existed to take advantage of wars among Christians in the most civilised lands during this century. When European peace was restored, Prussia, now called Germany, strengthened her national defences without attempting much colonial conquest. France, exhausted after her defeat by the Germans, rested under a republic, slowly recovering her former power, while retaining Algiers together with settlements in Cochin China and Madagascar. Germany has lately turned some attention to foreign colonisation, to which objects Britain and Russia still devote their energies with great success. Between them some rivalry may exist as to which is most successful in ruling distant subjects of different races and religions. The former power and vast supremacy of pagan Rome, especially in Asia, seems now transferred to Britain and to Russia. Though they rule many lands almost unknown to the ancient Romans, there is yet a resemblance between the former submission of the gorgeous East to Rome, and the homage now paid to London and to St. Petersburg by loyal Asiatic subjects, while Rome has long been and continues more distinguished for ecclesiastical than political supremacy.

> Thence to the gates cast round thine eye, and see
> What conflux issuing forth or entering in;
> Prætors, proconsuls to their provinces
> Hasting, or on return, in robes of state;
> From the Asian kings, and Parthian among these;
> From India and the golden Chersonese,
> And utmost Indian isle Taprobane,
> Dusk faces with white silk turbans wreathed;
> All nations now to Rome obedience pay.
> *Paradise Regained*, book iv.

The Spaniards and Portuguese, once successful, enterprising explorers and discoverers, retain few colonies, and have practically retired within their European dominions. Their colonists in America have largely intermingled with native races in Mexico and parts of south America. These colonists have mostly succeeded in emancipating themselves, and have established independent governments, all republics, while professing the religion of their European ancestry. They do not seem hitherto, however, to excel, or even to equal, their Spanish or Portuguese ancestors in either accomplishments or in naval and military exploits.[1] As yet they take little, if any, part in European affairs, and, though

---

[1] 'In north America we witness a prosperous state of things, civil order and firm freedom. In south America the republics depend only on military force.'—Hegel's *Philosophy of History*, Introduction.

preserving the faith and most of the habits and customs of their ancestry, apparently show little of the intellect or enterprise of European races. But the United States, whose inhabitants are chiefly of British descent, though not showing much desire to conquer or rule other nations, are rising greatly in the estimation of the Old World as well as of the New. They steadily, even proudly, preserve independence, without much seeking to extend their territories. They rule no foreign nations, and except with Mexican neighbours, whom they always defeat, have seldom been at war with other countries. The terrible civil strife between their North and South provinces after the middle of this century ended in the victory of the former, but caused neither loss nor gain to their dominions.

This civil war was in great measure caused by the desire of the Northern States to abolish negro slavery, which the Southern advocated and preserved. The influence of literature in this contest was peculiar and evident. The pathetic story of 'Uncle Tom's Cabin,' by Mrs. Stowe, had previously called European attention to the cruelties alleged to be still practised or legalised towards negro slaves in the Southern States. The power and pathos of this remarkable work greatly interested and probably influenced the public mind in Europe and America, among English-speaking people. The Southern States were altogether outnumbered by the Northern, and after an heroic resistance had to yield. It was remarked that the Irish in the United States, almost unanimously hostile to Britain, took opposite sides in this American civil war.[1] Its result left both parties somewhat exhausted by their struggle, but ever since the United States have enjoyed domestic peace, while gradually becoming more influential in the estimation of the civilised world.

It was very fortunate for them that no other country took advantage of their civil war. When it was over, the United States were territorially unchanged. Though the Irish element chiefly in the towns is usually hostile to England, and many Americans eagerly sympathise with the Cuban insurgents against Spain, yet the Government for some time restrained its subjects, but at length declared war with the Spaniards in behalf of Cuban independence. That the Americans during the middle of this century are greatly improved in domestic administration, social habits, and national institutions, was admirably noticed by Charles Dickens. His dislike to much he saw and heard during his first visit to America, and his changed opinions about the Americans during his second one some twenty-five years later, he admits most emphatically.[2] In a public speech at New York in 1868, which he republished in subsequent editions of

[1] McCarthy's *Ireland since the Union*.
[2] He mentions in *American Notes* (p. 291) their persistence in coarse usages and rejecting the graces of life, and in *Chuzzlewit* makes his hero Martin, doubtless representing his own opinions, sarcastically ask, 'Is smartness American for forgery?' to which a 'cute Yankee replies with unconscious self-condemnation, 'Well, I expect it's American for a good many things that you call by other names in Europe. But you

'Chuzzlewit' and the 'Notes,' Dickens avowed himself 'astonished' by the vast improvements he found around him in the States since his first visit. The extreme covetousness which he and other writers have imputed to the Americans in private life is not manifested by their foreign policy. In fact, no American country, whether inhabited by British, Spanish, or Portuguese descendants, seems desirous for foreign conquest. Among Europeans retaining parts of America or its islands, the British in Canada, Jamaica, and other West Indian islands, the Dutch in some settlements, and the Spaniards and Portuguese in a few places chiefly represent European rule. Nearly all other countries in America are independent republics since the overthrow of the Brazilian empire, some years ago, by an almost bloodless revolt against an amiable, peaceful monarch. No invading army, no designs of conquest in any other part of the world, proceed from the American colonies. The large island of Cuba, now in determined revolt against the Spaniards, seeks and has at last received American aid, but shows no desire beyond its own liberation. It is in Europe alone now where the desire and the capacity for foreign conquest, extension, or triumph in Asia and Africa seem still increasing at the close of this century.

can't help yourselves in Europe. We can.' 'And do,' thought Martin, 'you help yourselves with very little ceremony, too.'— Chap. x.

CHAPTER IX

Russian progress in Asia—Louis Napoleon's early ambition—Secular spirit of modern European policy—Conquests and supremacy of Europeans in Africa.

Asia has now for some years been the chief field for Russian invasion or increasing influence, while the conquests of the British and the French seem rather increasing in both Asia and Africa. The Russian mode of conquest or territorial extension is peculiar, being nearly always by land with little assistance from naval operations.

From the boundaries of Sweden and Germany to the north of China, Russian dominion is undisputed, and seldom any territory once acquired is abandoned. When politically supreme and obtaining the requisite tribute, the Russians, like the ancient Romans, rarely interfere with the habits, customs, or religious opinions of obedient subjects.[1] This true secret of Russia's enduring power is freely

[1] 'Russia is singularly free from the passion of reforming the world, a passion accountable for many of the most extraordinary aberrations of English policy. She never interferes with the creeds, customs, or modes of thought that hold sway in the regions she desires to appropriate, unless they seriously thwart her desires. She treats all these things as so many national forces, which it is much wiser and better to direct and utilise than to resist. Hard and inflexible upon all points that

admitted now by the most intelligent and observant of her British rivals. The subjects of Russia generally become adherents, and practically assistants. This is more observable, perhaps, in Asia than in parts of Europe, where for a long time Polish subjects detested her rule, and some of whom may yet entertain vague hopes of freedom from it. But throughout Russia's immense Asiatic territories, not only subjects, but over-awed neighbours, the Persians and Tartars, are apparently at least more friendly than hostile to her increasing influence. At the recent coronation of the present Russian Emperor Nicholas II., the Tartar princes of Khiva and Bokhara respectfully attended, while the partly friendly, partly submissive bearing of the Orientals present showed the profound respect, probably founded on fear, with which the Russian sovereign was viewed by his Asiatic neighbours as well as subjects. Though the Crimean war was a serious check to Russian progress in Europe, yet since that time it is in Asia fast regaining its former energy. It is remarkable that even after the defeat of the Russians and the destruction of their Black Sea fleet, no advantage was taken of these reverses by Asiatic neighbours or subjects. The Turks had to entrust their political interests to the European western powers, and remained entirely on the defensive. When peace, therefore, was concluded between these powers and

she regards as important, she is nevertheless pliant, accommodating, and tolerant in all non-essentials.'—London *Times* Leader, April 16, 1897.

Russia, the Turkish dominions in Europe and Asia were left as before. Russia was indeed forced to cease for a time from further encroachment in Europe, but her increasing power throughout northern and parts of eastern Asia seems never to have been diminished, nor her aggressive policy relaxed in either of those directions.

A few years after the Crimean war, the Russians beheld the signal defeat of their French foes by the Germans. Napoleon III., whose admirers might have thought he had to some extent avenged his uncle's fall by accomplishing French triumphs over Austrians in Italy and over Russians in the Crimea, finally declared war against Prussia, the third great foe of Napoleon I. Whether his imperial nephew, had he been victorious, would next have made war on Britain and thus tried to complete French national retaliation for the Waterloo disaster, can never be known. Yet, judging from his remarkable words when a young prisoner of Louis Philippe, it seems he then identified himself and his designs with his uncle's defeat, as well as with his political position and system.[1] It is true that his policy towards Britain was always friendly, but the same might be said of his policy towards the other powers till he declared war with them. He began his political career as President, Prince-President, and

---

[1] 'I represent a principle, a cause, and a defeat. The principle is that of the sovereignty of the people, the cause is that of the Empire, the defeat is Waterloo.' Speech of Louis Napoleon after his capture at Boulogne, 1840.—Alison's *History of Europe*, chap. xiv.

lastly Emperor, with peaceful professions; but if his reign is impartially studied, it is not unlike the gradual fulfilment of a retributive line of policy, indicated by his youthful speech when a prisoner at Boulogne. In his last war with Germany he had no avowed ally, while the Prussians were joined by Bavarians and other German states. His defeat, surrender, the deposition of his dynasty, and the establishment of a weak French republic, greatly strengthened the victorious Prussians. They became united with other German states, now acknowledging the King of Prussia as Emperor of Germany.

From this time the French never made war in Europe, but retain Algiers, while their power in Cochin China, Madagascar, and other parts of Africa seems on the increase. The extension of European influence in a manner apparently permanent, distinguishes the closing years of this century. There seems now neither aggressive power nor political ambition among Asiatic or African races, nor throughout the vast continent of America. In eastern Africa several European nations have during recent years effected singular conquests and explorations. In the north, British or French influence extends from Egypt to Morocco inclusive, while the western coast is also partly over-awed by the British and the French. In the east the Italians, with British and Germans, extend their power, and though often resisted by the natives, their success appears steadily if slowly progressing. In the south the outlook seems more

disappointing to the cause of civilisation. To the
north of the Cape of Good Hope, now peacefully
held by the British, hostile factions or conflicts
continue. These are no longer between Europeans
and native tribes, but among rival descendants of
European races. The German, Dutch, and British
colonists no longer dread the Kaffir natives, who now
probably to their surprise behold the enmity and sometimes the warfare between hostile descendants of their
European conquerors. These disputes or jealousies,
if not increasing, are still unsettled, though it may be
reasonably hoped that the influence of European
nations at peace with one another may soon produce
a pacific spirit in their descendants, who have more
to lose than gain by wars with each other in a
savage country. The practical result of warfare
during this century, especially its latter half, has
decidedly strengthened European nations, at the
expense of all others with whom they contended.

No Mohammedan or non-Christian power seems
capable of assuming a seriously aggressive policy.
The east African nations, who still occasionally
resist Europeans and at times with temporary
success, remain on the defensive, and are evidently
though slowly yielding more and more. The Arabs
of Algiers attempt no revolt against their French
rulers; Morocco is thankful to be at peace with
France and Spain, and never attempts to recover the
towns on her coast still held by the Spaniards.

Throughout Asia, the Russians in the entire
north and the British in many parts of the south

reign absolutely, or exercise supreme influence. In the extreme east of Asia the Japanese have lately been victorious in a short war with their numerous Chinese neighbours. The former seem far more inclined to adapt themselves to European manners and customs than the Chinese Celestials, who between the British in the southern island of Hong Kong and the Russians and Germans on their northern frontier are in reasonable dread of European aggression.

Throughout India, Burmah, the rest of south-eastern Asia and the Indian Ocean, the Dutch in some islands, the French in Cochin China, the British in nearly all India, and the Portuguese in a few settlements, assert European supremacy, though without either alliance with each other or any formidable resistance from their various native subjects. In central Asia, the Persians, though nominally independent under their Shah or native king, are greatly over-awed by Russia on their northern frontier, and the Caspian Sea is now practically a Russian lake. The same may be said of the Khiva and Bokhara Tartars, who can hardly be called independent of Russia, but seem quite under her influence, if not in her absolute power.

All these Mohammedan races seem unable to unite in resisting the steady advance of the northern Christians. The spirit, enterprise, perseverance, and success of the Russians opposing Asiatic Mohammedans seem decisively proved as well as rewarded by their present pre-eminence in central Asia.

Were it not for British and French interference, Russian triumph over the Turks in Europe and Asia, from every sign of probability, would soon be complete, and certainly be aided and welcomed by a large subjected Christian population of Greeks and Armenians. The western powers in this century, unlike their history in others, are the sole cause of preserving, even of strengthening Mohammedan rule over Christian subjects. By their efforts in behalf of Moslem rule the Turkish Empire is maintained, while all other Mohammedan neighbours or subjects of Russia, the Persians, Circassians, and Tartars, have had to deal with her alone. The result is that the resistance of the brave Circassians in the Caucasus has been overcome, while Persians and Tartars are falling more and more under Russian influence.

Yet no important religious change seems hitherto to attend the immense triumphs of Christian political power throughout Asia. In fact, nearly all the wars in this century, from those of Napoleon I. inclusive, were entirely political or secular in their motives and results. Napoleon's wars spread chiefly throughout those lands where Christianity had replaced paganism, and where subsequently the Protestant Reformation had contended with Roman Catholicism, yet during his campaigns religious motives or designs were scarcely named. Christians of differing and formerly hostile denominations were in strict alliance against Roman Catholic France, yet with the complete approval of the Papacy.

In most if not all subsequent European wars,

the secular spirit prevailed, except in the Greek revolution of 1824. In that peculiar, interesting contest, a spirit rather like the Crusades seemed to animate the European powers, but only for a short time.[1] Political apprehensions, jealousies, or interests gradually divided the Christian Governments, tempting them to view a weak Mohammedan rule with a contemptuous yet selfish preference, which still preserves its unpopular sway over a large and mixed Christian population. During recent wars in Asia, Africa, or America, religious interests were considered quite secondary to political. British, French, and Russian triumphs over Asiatics and Africans have made little if any change in the religion of subjected peoples. Throughout America the frequent revolts in its southern parts, and the recent civil war in the United States, had no religious designs and made no change in religious opinions.

When the political wars of pagan Rome are recalled, it seems that those of this century in this respect resemble them more than any of the subsequent religious wars in Europe and Asia during the Middle Ages. The replacement of European paganism by Christianity, the triumph of Mohammedanism over large parts of Asia and Africa, and many more recent European wars or revolutions, usually displayed more or less devout enthusiasm, which caused great changes in the religious position

[1] 'Again, as in the days of the Crusades, the Cross had been triumphant over the Crescent.'—Alison's *History of Europe*, chap. xiv.

of the world. This century presents a marked change in Christian policy, especially among the British, the French, and the Russians. Except these no other nation has recently achieved foreign conquests of much importance. No candid foreigners will deny that the British, more in the variety than in the extent of their possessions, far exceed other nations. In this respect they resemble the Romans rather than the Russians. The British rule not only a greater number of Mohammedans than any sovereigns of that faith possess, but also govern heathen tribes in Africa; Brahmins, Buddhists, and Parsees in Asia; while the most civilised of modern Jews are among their loyal subjects. It is a remarkable fact that till this century, many parts of Asia were more known to Europe before America was discovered than during the intervening centuries.[1] The interest, profit, and power aroused and obtained by so wonderful a discovery evidently engrossed for a period the physical and mental efforts of the most enterprising European races. The history of this century, especially since the career of Napoleon I., shows the re-direction of European interest, thought, and ambition to the most famous countries of the Old World. The vast territories of America and Australasia remain comparatively remote from the politics of Europe, as Napoleon involved the latter's chief countries in national wars, leaving the rest of the world almost undisturbed. His short campaigns in Egypt and

[1] Caldecott's *Civilisation*, chap. ii.

Syria were entirely for European objects while continuing his warfare with the nations of Europe, but had little if any effect on the policy or position of Asiatics and Africans. Since his time European enterprise and conquest have been chiefly in Asia and Africa.

At the beginning of this century and long before it, the Turkish Empire comprised many of the important countries mentioned by ancient history in Europe, Asia, and Africa. During its progress this extraordinary empire has been gradually rather than rapidly losing more of its dominions. Its position, however, still combines religious and political interests of an importance unequalled by any other country.

The Eastern question is chiefly, though not entirely, confined to Turkey, and evidently engages the anxious attention of European powers more than that of any Mohammedan nation. Though in this century secular interests predominate in almost every war or political dispute, the Turkish Empire alone revives the mingled antiquarian, religious, and political interests of classic and of Scriptural history. Again the ancient, time-honoured names, cities, and lands comprised in its varied dominions arouse the eager interest while tempting the political ambition of the chief European nations.

This question presents the peculiar difficulty of greatly dividing the opinions of those who ought to know equally well about it. While some Eastern travellers and politicians dread beyond measure any

Russian progress in Asia, others welcome it as practically aiding the British in diffusing European ideas and civilisation. It is a subject indeed which apparently interests Mohammedans less than it does the Christian powers, though, in fact, it concerns the former most of all. But such seems the present weakness of Mohammedans in a political, though not in a religious or a numerical sense, that the Eastern question is more examined and likely better understood in London and in St. Petersburg, than in any non-Christian capital. Its settlement may be said to lie really in the power of European rulers to whom most Asiatics and Africans are now directly or indirectly subject. The present time seems one which both religious zealots and political enthusiasts of former ages longed to behold. Yet the present race of men apparently turn it to a very different account from what their ancestry would have expected or sanctioned. Thus the objects of the Crusades abandoned by Christian rulers after long and sanguinary contests are virtually in the power of their successors, yet now only cause hostility or jealousy between them. They prefer and really maintain Mohammedan rule even in the land formerly called the holy one of the Christian faith, so completely have national apprehensions and political rivalry replaced religious enthusiasm or ancestral ideas of religious obligation in the Christendom of the present day.

CHAPTER X

Increasing success of British rule in foreign colonies and dominions—Historical enmity of Ireland to British authority—Eloquence of Irish revolutionists—Comparative absence of eloquence during British revolutions.

AMONG European races, the British have for some time usually taken the lead in foreign questions. They have national interests or possessions in all parts of the globe, while over their vast and varied empire the sun is said never to set.[1] Though they lost possession of the United States, and recently ceded the Ionian Islands to Greece, these losses and concessions did not diminish British power and influence, yet their possessions in Europe have not been increased for many years. They have lately obtained the island of Cyprus from the Turks, but this acquisition involves less territory than what they gave up in the Ionian Islands. Since the fall of Napoleon they retain Malta and Gibraltar, the latter rather to the irritation of the Spaniards. Among their varied subjects some non-Christians

[1] 'The English have undertaken the weighty responsibility of being the missionaries of civilisation to the world, for their commercial spirit urges them to traverse every sea and land.'—Hegel's *Philosophy of History*, sect. iii.

are among the most loyal. The Mohammedans,
Brahmins, and Parsees in India often show more
dislike to each other than to their Christian rulers.
In Canada, amid some discontent, the people on the
whole evidently prefer British authority to that of
their republican neighbours in the United States.

Of all British subjects, however, perhaps the
most deeply disaffected, and really opposed to
England at home and abroad, are derived from or
found in Ireland, though dwelling beside some
of the most loyal adherents of Britain. Three
centuries elapsed between the times of the poet
Edmund Spenser and the historian Macaulay,
yet there is a decided resemblance in the allusions of these writers to Ireland and the Irish.[1]
Each views that island from a British standpoint,
which, however true in some respects, can be
hardly free from national prejudice or predilection.
To the refined poet and the learned historian,
Britain represented progressive enlightenment, and
Ireland comparative ignorance or hostile prejudice.
But the English, and subsequently the British
invaders, representing England and Scotland among

[1] 'They say it is the fatal destiny of that land that no
purposes whatsoever that are meant for her good will prosper.
... It is a nation ever acquainted with wars, though but
among themselves. They have never been taught to learn
obedience unto laws, scarcely to know the name of law.'—
Spenser's *View of Ireland*.

Macaulay apprehensively writes: 'When the historian turns
to Ireland his task becomes peculiarly difficult and delicate.
His steps (to borrow the fine image used by a Roman poet) are
on the thin crust of ashes, beneath which the lava is still
glowing.'—*History of England*.

the native Irish, were mostly very different from these accomplished writers, who were only appreciated by a learned minority in Britain. It is not uncommon among politicians, when dealing with Ireland, to rather confound loyalty or disloyalty with the moral duties. Some openly declare it the bounden duty of Irishmen to detest or oppose British rule, while others apparently consider that attachment to it is a duty in itself. Political opinions, therefore, in Ireland are often placed among moral obligations, and the right of private judgment denied on a subject which specially claims it. Among the disloyal, those who favour British rule are often thought traitors to their oppressed country and forgetful of ancestral injury. Among the loyal those who deny the advantage of British authority are often thought unworthy of trust or confidence. In no country has British power been so unpopular as in the greater part of Ireland. Travellers returning from the Continent, or the British colonies, often express surprise at hearing British laws condemned in Ireland, which they compare favourably with those of the countries they have visited. Though Britain derives many most able and useful subjects from Ireland, it is evident that a large number, if not the majority, judging from their parliamentary members, dislike England to a degree unknown in any other part of her dominions. Thus during even recent foreign wars, Irishmen at home and abroad often sympathised with the foes of Britain, while some of their

bravest fellow countrymen ardently supported the
British against the same enemies. The Irish are
remarkably divided, whether Protestant or Catholic,
in their views of British government. The majority
of their representatives, and a large portion of the
press, denounce the British as Ireland's historical
oppressors, who never had, and some say never can
have, a moral right to Ireland's loyalty or obedience.
These men in speeches and newspaper articles continually denounce England, her rule and history, and
sometimes in as eloquent English as her warmest
admirers are able to command.[1]

It might surprise intelligent foreigners to hear
England often abused and censured with all the
force and energy of the English language. Yet
among other Irishmen, even among the relatives
and co-religionists of England's bitterest foes, arise
some of her most able, efficient, and trusty supporters
in the army, navy, police, and on the judicial bench.
Among the Protestant population the majority are,
as might be expected from history, sincerely loyal to
British rule.

Among the Catholics the majority seem to still
dislike it, especially in election times, when they
usually denounce or deplore its influence. The latest
Irish revolts since 1798 inclusive were apparently for

---

[1] 'Every popular government has experienced the effect of rude or artificial eloquence. The coldest nature is animated, the firmest reason is moved by the rapid communication of the prevailing impulse, and each hearer is affected by his own passions and by those of the surrounding multitude.'—Gibbon's *Decline and Fall*, chap. xx.

political rather than religious objects. The great Irish surrender or exchange of national separation for religious supremacy in the reign of James II. is emphatically described by the most eloquent British historian of this century, and is very instructive to those who wish to understand Irish sentiment even to the present time.[1] On that memorable occasion the Irish majority, for centuries the national foe of England, who had never really owned the authority of English sovereigns, became, by the command or influence of their clergy, transformed into the deposed British king's last army. Since the political triumph of British Protestantism, the Irish majority were inevitably subjected, and, they declared, cruelly oppressed, by a minority of fellow countrymen under the sanction of British power. The Irish Protestants, mostly in Ulster, descended from British colonists, had always shared or followed the political and religious changes in England and Scotland. To make Ireland their adopted country, as like Britain as possible, was always their object, and they to some extent accomplished it. The Irish majority had, of course, totally different views. All hopes of ancient Celtic nationality, to which they had vaguely

[1] 'The Reformation had been a national as well as a moral revolt. It had been an insurrection of all the branches of the great German race against an alien domination. The patriotism of the Irish had taken a peculiar direction. The object of their animosity was not Rome but England, and they had special reason to abhor those English sovereigns who had been the chiefs of the great schism, Henry VIII. and Elizabeth. The new feud of Papist and Protestant inflamed the old feud of Saxon and Celt.'—Macaulay's *History of England*, vol. i.

clung long after the disappearance of the ancient
heathenism, now yielded to the cause and interests of
Roman Catholicism. France, Italy, and Spain were
chiefly looked to for the education of their clergy
and for the relief of all who could afford to visit
those lands where their oppressed faith was the
prevailing, and sometimes the persecuting, religion.[1]

While the subsequent accession of German
Protestant princes to the British throne increased
the friendly intercourse between Britain and the
north of Ireland with Germany, the same cause
naturally inclined the Irish majority to visit and
communicate with the south of Europe, which
preserved Roman Catholicism. British rule in
Ireland, however, from the accession of William III.
continued undisputed till the rebellion of 1798. The
Jacobite insurrections of 1715 and 1745 in Scotland
caused no Irish rising in favour of the son or
grandson of James II. The 1798 revolt, though
depending on a Catholic majority, was chiefly planned
and headed by Protestant leaders. Their objects were
exclusively political, while those of the majority of
their followers were exclusively religious. The leaders
viewed the new republics of France and America
with admiration, longing to see Ireland follow their
example. Religious interests in this strange revolt

[1] 'The sectaries of a persecuted religion, depressed by fear,
animated with resentment, and perhaps heated by enthusiasm,
are seldom in a proper temper calmly to investigate, or candidly
to appreciate, the motives of their enemies, which often escape
the impartial and discerning view of those who are placed at a
secure distance from the flames of persecution.'—*Decline and
Fall*, chap. xviii.

BRITISH RULE AND MODERN POLITICS 103

were at first apparently ignored. Loyal Roman Catholics and Protestants were alike opposed to rebellious Catholics and Protestants, and for a short time religious motives were rarely manifested. British success in suppressing this revolt yet left Irish parties practically little changed. Ever since that time revolutionary speeches, books, and newspapers have been enthusiastically admired or condemned among Ireland's divided population. As in 1798, however, the mass of the disloyal are Roman Catholic, while some of their most able leaders are Protestant. The religious question in Ireland since 1798 inclusive has never been the chief motive of the most influential Irish laymen. The singular spectacle has occasionally been seen of Irish Protestant rebels to Britain arrested, tried, and sentenced by Catholic police, lawyers, and judges, a state of things almost unknown till the revolt of 1798.

During a long disastrous succession of revolutionary plots, meetings, and speeches, British supremacy in Ireland, though preserved to the present time, has never been really popular with the Irish masses. British victories abroad were not usually thought by them to be Irish victories, despite the valour and aid of many loyal Irishmen in achieving them. This partial alienation in national sentiment or sympathy is peculiarly remarkable in Ireland. Whilst many able Irishmen in almost every profession add to the glory and often to the power of the British Government, an Irish majority, or at least a very large number, never identify themselves with British triumph, but in speeches, newspapers, or histories, constantly denounce England, attributing to her rule directly or indirectly every injustice or misfortune. Ireland, therefore, has always been, and continues to be, viewed by the enemies of Britain as the chief, if not the only, instance of complete failure in ruling alienated subjects, eagerly abusing her authority in every foreign country with which their communication is possible. It may be specially observed in Ireland's history that political opinions or differences are often popularly viewed as questions of morality. By some Irish it is thought a patriotic duty either to praise or denounce the British monarchy. Among a great number, if not a majority, it is believed that what should be really a matter of private opinion or individual judgment is a question of morals. This party spirit, practically denying the right of private judgment, often inspires or actuates people who may not openly express it. Usually this intolerance of sentiment remains almost a concealed principle till political excitement such as a parliamentary election occurs. Then people, comparatively reasonable at other times, suddenly show a religious or political vehemence at the very time when moderation is most needed for the good of their country.

Throughout the wide and varied British dominions there is no country where English rule has always been so eloquently censured as in Ireland. The poet Edmund Spenser, in Elizabeth's reign, greatly admired Ireland's scenery, 'a most sweet and lovely country,' with its bays and harbours mostly opposite England, 'as if inviting us to come into them.'[1] Whatever may seem the silent meaning of inanimate nature in this respect, it is sufficiently evident that no corresponding invitation to British curiosity or enterprise was often given by the natives of the soil, whose hereditary enmity to England, and afterwards to Britain, has animated a large number of them from early history to the present time. Even now, Ireland's members in the British Parliament usually show intense enmity to British rule. It may surprise intelligent foreigners, unless profound historical students, to hear the noblest resources of the English language energetically turned not only against British rule, but against British interests, by eloquent Irish subjects. In fact, the whole history of Ireland's connection with Great Britain is specially remarkable for the brilliant eloquence rather than the martial valour with which British authority has been chiefly opposed by generations of able illustrious Irishmen. Eloquent words and heroic deaths in Ireland's history often distinguished rebels against England, who seldom showed much courage till at the last moment, a time when that of the bravest is put to the greatest test. The remarkable historical intercourse of England with Scotland and with Ireland may reasonably invite comparison respecting 'the predominant partner's' conduct to both the others. The friendly cordial union always existing between

[1] *View of Ireland.*

England and Scotland during and since the reign of James I., whose peculiar position made him lawful king of both, was never disturbed in either country by any design of restoring national separation.[1]

The civil wars in the next reign between Charles I. and the Parliament divided Scottish as well as English subjects. King and Parliament had their adherents and opponents among each. No idea of national separation was shown by either party. The final restoration of the British monarchy under Charles II. was eagerly welcomed by a British majority. In the subsequent civil war between James II. and William III. the Scottish and the English as before took opposite sides, but national division between them was never contemplated. In James II. the English and the Scottish alike recognised the lawful heir to an undisputed monarchy. It is true that a brief though gallant revolt of the Scottish Covenanters against Charles II. might have been vaguely connected with republican designs; but it was the rebellion of a small though brave conscientious minority, never expressing the feelings of the majority, who earnestly opposed the movement, which was soon politically suppressed.

[1] 'Scotland was now joined by her stronger neighbour on the most honourable terms. She gave a king instead of receiving one. She retained her own constitution and laws.'—Macaulay's *History of England*, vol. i.

CHAPTER XI

England's historical relations with Scotland and with Ireland —Religious intolerance in these countries during the time of Cromwell—Disputes among rival Protestant sects who all oppose Roman Catholicism.

THE policy of England towards Scotland and Ireland during and since the Reformation is an important subject for historical students. All their previous wars or transactions with each other are chiefly important or interesting to poets and to antiquaries. Since the religious divisions in western Europe, Britain and Ireland, representing Roman Catholics and Protestants of different sects, after a long period of bigoted animosity, became a united empire, extending and strengthening foreign conquests in distant lands, especially in Asia. Protestantism, politically established by James I. in the three kingdoms, prevailed in the reign of Charles I., that of the Commonwealth under Cromwell, and of Charles II., though in different forms. In England Episcopacy was the most influential, and in Scotland Presbyterianism, now its established faith, yet for a short time each had to yield to the Independent sect represented by Cromwell, who, soon superseding

the Parliament, though at first its general, governed
the three kingdoms with almost absolute power.
This extraordinary man, a born ruler by nature,
literally overcame all political opposition, and his
brave Independent soldiers were therefore for some
time completely supreme ; but they represented a
minority in England, a smaller minority in Scotland,
and in Ireland were almost unknown. Their illustrious literary champion, Milton, gloried in Cromwell's success. To him the triumphant Protector
was the avowed incarnation of a perfect ruler. All
opposing him, whether English Prelatists, Scottish
Presbyterians, Irish Roman Catholics, or even Irish
Protestants, he considered as alike enemies to the true
interests of England.[1]

Milton, almost alone in literary culture among a
warlike, bigoted minority, for a time abandoned his
noble poetry, devoting attention to political discussions, praise, or censure with an eager, even
coarse vehemence, little resembling the refined
sublimity of his immortal verses. His connection
with Cromwell in ruling or trying to influence the

---

[1] 'We have now to deal with another sort of adversaries.
These write themselves the presbytery of Belfast, a place better
known by the name of a late barony than by the fame of these
new doctrines, or ecclesiastical deeds, whose obscurity till now
never came to our hearing. By their actions, we might rather
judge them to be a generation of Highland thieves and Redshanks, who being neighbourly admitted, not as the Saxons by
merit of their warfare against our enemies, but by the courtesy
of England, to hold possession in our province, a country better
than their own, have, with worse faith than those heathen,
proved ingrateful and treacherous guests to their best friends
and entertainers.'—*Articles of Peace with Irish Rebels.*

English people is a remarkable incident in the national history. In these two great men, practical and imaginative Englishmen were represented in the highest degree perhaps ever known. Each was at the time unrivalled in his very different talents, and yet was singularly devoid of the other's peculiar gifts. Milton in thought, taste, and training was nothing of a soldier, while a more unpoetical and thoroughly practical person than Oliver Cromwell could hardly be imagined.

In their exciting period of British history, these illustrious men were firmly united in politics, and for a short time, directly or indirectly, ruled their country in the name of popular liberty. Yet they only represented a small and never popular minority of their fellow countrymen. It is remarkable how Dr. Johnson and Macaulay, taking such different views of Cromwell, yet agree that he quite superseded the 'liberties' of England by his sole, almost despotic authority.[1] Amid a party of eager zealots, brave, enthusiastic, and often very ignorant, the intellectual poet presented a marked contrast. Milton fully appreciated his glorious poetical predecessor, Shakespeare, whose works were generally condemned or

[1] 'Cromwell had commenced monarch himself under the title of Protector, but with more than kingly power. Nothing is more just than that rebellion should end in slavery.'—Johnson's *Life of Milton.*

Macaulay owns that: 'Cromwell was able to overpower and crush everything that crossed his path, to make himself more absolute master of his country than any of her legitimate kings had been. Few, indeed, loved his government, but those who hated it most, hated it less than they feared it.'—*History of England*, chap. i.

disapproved of by his party. He was usually a firm friend to mental freedom, yet allowed himself perhaps unconsciously to sometimes resemble his political foes in bitter, unjust intolerance. He sympathised with the persecuted Italian philosopher Galileo, whom he visited in a prison in Italy; and he deplored in beautiful verse the fate of some Piedmontese victims of religious bigotry. But when politically opposed even by fellow Protestants or fellow countrymen, Milton reveals much of the persecuting spirit which he so warmly condemned in others. His stormy period was indeed hostile, if not fatal, to real liberty of thought and expression. Thus, while Milton aided and vindicated what he believed the cause of national freedom and glory represented by Cromwell, a majority of his fellow countrymen took a different view of the Protector's vigorous rule. Accordingly, soon after Cromwell's death, his memory, instead of being honoured like that of William Tell among the Swiss, of Washington among the Americans, and of Napoleon among the French, became the object, especially in London, of popular execration, as even his warmest admirers admit, though with indignant surprise.[1] The British gentry detested Cromwell's very name, and the London popu-

[1] 'The Commons were more eager than the King himself to avenge the wrongs of the Royal House. All London crowded to shout and laugh round the gibbet where hung the remains of a prince who had made England the dread of the world. When some of those men who had sat in judgment on their king were dragged on hurdles to a death of prolonged torture, their last prayers were interrupted by the hisses and execrations of thousands.'—Macaulay's Essay on *Mackintosh*, pp. 86-7.

lace, in fact the people generally, showed no feeling but abhorrence towards his memory, and approved the executions of his chief parti ans.

'The execrations of thousands' in the London streets accompanied the deaths of these men, who, during Cromwell's life, were in his name almost absolute over Britain and many parts of Ireland. The enmity of British and of Irish Roman Catholics was hardly ever conciliated by Cromwell. He was openly hostile to their faith, and seems to have fully shared the most intense British prejudices against the Irish race. That his accomplished ally, Milton, should be unjust towards Roman Catholics, was perhaps inevitable considering the mutual intolerance animating them and all Protestants at this time. But when he writes with almost equal bitterness against fellow Protestants about the political question of the execution of Charles I. and in his turn accuses the defeated Royalists of the 'guilt of rebellion,'[1] he proves that his party desired supremacy without much reference to popular opinion. Hence at 'the wild Carnival[2] of the Restoration of Charles II.' the sight that the English, especially in London, presented, was that of a delighted nation, welcoming deliverance from tyranny, instead of really receiving a profligate young prince, whose only claim to their respect was his royal descent. It is evident, even were it not owned by Cromwell's admirers, that his military rule was most unpopular except among his devoted soldiery.

[1] Prose works. [2] Macaulay.

While he lived, to cheer, lead, and reward them, he had nothing to fear but the danger of assassination, of which he was latterly in constant dread.

When he was gone, the rule of his soldiery vanished with him, and Charles II., gay and merry, 'witty himself, and the cause of wit in other men,' to quote the words of Falstaff, seemed a delightful change from the stern gloom of Cromwell's military dictatorship.[1]

It seems specially reserved for the British intellect in this century to consider Cromwell and Milton as promoters and lovers of their country's freedom. Yet, judging from the manifestations of Britain at their period, Cromwell's death almost caused a national thanksgiving except among a small minority, probably composed of his former soldiers, while the restoration of the monarchy was welcomed in Britain by an immense majority. Though most Irish Catholics may have disliked British authority when wielded by kings, it was far more odious to them when wielded by Cromwell, who was always their inveterate enemy. He, in the name of British civilising liberty rather than of national conquest like his royal predecessors, made an almost exterminating war upon the Irish. This

---

[1] 'The temper of soldiers, habituated at once to violence and to slavery, rendered them very unfit guardians of a legal or even a civil constitution. Valour will acquire their esteem and liberality will purchase their suffrage, but the first of these merits is often lodged in the most savage breasts, the latter can only exert itself at the expense of the public, and both may be turned against the possessors of the throne, by the ambition of a daring rival.'—*Decline and Fall*, chap. vii.

warfare Macaulay describes in a rather singular manner.[1] He denies nothing of its atrocity or bigoted motives, yet appears so overcome by 'hero-worship' or personal admiration for Cromwell that he can hardly blame a relentless policy which in opponents he would denounce with powerful eloquence, and his classing Irish Catholics with ancient Syrian idolaters seems like a re-echo of the fanaticism of Cromwell's soldiery, and equally inconsistent with the state of Europe at that time or with his own historical knowledge. Roman Catholicism, though repudiated by the most intellectual minds in Britain and north Germany, remained the faith of the most learned men throughout France, Spain, Italy, and Austria. These countries often afforded literary as well as religious instruction to the Irish clergy. Theological opinion in Europe was remarkably divided at this time ; learned and ignorant men were found in all its divisions. It was no contest between education and ignorance, but between educated men in the most civilised countries, who were alike followed or trusted by a comparatively ignorant majority. The religious dispute was carried on by both sides with a bitterness even among intellectual men which often, if not usually, overcame justice

[1] 'He waged war resembling that which Israel waged on the Canaanites, smote the idolaters with the edge of the sword, so that great cities were left without inhabitants. Under that iron rule the conquered country began to wear an outward face of prosperity.'—*History of England*, vol. i.

Yet rural improvement might hardly compensate for the utter desolation of great cities, which Macaulay owns was one result of his hero's policy.

I

and charity in their conduct, motives, and legislation. Some, even learned Roman Catholics, hardly scrupled to class or confound 'heresy' or 'schism' with utter atheism, equally unpardonable by the Creator, while some learned Protestants, among their many divisions, ranked the faith of their ancestry among the heathen idolatries of ancient times.

This last classification practically influenced Cromwell, as admitted even by his modern admirers. Milton's similar abhorrence of Catholicism seems yet more extraordinary in so accomplished a man, who must have known better than Cromwell that this form of Christianity was still the belief of some among the highest intellects in Europe. It also remained the religion of a British minority in all classes. The feelings of the Dukes of Norfolk and other aristocratic families among British Roman Catholics must indeed have been severely tried at hearing their ancestral faith classed with heathenism by these illustrious Englishmen, the one representing the power, and the other the intellect, of England in the highest existing degree. During the Reformation in Britain and on the Continent, it is a remarkable fact that well-educated men, endowed with superior learning, knowledge, and information, rarely used these gifts in favour of toleration or calm reasoning whenever religious differences were aroused. Their mutual prejudices naturally influenced political legislation, which at such a time practically enforced their bigoted ideas. The ignorant majority in all parties amid these doctrinal contests were often induced or encouraged by the more educated to view religious opponents with a prejudiced aversion, the result of partial knowledge and sectarian bitterness.

The cruel legislation sanctioned for a time by most, if not by all, the Christian powers in matters of religious opinion was clearly the work of the most educated men of the time, enforced or obeyed by ignorant or fanatical subordinates. Years after the actual conflicts of the Reformation ceased in Europe, when its various countries had either established Protestantism or successfully retained Roman Catholicism, men's minds began, it must be owned very gradually, to calmly examine during a national peace the conduct of their respective ancestry in times of religious dispute and theological argument. The result of this examination in its slow development in European history is described by an able living historian as the secularisation of politics more or less throughout western Europe.[1] This change was virtually the peaceful transfer of legislative power from theological to political influence. It was naturally dreaded by some devout men and welcomed by the sceptical. The result, even to the present time, in the religious position or philosophy of Europe, has in great measure falsified the predictions of both. Differing versions of religion, once utterly hostile to one another, now peacefully co-exist in the same countries and nations. Among theological divisions, sceptics and religious zealots

[1] Lecky's *Rationalism*.

alike enjoy liberty not only of thought but of expression. Yet this liberty has in no country obtained political nor probably numerical supremacy.

This result contradicts the expectation of both the religious and the irreligious, who remember the zealous intolerance of early Christian political history. This century has proved, more especially towards its close, that their anticipations have hitherto, at least, been mistaken. Nearly all the religions ever known except the Paganisms of Greece, Scandinavia, and Arabia are found to coexist sometimes in the same lands, neither converting nor being converted to any decisive extent.

This secure position of various religious beliefs at a time when international intercourse is so general and political freedom so largely extended, may well claim the attention of thoughtful men. It is a remarkable contradiction to previous religious history, even since the political establishment of Christianity. The former anxiety of most religious minds not only to preserve their own faith, but to eradicate by every means what they thought the false faith of others, was a leading principle in civilised history for centuries. Any apathy on this subject was often thought by the devout as sure to produce either dangerous superstitions or complete atheism. Yet of recent years, especially during the last half of this century, this religious fervour has practically almost vanished from Christian lands. Doctrines ignoring, altering, or opposing Christianity, like Buddhism, Mohammedanism, and Judaism, are professed by some estimable, well-educated men. Yet Christianity in its moral and political position appears to lose nothing in consequence. It is the prevailing political ruler of all the civilised and a great part of the uncivilised world. But it has lost or voluntarily abandoned nearly all its former persecuting or exacting character. It is now the fountain of national justice—in fact the arbiter of this world's political destiny; while protecting doctrinal foes or unbelievers with the same firmness, justice, and discrimination with which it protects its most faithful and obedient votaries.

CHAPTER XII

Religious differences in Britain and Ireland after the restoration of the British monarchy—Northern Europe, except Russia, which adhered to the Greek Church, became Protestant, while its southern countries except Greece remained Roman Catholic.

THE restoration of Charles II. and the first part of the reign of his brother James II. beheld Britain and Ireland comparatively free from religious persecution. In Scotland, indeed, a partial revolt of the extreme section of Presbyterians proclaimed their apprehension of the political influence of the Church of England. This rebellion, soon suppressed, though disgraced by murder and cruelty on the part of both the Government and of the insurgents, was one of those strange contests in which neither party was really on the side of rational liberty, but alike wished to deny to others what they demanded for themselves. The insurgents in this respect were avowedly more intolerant than the Government. One of the chief causes of their revolt was their anger at the mere toleration of any other form of faith but their own in Scotland. In the end of the reign of James II. these religious discontents and jealousies in the three kingdoms rose to a height before unknown, but were no longer involved with the political divisions of the reign of Charles I. No republican champions appeared in either Britain or Ireland. This form of government was evidently not popular in these countries. All parties at this time advocated monarchy, and the question of sovereignty lay between rival claimants to a throne, without any idea of a republic. Cromwell's arbitrary power, his imperious dismissal of the republican parliament of which he was the paid general, and his subsequent almost absolute rule over Britain and Ireland, had practically prevented republicanism obtaining a fair trial in England. Men approving that system might well say that Cromwell, though not 'propped by ancestry,' was yet, as Macaulay admits, a more arbitrary monarch than any of his royal predecessors. British republicans, however, seem to have politically disappeared. Indignation, deep and permanent, was constantly expressed against the Protector's deeds and memory by ardent Royalists, but real republicanism made little sign of life. The fact owned by Macaulay of Cromwell's seeking popularity with the army alone, and 'breaking' or quarrelling with all other sections of his fellow countrymen, may recall Gibbon's account of a like policy in the Roman Emperor Caracalla.[1]

No one, unless influenced by party spirit, would

[1] 'One dangerous maxim worthy of a tyrant was remembered and abused by Caracalla, " To secure the affections of the army, and to esteem the rest of his subjects as of little moment." As long as his vices were beneficial to the armies, he was secure from rebellion.'—*Decline and Fall*, chap. vi.

for a moment class the illustrious English Protector with one of the worst Roman emperors. But their policy as described by Gibbon and Macaulay displays in this respect some resemblance, as Cromwell had really violated republican principles as much as he had those of the Royalists. There was nothing republican in his deeds or sentiments directly he ceased to be the nominal champion of that party. His wishing his son Richard to succeed him as Protector, a man who had neither the ability nor the inclination for ruling, showed that he desired the monarchical spirit should be transferred from the House of Stuart to that of Cromwell. Oliver practically wished his son to be viewed as a new Prince of Wales, heir apparent by virtue of birth alone to supreme authority. In Richard Cromwell's peculiar case, however, his personal feelings evidently agreed with those of the British nation generally. He had no desire for power, and of his own free will became one of the most peaceful among the subjects of the restored monarchy, which the wonderful genius of his father had mainly contributed to overthrow for a time. The troubled reign of James II. gradually became as interesting from a religious as from a political point of view. It was a time when Scotland and Ireland from different causes had substituted religious interests for political or national designs. The Scottish nation, except a small minority, acknowledged James. He was generally considered their lawful king, descended from a long line of national ancestors, as well as King of

England. Like his three predecessors, grandfather, father, and brother, he represented the same royal house acknowledged by both England and Scotland. Thus British loyalty was his birthright, and his becoming a Roman Catholic finally obtained for him the hitherto unknown national loyalty of Ireland to a British sovereign.

The Irish majority in his time had begun more than ever to entrust their political views or interests to their clergy. Ideas of ancient Celtic independence dearly cherished in songs and traditions gradually became less attractive among them. Distrusted and, as they alleged, oppressed as a conquered race by British Protestants, the Irish Catholics ever since the Reformation found their chief aid and consolation in south-western Europe owing to religious sympathy.[1] Thither many of their clergy habitually resorted. They could thence communicate to friends at home that Protestantism was either unknown or repudiated in France, Spain, Italy, and Austria, and that their own faith prevailed in those countries. As religious contests increased throughout western Europe, the Irish became more and more interested in this result.

Almost like Christian Rome, the Irish majority became inclined to exchange political for religious

[1] 'One Irish exile became a Marshal of France. Another became Prime Minister of Spain. In his palace at Madrid he had the pleasure of being assiduously courted by the ambassadors of George II. and of bidding defiance in high terms to the ambassador of George III. Scattered over all Europe were to be found brave Irish generals, dexterous Irish diplomatists.'—Macaulay's *History*, chap. i.

interests. Ancient Celtic traditions, glories, and hopes yielded in their minds to enthusiasm for the cause of endangered Roman Catholicism. With the devoted ardour of their race they firmly maintained it against every threat, risk, and temptation. Britain now seemed to them a nation of heretics as well as invaders, and as they became more closely connected with or interested in the Catholic nations of Europe, they naturally were more united with them in political desires. The Celtic independence of remote times, like its yet more ancient and vanished faith, was no longer advocated by eager warriors or impassioned poets. It had become a vague, though pleasing, tradition of an unknown period, which had and could have no reference whatever to the existing political or religious state of Europe.

Yet the unpopularity of British rule still weighed heavily upon them. In this extremity the sympathies of southern Europe with Irish Catholics were perhaps more sincere than those of their English co-religionists. The latter, despite religious differences, preserved many national feelings in common with Protestant rulers and fellow countrymen. They could hardly forget the deep national enmity which before the Reformation had always inspired the Irish natives and the English invaders against each other.

But Continental Catholics recognised in the native Irish fervent co-religionists, governed, if not oppressed, by a common foe, and struggling desperately to preserve their own version of Christianity. Hence their sympathy was more religious than political or national. No European country at this time desired the national independence of Ireland. The preservation, if possible the triumph, of its Roman Catholic faith was the chief object among foreign Catholics, from the Pope to the peasant and artisan. On the other hand, the British colony, chiefly in the north of Ireland, viewed England and Scotland as their models. To them their mother countries represented all that was exemplary in religion, legislation, habits, language, customs, and thoughts. To make the land of their adoption as much like them as possible was therefore the natural desire of the colonists, especially after the Reformation. Previous to this event it was, however, said that English colonists in the south of Ireland adopted many Irish ideas and habits, and became 'Hibernis ipsis Hiberniores'—more Irish than the Irish themselves.

But this adaptation, probably limited to certain localities, quite ceased at the Reformation. After this event, the lines of religious and political demarcation became more clearly defined than ever. Thus when James II. was deposed and disavowed by British and Irish Protestants, he immediately became the champion of the Irish Catholic majority, as if he were some Celtic chief of former times. The chief reason for his deposition by the British majority being devotion to Roman Catholicism, it became his chief claim to popularity among Irish Catholics.

His Saxon origin and descent from a race of
invading kings were practically ignored or for-
given, and, for the first time in history, an English
king became the chosen monarch of the Irish
majority. The ensuing civil war, ending in the
political triumph of Protestantism by the accession
of William III., left British and Irish unchanged
in a religious point of view, but politically in an
altered position. Protestant triumph in Ireland
seemed, in some respects, more complete than it
really was. The full power of Britain, aided by a
small yet valiant Irish Protestant minority, maintained its real success in Britain, and its political
supremacy in Ireland. But the religious convictions
of the majorities in the three kingdoms have remained to this day practically unchanged by the
fortune of war. William III., though permanently successful, became personally almost as unpopular among many British Protestants as among
Irish Catholics. It was his remarkable destiny to
overcome Scottish and Irish foes in battle, to suppress subsequent English conspiracies against him,
and to peacefully end his days as the acknowledged
sovereign of the three kingdoms. Their religious
divisions, however, have hardly changed since his
time. Then, as now, Protestantism in differing forms
prevailed in Britain, and Roman Catholicism among
a majority in Ireland. During the present century,
a time specially distinguished for religious toleration
not only among fellow Christians, but for its extension to other faiths, the historical bigotry of former

days is generally repudiated by civilised governments. It is now thought only consistent with Christianity to allow subjects perfect freedom in religious opinions, provided they are not induced by this concession to violate the established laws.

During a long period throughout western Europe, including Britain and Ireland, such results of calm reasoning were seldom avowed by any ruling party, or acknowledged in legislative enactment. Doubtless, some thoughtful, charitable minds among all parties secretly deplored the persecuting injustice of partisans as well as opponents; but such men were for a long time not found among the influential, as the evidence of persecuting laws, deliberately established and maintained, only too clearly testifies. This was a time, amid Christian intolerance to co-religionists, for subjected Jews to wonder, if not rejoice, at the religious contests or hostility among their Christian rulers, to which, during many previous years, they had themselves been so relentlessly exposed. To Christians had passed the sovereignty of the pagan world in Europe except Turkey, and the Jews gradually perceived their executed fellow countryman becoming the object of their conquerors' enthusiastic worship. He was exalted into their guide, teacher, example, and future hope. The political triumph of Christians throughout the civilised world had been almost as complete as they could have desired, and was certainly beyond anticipation. The vast Roman Empire in Europe becoming Christian, the noble capital of imperial paganism also became the venerated residence of the head of the Christian Church. The subsequent Reformation unequally divided Christendom in western Europe. It was no contest between civilisation and barbarism, but between the most learned Christians of the age about what were true doctrines in the same faith. Fortunately for its future interests no advantage was taken by non-Christians of these divisions in the very heart of its civilised dominions. When actual strife ceased, European nations again enjoyed religious peace, though not agreement. Some exulted in Protestant triumph, others in the successful retention of Catholicism, yet Christianity itself had lost nothing of its vigorous deep-rooted conviction and world-wide influence. The divided house, instead of falling, according to the proverb, still remained established in the most civilised countries, firmly founded on a venerated history. Many years elapsed, however, since the Reformation before the European mind generally could recover its fair judgment, after so much religious controversy about tolerating even divisions of the same faith. By slow degrees, kings, governments, and the ruling classes in western Europe, practically owned what they might have previously known, that good and true men, with their opposites, are found in every sect, and that the only moral safety for a civilised community was to legalise freedom of expression, as well as of thought, upon all questions which transcend human comprehension.

Political interests or influences have often suppressed the free utterance of religious opinion. But the history of civilised nations, before and since Christianity, proves that neither political power nor social supremacy can extinguish religious convictions, transmitted as among the Jews through successive generations with equal sincerity and enduring strength, whether their adherents were in subjection or in authority.

Judaism among all other religions has specially proved this fact in its extraordinary history during political subjection. In some respects Parseeism appears to resemble it in the heroic survival of a persecuted faith. It was the fate of the Parsees to incur the peculiar enmity of the Mohammedans under whose political rule they all fell. No toleration for them appears in the Koran, mentioning the three religions of the Book—Judaism, Christianity, and Mohammedanism as alone meriting either favour or protection. This century, however, has seen a most remarkable revival of both Judaism and Parseeism, not only in the increasing number of their votaries, but in their education, wealth, and social, even political influence. While the rich Jews of western Europe, of England especially, enjoy social advantages unknown since their conquest by the Romans in Judea, those among the Parsees who took refuge in western India from Mohammedan oppression in Persia, are rapidly acquiring social and, to some extent, political influence under the firm protection of British rule. These votaries of the two most ancient of all religions have witnessed the extinction of the European and Asiatic Paganisms of Greece and of Arabia ; the rise of Christianity and of Mohammedanism, their enormous triumphs and internal dissensions. No Jewish or Parsee revolt has disturbed or even menaced the long continued supremacy of Christians and Mohammedans, the territorial as well as the doctrinal successors of Pagan Greece, Rome, and Arabia. It is as loyal, peaceful subjects seeking no national independence or political authority that the votaries of the two oldest faiths in the world—the Jews and Parsees—are now rising more and more in the full light of modern civilisation and recognition.

CHAPTER XIII

The Jacobite revolts in Scotland arouse no Irish sympathy—The rebellion of 1798 in Ireland unlike all other revolts in that country—Increase of British influence in Europe after the fall of Napoleon.

THE most important of British wars and revolutions connected with subsequent history were those of the Commonwealth and Charles I., of James II., and William III., and the Jacobite revolts in 1715 and 1745. The previous civil war of the Roses in England was essentially a contest between the English gentry themselves in behalf of rival princes of the same royal family. The English peasantry and lower classes suffered but little from its effects, which fell with destructive force on the divided nobility and gentry of England. The frequent warfare between the English and Scottish, usually about the Border, made little or no territorial change, though preserving a national alienation or distrust for many years. The Commonwealth contending with the established King of Britain and Ireland at first seemed like a strife between monarchy and republicanism. But the ambition and genius of Cromwell were alike fatal to the true principles of

K

either. Though the trusted general of the Commonwealth, he eventually supplanted both the king and his own partisans by making himself, in the words of Macaulay, more absolute master of his country than any of her legitimate kings. Yet his vigorous successful rule never made him popular, as his admirers have admitted. The monarchy, restored in the person of a selfish, profligate representative, Charles II., immediately obtained the joyful, welcoming loyalty of an immense majority of British subjects. The following reign of his brother, James II., however, occasioned a most important religious contest of a British minority allied with an Irish majority in behalf of Roman Catholicism, and against a British majority and an Irish minority allied in favour of Protestantism.

The result left the latter triumphant and popular in Britain, but unpopular though triumphant in Ireland, under the rule of William III. The succeeding reign of his sister-in-law, Queen Anne, was comparatively peaceful throughout the three kingdoms, but after her time occurred the last efforts of the deposed House of Stuart in 1715 and 1745 against the new Protestant House of Hanover. In these two contests Britain alone was concerned. The exiled princes, son and grandson of James II., found their chief adherents among Scottish Highlanders, while the established government was supported by an English majority allied with most of the Scottish Lowlanders in behalf of the successive Protestant kings George I. and George II. During these wars Ireland remained passively or sullenly tranquil.¹

The sympathies of the Irish majority were naturally with the Stuart family, while those of the minority favoured the existing Protestant government. But the island, despite the martial excitable nature of its people, took no part whatever in either of these contests. After their termination the successful revolts of America against Britain, and of France against its national monarchy, aroused the extraordinary Irish rebellion of 1798, which Macaulay terms² the third and last rising of the aboriginal population against the colony.

Of all his statements about Ireland, this is perhaps one of the most erroneous and misleading. The revolt, instead of continuing or resembling the former Irish wars against Cromwell and William III., was a complete contrast to them. So far from being a revolt against the Protestant colonists, its chief leaders, and some of its bravest champions in Ulster, were Protestant colonists. The Irish Catholic aristocracy, though few in number, were decidedly opposed to the movement, as were the chief prelates of the Romish Church. The rebellion was totally different in its nature and professed objects from

---

[1] 'Two rebellions were raised in Great Britain by the adherents of the House of Stuart. In '45, when the Highlanders were marching towards London, the Roman Catholics of Ireland were so quiet that the Lord Lieutenant could, without the smallest risk, send several regiments across St. George's Channel to recruit the army of the Duke of Cumberland.'—Macaulay's *History*, chap. xvii.

[2] *History of England*, chap. xvii.

any previous Irish resistance to Britain. Protestants and Roman Catholics were now allied both for and against British authority, a spectacle hitherto unknown in Ireland's history. The designs of its leaders were exclusively political, though the majority of the Catholic rebels finally showed a desire to change the contest into a religious warfare. To the dismay of the chief leaders, who were mostly Protestant, the majority of their followers turned against their Protestant fellow countrymen, who accordingly tried to represent the revolt as in reality a Roman Catholic movement. Its final suppression by British power left the Protestant minority, who were chiefly ardent loyalists, apparently triumphant, yet their triumph was scarcely regretted by most of the Catholic clergy or gentry, whose Continental knowledge taught them that the object of the insurgent leaders was not the restoration of Catholicism, but a fraternal union with its mortal foes, the infidel republicans of France. Thus enlightened Irish Catholics saw with comparative equanimity the preservation of British power; believing that, though unpopular, it was preferable, even from their point of view, to the triumph of an infidel philosophy.

That such would have been the immediate result of successful revolt was evident from the admissions of the rebel leaders, Wolfe Tone especially, as shown in his remarkable Diary, published after his suicide when captured by the British. In this extraordinary disclosure Tone reveals intense hatred of Roman Catholicism and thorough sympathy with its vindictive enemies, the French Republicans, who not only tried to abolish it in France, but had expelled the Pope from Rome. Tone's revelations, with other testimony, induced well-informed Irish Catholics to prefer even Protestant rule to the destructive enmity of the new French Republic, the avowed model and ally of the chief Irish rebels in 1798.

Though Wolfe Tone was the prime mover in this revolt, Lord Edward Fitzgerald, from his rank and reckless courage, was more of a popular favourite, and since his death more praised and admired than during his life. Poets and novelists have described this man as a national hero, almost an Irish Washington or Kosciusko, in devotion to his country's freedom, but historical facts tell a somewhat different story. He had been an officer in the British service, which shows he had no dislike to British power at one time of his life, had afterwards visited France and became an enthusiastic Republican. Unlike most of his fellow insurgents Lord Edward was no orator, but always a man of action. Yet neither he nor Tone represented in feeling or design the Irish majority whom they aspired to lead. They simply took advantage of their dislike to British rule, to instigate revolt against it, and promote principles peculiarly odious to most of their fellow countrymen. In fact, enmity to British supremacy was almost the only bond of union between the chief rebel leaders in '98 and their followers. But this enmity in such different men was not of the same nature. It must be owned that the ignorant majority among the Catholic rebels were far more consistent and practical than their fanciful, dreamy leaders, who were completely under French Republican influence.

The former not unnaturally desired the triumph of their faith over a minority of Protestant fellow countrymen. This desire had been their historical inheritance, while their leaders, who altogether ignored the lessons of Irish history, only longed to make Ireland a second France of their period. But this was no longer the France of a religious monarchy favoured by the Papacy, and to a great extent morally ruled by a venerated clergy. The France admired by Tone and Fitzgerald, who both liked to call themselves 'Citizens,' was a changed country, abolishing established religion, while deposing established monarchy. It was a country which suddenly became the prey of a reckless political experiment in the art of ruling, distinguished finally by peculiar ferocity, by the abolition under legal penalties of any form of religious worship, and the practical suppression therefore of individual liberty.

In some measure this Irish revolt collapsed of its own accord, most of its chiefs being arrested before the outbreak, and the whole movement being comparatively destitute either of able leaders or munitions of war. Many of its chiefs were executed and died heroically, but usually the insurgents in the field showed little of the national courage. After the suppression of this revolt, the disappearance of the French Republic, and the accession of Napoleon I. in its place, the religious and political position of Europe was, in some respects, singularly changed.[1] Though professing Roman Catholicism, Napoleon was politically opposed by the Papacy, which consistently continued to acknowledge the rights of the deposed French royal family.

The ambition and genius of Napoleon, together with his marvellous power over the French nation, gradually involved nearly all Europe in national warfare. The position of this wonderful man, his eventful career and ultimate fate, caused great changes in European policy. At the head of the warlike French nation, still agitated by recollection of a terrible domestic revolution, he united it, as it were, into one vast army under his sole control.[2] He became at once the head, the ruler, and the hero of the French nation. Neither Royalists nor Republicans dared to oppose him. All the ancient military glory of France faded into insignificance when compared with the wonderful national triumphs and extensive conquests of this most victorious of modern generals.

[1] 'The eminent man of the time was Napoleon Bonaparte, the revolution-queller, the burgher-sovereign, the imperial democrat, the supreme captain, the civil reformer, the victim of circumstances, which his soaring ambition used, but which his unrivalled prowess could not control; his was the most tragic figure on the stage of modern history.'—Sloane's *Life of Napoleon*, Preface.

[2] 'Bonaparte was a child of the Mediterranean. The light of its sparkling waters was ever in his eyes, and the fascination of its ancient civilisations was never absent from his dreams of glory. His proclamations ring with classic allusions, his festivals are arranged with classic pomp.'—Sloane's *Life of Napoleon*, vol. ii. chap. ii.

Unlike former times, when French troops were chiefly led against Asiatic Mohammedans or English neighbours, they were now successively involved in war with the chief powers of Europe. Napoleon thus turned the energy of the French people, whom he ruled with almost absolute power, from domestic discord to foreign warfare. No longer advocating either Royalist or Republican principles, nominally professing Roman Catholicism, while politically opposing its spiritual head, the French soldiery under their new general became his devoted, unreasoning instruments. His personal popularity was so great, and his knowledge of the French so profound, that his power over them was as complete as if he had belonged to a world of superior beings. His will was literally French law, and no matter how costly or destructive were his enterprises, or how great the misery caused by his ambition, he continued to be their popular idol and glorified hero till long after the end of his career.

The French clergy alone in their martial country were passively opposed to him, secretly desiring the restoration of the monarchy, yet they apparently followed the national will and never openly aroused their hearers against Napoleon's empire.[1] His terrible and for some time successful career against a united Europe was always opposed by the British.

[1] 'Napoleon passed through a stage of rampant infidelity in his youth. But with advancing years the dimensions of the Papacy impressed his imagination, while ripening political wisdom convinced him of its power.'—Sloane's *Life of Napoleon*, chap. xviii.

In intrigue or in war Napoleon was constantly thwarted by them from first to last. The decisive battle of Waterloo placed the British, therefore, in a peculiarly strong position among foreign Powers, as none had opposed Napoleon with the same persevering success. All other opponents he had conquered except the Russians, whose singular resistance to his invasion owed success more to the rigours of their climate than to their valour in the open field. The disastrous retreat of the French from Russia in winter had experienced the fatal effects of its severe climate, of which the Russians, chiefly acting on the defensive, availed themselves in every way. But the British, by sea and land, whether in Spain, Egypt, or Syria, had steadily defeated Napoleon, whose very name became specially detested in England.[1]

When, therefore, the European alliance against him effected his final defeat, the British held the foremost place among his victorious foes. The restored French monarchy was for some time in a rather humiliated position among European powers, who by their united action had forcibly re-established its unpopular authority over a vanquished people. The political result of Waterloo left the British and the Russians, however, all the more fitted and disposed for foreign conquest and annexation. The

---

[1] To this national antipathy Thackeray makes comic allusion when Becky Sharp shocks Miss Sedley by exclaiming, 'Vive l'Empereur, vive Bonaparte!' 'O, Rebecca, for shame!' said the latter, for in those days in England to say 'Long live Bonaparte' was as much as to say 'Long live Lucifer.'— *Vanity Fair*, chap. ii.

Germans, who have recently become a colonising power, had at this time less desire for such enterprises, which the Austrians have never undertaken to much extent. But Britain and Russia pursued their foreign enterprises and increased their foreign influence with more success than ever after the signal defeat of Napoleon in 1815.

At this time, and for some years after, Britain and Russia were on friendly terms. In the subsequent war for Greek liberation from the Turks, the Russians with the British and French alike assisted the Greeks, and agreed in establishing their small kingdom, forcing the allied Turks and Egyptians to leave Greece, and to acknowledge its independence. The hopes of Christian subjects under Mohammedans in Asia and in Europe, longing for deliverance, were naturally roused and encouraged by this remarkably interesting contest. In some degree it seemed to recall the spirit of the Crusades when the allied Christian powers of Europe had waged war with Mohammedans. Yet after the Greek revolution a great change occurred and has ever since continued in European policy towards the Turks. The Russians by their vast conquests and extension throughout northern and parts of central Asia, and the British by their firm consolidation of their great Indian Empire, even the French through their conquest of Algiers, have not only vastly increased their number of Mohammedan subjects, but gradually made many of them obedient, loyal, and serviceable. But the Russians and the British alike ruling more non-Christians than any other nation, especially in northern and in southern Asia, are now constantly opposing, thwarting, or intriguing against each other. While in continual rivalry, watching one another's success with increasing apprehension, Turks, Persians, Tartars, and Chinese are comparatively helpless before them. A complete Christian political triumph throughout all Asia, the dream of mediæval Christendom, seems now fully within the range of practical politics. Yet, hitherto, it is checked or restrained no longer by the bravery or religious enthusiasm of non-Christian nations, but by the deep political jealousies of the European Christian powers of the present time.

CHAPTER XIV

Influence of literature in celebrating British civil wars and revolutions—Shakespeare and Milton on British history, in historic plays and political essays.

During and since the political, social, and religious wars or rebellions in Britain and Ireland, literary talent in prose and verse has brilliantly illustrated the ideas and conduct of differing men. Dramatists, novelists, and poets, from their peculiar interest in and profound knowledge of character when personally free from misleading party interests, sometimes describe real events and men with an impartial accuracy, rarely found, perhaps not easily preserved, among many professed historians. Shakespeare, for instance, in 'King John' and 'Henry V.' shows himself free from those prejudices against the French which before, during, and long since his time often misled even intellectual Englishmen. He seldom mentions the politics of his own time, and with extreme caution those in the reign of Henry VIII. Mary of Scotland, the great rival of his own Queen, he never mentions, though a person more attractive to poet or dramatist could hardly be imagined, and who was doubtless often talked about among his acquaintances. Mary of England, Philip of Spain, Sir Walter

Raleigh, and Lord Essex, whose names were probably 'familiar as household words' among Shakespeare's friends, he never introduces or describes, except in one brief allusion to the Princess Mary when an infant.

As these persons were living at or near his own time, to describe them would not have been advisable, if safe, for so able and yet socially so humble a writer. Even personages who lived somewhat earlier, Katharine of Aragon, Anne Boleyn, Henry VIII., Cardinal Wolsey, and Buckingham, Shakespeare cautiously contrives to render alike so interesting in different ways that though some of them would hardly have been so favourable in their views of each other, yet all would probably be satisfied, if not gratified, by his descriptions of themselves.

Shakespeare was certainly a thorough monarchist in his ideas and sympathies. 'His ideal England is England grouped around a noble king.'[1] The same spirit has usually animated a majority among British writers, Milton being an illustrious exception to a general rule, though his admiration of Cromwell's *sole* authority is hardly consistent with Republican sentiments. Of all modern civilised nations, the British are probably the most amenable or attentive to literary influence, reasoning, and enlightenment. Though their vast Protestant majority abandoned nearly all faith or interest in the legends of Christian saints, they were respectfully preserved among devout British Catholics. While learned

[1] Green's *History of the English People*.

Protestants cultivated with special care the classic writings of Greece and Rome, together with Jewish Scriptural traditions, learned Catholics added to these studies an undiminished interest in the lives or works of Christian saints and martyrs.

Perhaps no country has more encouraged or favoured historical knowledge than England, or was so conversant with the contemporary as well as former state of foreign nations. British travellers in Greece, Italy, Palestine, Egypt, and Assyria are usually more interested and better informed about their ancient times than their present inhabitants are, or profess to be. While, however, Great Britain was distracted by civil wars, or religious controversy, her chief energies were inevitably engrossed by them, and serious domestic contests had to terminate before the fruits of British learning and enterprise could be realised. The success of William III. was naturally regretted by British and Irish Roman Catholics, and also by some British Protestants, the objections of the former being religious, those of the latter political, as William's accession to the throne was in their opinion a usurpation of royal rights. Two civil wars after the death of his successor Queen Anne agitated Great Britain, Scotland especially, but had no effect in Ireland. Again, the British were divided by civil war, in which the Scottish Highlanders took a rather romantic, though hopeless, part; but no mention of a Republic was heard on any side. Most of these brave mountaineers supported the son and grandson of the deposed James II. in the successive Jacobite revolts of 1715 and 1745. They were allied with some English Prelatists and Catholics; but the chief support of the banished princes was among the Scottish Highlanders.

These clans, under Charles Edward, styled the young Pretender, while his father was termed the old Pretender or James III. by opponents and partisans, invaded England in 1745. They seemed to the English peasantry rather like a foreign army, and Charles Edward, often attired in Highland costume, more resembled a Scottish chief than an English prince. His royal claims were firmly resisted by the English majority, while a strong party in Scotland also opposed him. Ireland, usually the most excitable of the three kingdoms, remained singularly tranquil during both these revolts. The Scottish Jacobites in Scotland, however, in 1745 prevailed for a time in that country, but were finally defeated. Charles Edward fled to the Continent, a price being actually set upon his head, as if he were a dangerous criminal, while his followers were treated with a deliberate legalised cruelty, little consistent with the principles of Christianity or of the British character.

The only way to explain, though hardly to excuse it, was the fear in Britain of the revival of James II.'s tyranny in the dreaded triumph or restoration of his son or grandson. The severity authorised by that king and by his subordinates to their political prisoners or rebels had sunk deep into the minds of the British people. When, therefore, they found themselves threatened by foes terming James II.'s deposition an act of guilty rebellion, they naturally apprehended that the restoration of his family would recall ancestral tyranny with additional vindictiveness. Both Jacobite revolts were, therefore, eagerly crushed with stern severity by the British Government, and little pity shown or expressed towards the vanquished party, till a more peaceful age enabled their motives or personal characters to be viewed with comparative impartiality. In these most recent British civil wars, it must be owned that victors treated vanquished fellow countrymen with a severity not only equalling that of former ages in Britain, but exceeding that which the British have since usually shown to conquered foreign foes.

In the wars of the Roses the English aristocracy, whom they chiefly concerned, were utterly implacable towards each other, executing even near relatives with relentless cruelty as traitors to their respective political parties. During the subsequent partly political, partly religious, contests or conspiracies in the reigns of Henry VIII., Mary, and Elizabeth, the Commonwealth, James II., William III., and the first two Princes of the House of Hanover, the established laws punished fellow countrymen with implacable severity for political offences. Thus the defeated party, whoever they were, usually suffered precisely the same legal penalties which they themselves would have been eager to inflict had they been victorious.

In fact, mercy towards 'treason' was thought, perhaps with truth, really dangerous to the safety of those extending it. Impartial readers of British history will hardly perceive much advance in legislative clemency towards ' traitors ' till comparatively recent years. The legal penalties inflicted on captive Jacobites in 1715 and 1745 for treason were nearly, if not quite, as cruel as those which during previous periods of English history had been inflicted for the same offence. Shakespeare's English historic plays, clearly though indirectly aimed to mitigate the sternness of 'party' feeling, when in describing English civil wars he represents good and evil men on opposing sides. In a very different spirit from that often shown by eager political historians, he makes, for instance, the chiefs of the York and Lancaster parties alike interesting in triumph and in defeat. In the case of Richard III., he had to describe that king as he was usually represented, though he has met with more recent apologists than have honoured the memory of King John. But from the historic plays, ' Richard II.' to 'Henry VIII.' inclusive, readers are usually more induced to admire, or make allowance for opposing princes and statesmen, than to be embittered against any of them.

To influence people in his own lifetime, however, was not in Shakespeare's power, and like his philosophic contemporary, Bacon, he might have predicted that his real appreciation was reserved for a more remote period of his country's history. His works gradually proved a strong inducement for men to examine history with mingled love of truth and real philanthropy, not always taught or aroused by some religious and political historians. The ignorance or prejudice which for some time delayed Shakespeare's proper appreciation had slowly yielded to a more enlightened spirit throughout Britain when Walter Scott's historic novels appeared. Resembling Shakespeare in profound knowledge of men, Scott was also like him in the rare practical patriotism of wishing his fellow countrymen, of whatever creed or party, to do justice to one another. This grand moral purpose has often been opposed rather than cherished by either enthusiastic or prejudiced writers, and Scott's most useful novels in this sense are those describing British history.

It is a strange fact, partly sad and partly ridiculous, that while Jacobite prisoners were treated with legalised cruelty, executed, exiled for life, or ruined by confiscation for political offences, the British public, more literary than in former times, were often sentimentally deploring the woes of fictitious persons in novels or romances. The imaginary griefs of heroines in novels roused more compassion than was apparently shown to the sorrowing relatives of noble, heroic men executed as traitors about the same period. It was Scott's great object to gratify the taste for novel-reading by freeing it from mere fancy and associating it with historic truth and practical charity. In this design it is delightful to see that he succeeded, if not as much as he could have wished, at least more than he probably anticipated. By the attractive power of his literary genius, the historic dead seemed to revive involved with imaginary events and characters, and to thus vindicate themselves from the aspersions of religious or political opponents. Among British writers of plays and poems most successful in dealing with political history, Shakespeare, Milton, Dryden, and Scott are pre-eminent. Shakespeare and Scott lived in times of comparative domestic peace; Milton and Dryden amid the excitement of domestic, religious, and political contention. Accordingly the calm impartiality of the two former, and the vindictive or satirical bitterness of the two latter, seem to rather represent the spirit of their respective times.

Queen Elizabeth, though threatened by foreign nations and by an oppressed minority of her own, was one of the most popular of English sovereigns, and in friendly alliance with the ruling majority in Scotland. To predict every happiness for her when an infant was sure to be popular in England, and so Shakespeare ends 'Henry VIII.' with her christening, while cautiously writing with forbearance, if not courtesy, of nearly all historical personages at or very near his own time:

> This royal infant (heaven still move about her!)
> Though in her cradle, yet now promises
> Upon this land a thousand thousand blessings.
> Holy and heavenly thoughts still counsel her:
> She shall be lov'd and fear'd; her own shall bless her.
> In her days every man shall eat in safety

Under his own vine what he plants, and sing
The merry songs of peace to all his neighbours.
She shall be, to the happiness of England,
An aged princess; many days shall see her,
And yet no day without a deed to crown it.
Would I had known no more! but she must die,
She must, the saints must have her; yet a virgin,
A most unspotted lily shall she pass
To the ground, and all the world shall mourn her.
Henry VIII. act v.

Among the historical plays 'Henry VIII.' seems the most politically important, as it alone describes events and persons about the author's own period, or within living memory. Thus, in describing people hostile to, or rivalling each other, Shakespeare is peculiarly cautious in this play. Cardinal Wolsey is haughty and intriguing, yet kind and generous. Not a word of complaint does he utter against his imperious master save when he deeply regrets that he had not served his God with equal fidelity. But these words are strictly historical, well known doubtless in Shakespeare's time, and the poet, therefore, could give no possible offence by recording what was no invention of his. To their implied reproach against the king, Shakespeare adds nothing similar of his own composition. In fact, everything he says of the arbitrary king is more or less in his favour. All loyal subjects of Elizabeth, therefore, might enjoy this royal play, though full of inflammable materials, without the least irritation against any of the contending parties in her father's terrible reign.

Shakespeare's great poetical successor, Milton,

lived in changing times of triumph and defeat among English parties. At first his prose political essays expressed devotion to Cromwell, and scorn as well as detestation of both British and Irish opponents, whether Protestant or Catholic. When in political adversity after the restoration of Charles II. his few sad lines deplore the Royalist triumph of his fellow Englishmen with an abhorrence as complete as if they belonged to a different race or nation:

> More safe I sing with mortal voice, unchanged
> To hoarse or mute, tho' fallen on evil days,
> On evil days tho' fallen, and evil tongues;
> In darkness, and with dangers compassed round.
> But drive far off the barbarous dissonance
> Of Bacchus and his revellers, the race
> Of that wild rout that tore the Thracian bard
> In Rhodope; nor could the Muse defend her son.
> So fail not thou, who thee implores;
> For thou art heavenly, she an empty dream.
> *Paradise Lost*, book vii.

This national alienation Milton's genius had rather tried to embitter than to pacify. Like some men at his period, though chiefly in Scotland, he classes in prose or poetry religious and political opponents with the heathen of remote times, or with evil spirits, malevolently influencing human thought. Such fanatical prejudices in so learned and illustrious a man prove decisively how the maddening excitement of civil war or rebellion may degrade the mind, pervert the judgment, and harden the heart of the most gifted men when under its pernicious influence.

CHAPTER XV

Sir Walter Scott and Thomas Moore on Scottish and Irish history—Shakespeare's caution in describing historical personages of his own time—His impartiality in historical allusions.

The last revolutions in Scotland and in Ireland occurring in times of comparative enlightenment naturally elicited descriptive allusions in poetry and in prose fiction. Scott and Moore were perhaps the most attractive writers who in prose and verse illustrated the terrible contests in their respective countries during the eighteenth century. Moore, though in poetry encouraging or sharing Irish popular dislike to British rule, yet personally liked England and often lived there. His anti-Saxon sentiments, however, instead of being expressed in hostile Celtic, are beautifully worded in the language of the nation he denounces. He is thus unlike a former Irish chief O'Neill, who, according to Macaulay, boasted it did not become him 'to writhe his mouth to chatter English.'[1]

Macaulay's learned contempt for this chief is rather amusing when ridiculing him for despising 'a jargon

[1] *History of England*, chap. vi.

in which the "Advancement of Learning" and "Paradise Lost" were written.' Yet, in historic justice to O'Neill, it might be pleaded that few of the English he had seen probably knew more of those great works than he did. English and subsequent British invaders were not likely to discuss or explain English literature to Irish chiefs at a time when only a small minority in England knew anything about it. But Moore expressing Irish hatred to England in beautiful English was nearly as much admired by descendants of the abused Saxon as by those of the lauded Celt. He probably, unlike Scott, never considered the existing feelings of his excitable fellow countrymen. His personal liking for England and the English seems little consistent with his poetic denunciation of 'cold-hearted Saxons' &c., which to this day seems sullenly endorsed by a majority of Ireland's chosen representatives in speeches and newspapers. While honouring the memories of Irish revolutionists as the injured victims of British tyranny, Moore terms the Saxons the national oppressors of Ireland :

> I will fly with my Coulin, and think the rough wind
> Less rude than the foes we leave frowning behind ;
> And I'll gaze on thy gold hair as graceful it wreathes,
> And hang o'er thy soft harp as wildly it breathes.
> Nor dread that the cold-hearted Saxon will tear
> One chord from that harp, or one lock from that hair.
> *Irish Melodies.*

Many an Irish political exile has likely repeated Moore's anti-Saxon or anti-English verses, and found in them both incentives to revolt against British rule and a consolation for its legal penalty. In some remarkable lines Moore, evidently finding England a more agreeable abode than Ireland, offers a beautiful, though hardly a patriotic, excuse for voluntary absenteeism :

> O blame not the bard if he fly to the bowers
>   Where Pleasure lies carelessly smiling at Fame ;
> He was born for much more, and in happier hours,
>   His soul might have burn'd with a holier flame.
> But, alas for his country ! her pride is gone by,
>   And that spirit is broken which never would bend,
> O'er the ruin her children in secret must sigh,
>   For 'tis treason to love her, and death to defend.
> *Irish Melodies.*

Since his beautiful and pathetic verses were written, the crimes and penalties of Irish sedition form the saddest page in the brilliant history of Great Britain during this eventful century. While British readers may from poetic taste admire the charm of Moore's verses, only residents among Ireland's population could know the dangerous political, if not moral, influence they have often exercised upon them. Moore apparently believed that sad allusions to Ireland's subjection to England would be viewed as a mere historical remembrance on both sides of the Irish Channel. But though geographically near each other, they preserve very different feelings in their inhabitants. Many enlightened British statesmen, or writers, have since perceived how recent mediæval history still remains in Irish minds, and with what glowing interest they preserve the remembrance of its glories, its sentiments, and its sorrows. To do Moore justice he never irritates his readers against living statesmen, nor practically advocates future rebellion. He fancifully classes modern Irish revolts against Great Britain with their traditional wars against Danish invaders. According to him, Danes and Saxons were alike barbarous foes or oppressors of a peculiarly intellectual as well as heroic nation. Yet he practically views the Saxons of old, whom he poetically denounces, very differently from their English descendants among whom he liked to dwell.

Many of his fellow Irishmen were by no means able or inclined to make such strong distinctions between ancient Saxons and modern Englishmen— between former invaders and existing rulers of their country. Among many of them recent history proves that their hatred of prevailing British power much resembles ancestral enmity to Saxon invaders. Among many home-staying Irish, Moore's sentiments were not only thought historically true, but a practical justification of national hatred to British rule, which in their opinion was the result or continuation of Saxon conquest in former times. It is remarkable that Moore seldom, if ever, mentions the Christian divisions of modern Ireland. He says little or nothing about the mutual antipathy of Protestants and Catholics. He prefers to keep the Danes, the Saxons, and the native Irish before his readers, with little reference to the religious disputes which have so materially influenced his divided fellow countrymen.

The comparatively modern strife between Ireland's religious divisions has for a long period almost replaced national animosities. Accordingly Irish revolutionists, whether Protestant or Catholic, by classing existing British and former Saxons together as alike oppressors of Ireland, practically try to ignore the more recent cause of Irish alienation from Britain. The Catholic clergy, who, despite British power, always politically ruled the Irish majority since England became Protestant, have recently proved that they understand Irish public opinion better than any political leader who has hitherto attempted to guide it. In fact, Tennyson's lines on the ever-running brook might be paraphrased to describe the enduring influence of the Catholic clergy, compared to the fleeting popularity of temporary leaders who may indeed come and go, while the priesthood 'go on for ever.' Moore's sentiments could not fail, however, to stimulate or preserve Irish enmity to England. But this hostility became no longer shown in ardent praise of ancient national heroes, but in eagerly maintaining the dislike of an Irish majority to a Protestant minority in Ireland allied with a Protestant majority in England. Some Irish Protestant leaders, therefore, despite a brief, though sincere, popularity, found themselves at last surpassed in attaining that coveted object by the religious leaders of the Irish majority.

This recent phase of Ireland's politics Moore must have known, as the lessons of 1798 have in this respect been often repeated; but he scarcely mentions priestly influence, while often praising Irish resistance to Danes and Saxons, as well as sympathising with the '98 insurgents. The old traditions he often mingles with sympathy, either expressed or implied, with existing Irish dislike to British authority. This strange historical classification was amply sufficient to fire the excitable and poetical Irish to a degree which probably Moore neither wished nor expected. His poetic anti-English sentiments were eagerly read and admired by many ardent foes of that country in which her gifted Irish denouncer voluntarily spent much, if not the happiest time, of his life. Without probably anticipating results, Moore certainly, like some other Irishmen, turned the full eloquence of the English language against England's rule, if not against the English nation in its relations with Ireland.

His great contemporary, Walter Scott, took a very different view of the moral duty enjoined by literary genius. Though neither of these writers took an active part in politics, their works were evidently, if indirectly, very influential among fellow countrymen. But they showed a totally different spirit in addressing them, as Scott, to an extent almost unknown in his time, or before it, rose above all the limits, prejudices, or restraints of party spirit and religious bigotry.

In his instructive, as well as delightful, ' Waverley

Novels,' he keeps historic fairness and the principles of strict justice above every other consideration. In the 'Talisman' and 'Ivanhoe' British ideas about Mohammedans and Jews are examined with an impartiality which learned historians and theologians, often excited by political or religious enthusiasm, rarely display. Mohammedan generosity and Jewish virtue and heroism are conceived, though by a Christian mind, in a spirit worthy of the highest qualities imputed to, or inspired by, that faith. But in describing British civil wars, or rebellions, Scott confers a special benefit on fellow countrymen and fellow subjects of this century to whom his works were presented.[1]

Shakespeare's previous account of England's wars with France and her domestic strife evinces no very decided political sympathy. The French are not ridiculed or described in a hostile spirit. The troubled reign of King John in his play arouses no feeling for or against the Papacy or the mutinous English nobles, while the unworthy king, 'a trifler and a coward,' according to Macaulay, is made at last almost a subject for pity, despite his many crimes. In 'Richard III.' Shakespeare shows partiality for the

[1] 'Scott was one of the greatest men of letters that have ever lived in any country, and as time goes on, so far from his fame becoming dimmed or the knowledge of him becoming the property only of the few, it seems to me, so far as I can judge, that he is more likely to defy the ravages of time than almost any other of the writers who have adorned the present century.'—Mr. Balfour's speech in Dumfries, *Times*, of August 25, 1897.

future Henry VII.; but none of Richard's partisans are described with the bitterness which perhaps some deserved. Indeed, Shakespeare's caution or forbearance in describing historical characters is one of his characteristics. Thus even his account of Richard III., in his deeds, habits, and soliloquies, is in great measure borne out by, probably founded upon, Sir Thomas More's life of that prince as well as other histories of him. His sketch of Joan of Arc, however, is an exception, being coarse and extravagant. It is thought by many people not to be written by him, and is certainly unworthy of his genius. Richard III., as an undoubted usurper and alleged murderer, is certainly held up to odium and made to condemn himself in soliloquy, but none of his adherents are exposed to popular indignation.

In the long, important play of 'Henry VIII.' Shakespeare shows peculiar skill in dealing with dangerous materials during the reign of that imperious king's daughter. The recollection of Henry's terrible times was doubtless fresh in English minds when he wrote this play; but he succeeds in making its chief personages, though often opposing each other, extremely interesting to the English public of his time and since. Pity is mainly excited for Queen Katharine of Aragon and Cardinal Wolsey, and much interest aroused for Anne Boleyn; while Henry himself is only described in his best days, frank, generous, and eager for his subjects' welfare, before his violent passions and bodily infirmity had made him the implacable tyrant of his later years.

The way in which Shakespeare introduces historical facts in noble language, while adhering to truth, eminently distinguishes him above other poets. His speech of Henry VIII., when refusing to sanction oppressive taxation of his subjects, is drawn in a very different spirit, however, from subsequent historians, yet in the main points they practically agree.[1]

The alarmed, apologetic king of the liberal historian becomes in the hands of the royalist poet a noble sovereign earning national gratitude by generous use of supreme power. This instance is

---

[1] 'When, without the consent of Parliament, he demanded of his subjects a contribution amounting to one-sixth of their goods, he soon found it necessary to retract. Henry, proud and self-willed as he was, shrank, not without reason, from a conflict with the roused spirit of the nation. He not only cancelled his illegal commissions, he not only granted a general pardon to all the malcontents, but he publicly and solemnly apologised for his infraction of the laws.'—Macaulay's *History of England*, chap. i.

The poet's version of this matter is more respectful to His Majesty:

K. Henry. We must not rend our subjects from our laws,
And stick them in our will. Sixth part of each?
A trembling contribution! Why, we take
From every tree, lop, bark, and part o' the timber;
And, though we leave it with a root, thus hack'd,
The air will drink the sap. To every county
Where this is question'd send our letters, with
Free pardon to each man that has denied
The force of this commission.
　　　　　　　　　　　　Henry VIII. act i.

among many in Shakespeare's historical plays where his monarchical feelings, if not partialities, are evident. Such sentiments when he wrote would, perhaps, elicit eager applause from London theatrical audiences, but might be keenly controverted by historians of a subsequent period.

All Roman Catholics viewed Henry VIII.'s divorce from Katharine with disapproval, while Protestants expected real advantages from his marriage with Anne Boleyn. Shakespeare, therefore, contrives to please the adherents of each; his account of Katharine would surely gratify her co-religionists, while that of Anne would interest and delight the Protestants. The latter's coronation, and the former's pathetic last message to Henry commending their daughter Mary to his protection, are equally pleasing to readers of taste and feeling.

Describing Anne's coronation at Westminster Abbey, the poet writes:

> At length her grace rose, and with modest paces
> Came to the altar; where she kneel'd, and, saintlike,
> Cast her fair eyes to heaven, and pray'd devoutly.
> Then rose again, and bow'd her to the people:
> When by the Archbishop of Canterbury
> She had all the royal makings of a queen;
> As holy oil, Edward Confessor's crown,
> The rod, and bird of peace, and all such emblems
> Laid nobly on her; which perform'd, the choir,
> With all the choicest music of the kingdom,
> Together sung 'Te Deum.'

During, or about the time of, this celebration Anne's unfortunate predecessor thus besought the arbitrary drince, who was indeed the ruin of both :

Q. Kath. I have commended to his goodness
    The model of our chaste loves, his young daughter :
    The dews of heaven fall thick in blessings on her !
    Beseeching him to give her virtuous breeding ;
    She is young, and of a noble modest nature ;
    I hope she will deserve well, and a little
    To love her for her mother's sake, that lov'd him,
    Heaven knows how dearly.
           Henry VIII. act iv.

In Elizabeth's reign the play of 'Henry VIII.' was well suited to soothe the feelings and to delight the fancy of most English people. The Catholic party might pity and admire Queen Katharine and Cardinal Wolsey, while Protestants would enjoy the beautiful descriptions of Anne Boleyn's coronation and of the Princess Elizabeth's christening. The poet in this, as in other English historical plays, is a thorough, patriotic Englishman in ideas and sympathies. He earnestly admires distinguished and illustrious personages, despite their differing religious professions or opposing political opinions.

Shakespeare's account of the opposing theologians Wolsey and Cranmer was also calculated to have a pleasing effect upon enthusiastic Protestants and Catholics alike. The highest admiration is due to these illustrious Englishmen, whose religious partisans were destined to engage in lamentable strife during the successive reigns of Henry's daughters, Mary and Elizabeth. In religious impartiality Shakespeare and Scott may be well compared, and Britain congratulated for producing two of the most patriotic writers on historical subjects that ever lived. They were alike able by their genius, love of truth, and wonderful knowledge of character to teach millions of fellow countrymen the inestimable value of impartial truth in the description of historical events, and in the delineation of real personages.

While Shakespeare describes good and evil men alike among the Yorkist and Lancastrian factions; while Cardinal Wolsey and the Protestant bishop, Cranmer, are each made noble and interesting to religious opponents and to partisans, Scott shows similar impartiality in a yet more decided and elaborate form. In writing about Scottish civil wars or revolts, times, men, and scenes in which his own feelings were doubtless specially interested, he thoroughly appreciates the noble characters of his own invention as well as those in history who oppose his religious and political views. This love of truth and calm judgment he shows remarkably in 'Ivanhoe,' 'Old Mortality,' and 'The Abbot,' where the religious element is involved with the political. In this respect it must be owned that few, either historians or practical politicians, have attempted or been able to equal him. Through the medium of fiction with historic reference, Scott, indeed, 'holds the mirror up to nature, and shows virtue her own feature.' Among the practical results of such a literary genius obeying so lofty a mind appears the encouragement not only of complete harmony between England and Scotland, but the

M

thorough religious toleration in feeling as well as in legislation ever since prevalent in Scotland among the Scottish people themselves. The fierce disputes, the almost ferocious denunciation of opposing fellow Christians in Scotland were perhaps more thoroughly eradicated from Scottish minds, through the elevating influence of so keen, yet so pleasing a judge of human nature, than could have been effected by the penalties or rules of legislation.

CHAPTER XVI

Instructive nature of Shakespeare's historical plays—Their monarchical tendency—Loyalty of London people to the monarchy—Beneficial influence of Scott's historical novels.

THE political tendency of Shakespeare's historical plays was certainly to confirm and increase attachment to the English monarchy. This feeling had always prevailed from the earliest records, and occurs even in legends of remote times. England, when Shakespeare wrote, was more opposed by Spain and France than by any other power. In this enmity new religious differences were added to national jealousies. England, of comparatively small size, was peculiarly strengthened and protected by her insular situation. In many respects at this time the sea was England's best ally, effectually guarding her from sudden attacks of those two maritime nations with whom she was at frequent variance, and in almost constant political rivalry. Shakespeare, impressed with this knowledge, makes the prince, John of Gaunt, while praising England with his last breath, specially declare the surrounding sea to be her chief natural ally and protector :

> This royal throne of kings, this sceptred isle,
> This precious stone set in the silver sea,
> Which serves it in the office of a wall,
> Or as a moat defensive to a house,
> Against the envy of less happier lands.
> *Richard II.* act ii.

The poet found his country under the rule of Queen Elizabeth, a sovereign specially popular with the English majority, and in firm alliance with the ruling party in Scotland, which, having deposed Mary Stuart, was now ruled by her illegitimate brother, the Regent Murray, in the name of her infant son, the future James I. Mary, as Elizabeth's legal and Roman Catholic successor, was thought a constant danger to the English Queen and to the Protestant faith. The chance of her succession to the throne they apprehended might yet revive the fearful persecutions of English Protestants during the previous reign of Mary Tudor, Elizabeth's sister. The most intellectual English Protestants at this time vied with Roman Catholic fellow countrymen in showing an intolerance which proved their practical resemblance in feeling, despite differences in religious belief.

The execution of Mary Stuart—an event which to this day rouses pity and regret among English readers of all persuasions—was at the time a matter of public and general rejoicing in England. It seemed to many people a deliverance or security from a probable future danger.¹

It is vain for any religious denomination to lay claim to mercy for opponents at this period, as all parties, Protestants and Roman Catholics, dreaded and distrusted each other with about equal reason. In the present century people were easily induced by Scott and other writers to admire or pity Mary Stuart, Charles I., Oliver Cromwell, and the Jacobites as interesting or noble in various ways. But if the literary men in their times are referred to it is sufficiently evident that these historic celebrities, so interesting to posterity, were in their lifetime only attractive to political partisans.

Edmund Spenser, devoting his genius to an imaginary 'Faery Queen,' had evidently no compassion for the unfortunate living one in his time, now thought among the most interesting and attractive of historic female sovereigns.

Each of the royal Maries, the past and the apparent future Queen of England, represented the faith of the once persecuting, but in Elizabeth's reign, the persecuted faith of a British minority and of an Irish majority. In many ways Mary Stuart was peculiarly odious to her reigning cousin Elizabeth. Mary's extraordinary beauty, which since the days of Cleopatra had scarcely been equalled in

¹ 'The streets of London blazed with bonfires, and peals rang out from steeple to steeple at the news of Mary's condemnation. Edmund Spenser presses strongly and pitilessly for the execution of Mary Stuart.'—Green's *History of the English People*, book vi.

the description of any reigning queen, was a well-known constant mortification to Elizabeth, who, despite the flattery of a peculiarly admiring or submissive Court, could never believe herself in this respect Mary's equal or rival. Though Mary was indeed a most attractive subject to any poet, from her wit and grace as well as beauty, Shakespeare avoids allusion to her or to Scottish politics. Elizabeth herself is only mentioned as an infant, the future hope and glory of England, and this loyal prediction closes the play of 'Henry VIII.'

The expected, perhaps inevitable, union of England and Scotland, which doubtless occupied many British minds in Shakespeare's time, he once mentions in the partly fanciful, partly historical, play of 'Macbeth.' In that noble tragedy the witches show the murderous king, their dupe and victim, a vision representing several British monarchs carrying 'twofold balls and treble sceptres,' indicating future sovereignty over the three kingdoms. All the glories and perils of Elizabeth's extraordinary reign are avoided by Shakespeare, while eagerly recording and illustrating the reigns of many among her predecessors.

In a long subsequent period some eminent Englishmen, Lord Chatham among them, owned that they learned their country's history chiefly from Shakespeare's historical plays, and it could not perhaps have been derived from a source less tainted with religious or political prejudices. The special value of Shakespeare and Scott in historical descriptions lies chiefly in their rare impartiality and love of truth in the delineation of character.

The former's grand words acknowledge the permanent value of truth so often violated or perverted in this brief world, yet which must prevail in that which is to come, according to religious belief:

> In the corrupted currents of this world,
> Offence's gilded hand may shove by justice;
> And oft 'tis seen the wicked prize itself
> Buys out the law; but 'tis not so above:
> There is no shuffling, there the action lies
> In his true nature; and we ourselves compell'd,
> Even to the teeth and forehead of our faults,
> To give in evidence. . . .
> *Hamlet*, act iii.

This great merit of thorough impartiality is seldom found in the works of statesmen or among zealous theologians. The enthusiasm of 'hero-worship' has, moreover, proved the special bane of able historians, being little compatible with strict veracity in recording the dealings of fallible men with each other in a world of trial and temptation. Writers, when yielding to this singular influence, are likely to induce readers to admire men for their success or genius alone, without carefully examining the conduct which may achieve the one or disgrace the other. It is a characteristic merit of Shakespeare and Scott to describe both real and imaginary persons sometimes endowed with great genius and every quality to ensure success or command influence, yet to be so wicked or debased as to deserve no admiration beyond a limited point.

Shakespeare, in sketching historical persons, certainly endows them more or less with a power of language and beauty of expression exclusively his own. Yet in the main points his account usually agrees remarkably with that of historical record. He represents King John and Richard III., despite their eloquent or dramatic language in actual deeds, much the same men whom Hume, Hallam, and other historians describe in calm, measured language. Shakespeare thus endows historical characters with dramatic attraction, but their real actions he mentions in accordance with history.

Scott does the same in historical novels describing British civil wars or rebellions. While mingling real persons with those of his fancy, the latter, perhaps, sometimes of a loftier type than shown by history, he gives a surprisingly correct impression of their times. Most of his historical novels appeared soon after the battle of Waterloo, when recollections of the Jacobite revolts of 1715 and 1745 had comparatively ceased to agitate British minds. Descendants of executed or exiled Jacobites were enlisted, as well as those of former opponents, in the service of the British monarchy representing a reigning House without a rival. To induce readers to admire and pity the Jacobites without regretting their failure, to loyally obey the ruling party while respecting the motives of the defeated one, was the truly patriotic object indicated, especially in 'Waverley,' 'Rob Roy,' and 'Redgauntlet.' In 'The Abbot,' 'Old Mortality,' and 'Woodstock,' Scott dealt with those opposing religious interests among fellow countrymen which were for a time closely involved in political rivalry.

The different sections of Protestants, first warring with Roman Catholics and afterwards among themselves, had roused almost incredible hostility between fellow countrymen. Eager politicians and zealous theologians alike vindicated or glorified their partisans often at the expense of maligned or oppressed opponents. The British public were perhaps never so much inclined to historic impartiality as by the works of Scott. People whose remote or recent ancestry had slain each other in religious or political contests were induced to recognise moral merit, both in opponents and in partisans. A more patriotic benefit to the subjects of an empire divided in religious and political opinions could hardly be extended through the peaceful medium of literature. Other poets and dramatists have described British religious and political parties, but seldom with truthful impartiality. Among the most attractive, Dryden, in 'The Hind and the Panther' and other works, was much admired. In that able, satirical poem he censures or ridicules the chief Christian divisions except Roman Catholicism, which he praises, while never mentioning the Greek Church. The Romish faith, protected by the royal lion James II., is the pure, milk-white hind, persecuted by ferocious beasts representing the most influential Protestant divisions; and Atheism is personified in the monkey, 'the mocking ape, who mimicked all sects and had his own to choose.'

The Jews are not named by Dryden, probably because in his time they took no part in British politics, being naturally indifferent to the quarrels of rival Christians among themselves. Mohammedans are not mentioned either, as they, at this period, were of less interest to the British than the Jews.

When this remarkable poem appeared the Romish Church in Britain was in the strange position of a faith represented by a British minority, yet accepted by an Irish majority and also by the reigning sovereign of the three kingdoms. Dryden seldom apparently tried to reconcile or pacify disputing parties, whether religious or political. Conciliation, indeed, was no object of his brilliant genius, for his keen ridicule of all faiths but the Catholic was in his time more calculated to irritate than to pacify. His popularity as a religious or political partisan was fortunately never very extensive among the masses. His works were chiefly read in England, probably more in London than anywhere else, while his scorn of Puritanism would surely have offended a large majority in Scotland.

Ireland has produced many writers showing yet more bitterness or prejudice in religious and political views. Eloquence, energy, zeal, and talent have usually in that unfortunate country been devoted to eager eulogy or implacable invective, extravagant praise, or unscrupulous denunciation of differing religions and opposing politics. Even in Dublin enmity to England and the English, if not a general, still seems a popular, sentiment.[1] If Dublin in this respect represents an Irish majority, the peaceful prosperity of London amid troubles and revolts in nearly all European capitals during the middle and end of the nineteenth century seems to well represent, within a larger compass, the almost universal loyalty of Britain. It seems still prospering in the candid estimation of foreigners and colonists who visit or know about it. A recent impressive instance of London's civilised pre-eminence was shown in the present Queen's Jubilee, June, 1897. On that interesting occasion the loyalty of Britain's colonies, the friendship of her foreign allies, and the warm attachment of British subjects to the monarchy were unmistakably displayed. London appeared in full glory at this celebration, proving itself a city in which the practical and the romantic, the real and the imaginative are blended in a most remarkable manner. Artists of all kinds, besides historians, statesmen, warriors, and theologians, have long contributed to render London the chief capital of modern civilisation and intellectual influence. The London of Shakespeare shows its population always deeply attached to monarchy, even amid Court intrigues or when under the temporary influence of an unworthy king or his favourites.

In all Shakespeare's sketches of London's population, a strong affection for the royal family is shown decisively. The monarchy, sometimes divided between rival representatives, is always the chief

[1] See Lecky's remarks, *Democracy and Liberty*, chap. vi.

interest in Shakespeare's English historical dramas. Thus the strange period of Jack Cade's revolt is described in a thoroughly royalist spirit. Cade and his partisans are keenly ridiculed, as well as censured, in the evident wish to prevent sympathy for them, their designs, or their fate. Though Cade is evidently a brave man, he is no favourite with Shakespeare, who ridicules him and his revolt with the scornful sarcasm of an ardent monarchist. He makes his followers secretly ridicule Cade while the mutinous leader is addressing the mob—a theatrical scene which doubtless delighted a loyal London audience :

> *Cade.* We John Cade, so termed of our supposed father,—
> *Dick [the butcher, aside].* Or rather, of stealing a cade of herrings.
> *Cade.* I am able to endure much.
> *Dick [aside].* No question of that; for I have seen him whipped three market-days together.
> *Cade.* I fear neither sword nor fire.
> *Dick [aside].* But, methinks, he should stand in fear of fire, being burnt i' the hand for stealing of sheep.
> *Henry VI.* part ii.

Even Cade's fate, when a half-starved fugitive slain by the loyalist, Squire Iden, elicits none of Shakespeare's sympathy. Yet the unfortunate leader dies bravely, while his triumphant slayer glories in his victory, as if he had delivered England from a dangerous enemy, and is well rewarded by his approving sovereign, Henry VI.

Among Shakespeare's most pleasing London scenes, Anne Boleyn's coronation and the christening of the Princess Elizabeth are perhaps the most impressive. In some respects the loyal enthusiasm of the London people resembled that of their existing representatives during the joyous popular excitement of royal celebrations in London, and of which Queen Victoria's Jubilee in 1897 was a remarkable instance. Allowing for many changes, inevitable in a long period of time, the enthusiasm of London people described by Shakespeare in applauding royal festivities much resembles the spirit shown at the present time during similar occasions for loyal rejoicing and congratulation.

The most remarkable difference perhaps between London's loyal demonstrations of past and present times is the large addition of Asiatic, together with colonial friendship lately so conspicuous. In Shakespeare's time the friendship of the ruling Scottish faction, the enforced submission of the Irish majority, the doubtful relations with France, and the enmity of Spain alike formed the encouragement and aroused the apprehensions of the English government. The friendship or loyalty of Asiatics, and the faithful adherence of immense colonies sprung chiefly from British ancestry, were altogether unknown. They are the peculiar and interesting results of subsequent history, and are evidently more developed than ever at the end of the present century.

CHAPTER XVII

Differing views of London expressed by Johnson, Cowper, Scott, and Dickens—Scottish and Irish rebellions differently treated by their respective historians—Unfairness in blaming men of former times for enforcing laws still unrepealed.

THE London described by Dr. Johnson and by the poet Cowper in prose and verse shows the feelings of thoughtful Englishmen alike proud of their capital, yet deploring its many social evils. Johnson's profound mind was devoted to promoting, encouraging, and improving literary effort, taste, and culture among his acquaintances. His experience of genius and talent, struggling in London against adversity, appears in his expressive lines:

> The mournful truth is everywhere confessed,
> Slow rises worth by poverty depressed.

Cowper, more sad or sentimental and less practical, describes the London of his days with a melancholy interest:

> O thou, resort and mart of all the Earth,
> Chequer'd with all complexions of mankind,
> And spotted with all crimes;
> In whom I see
> Much that I love, and more that I admire,
> And all that I abhor . . .
>   *The Task*, book iii.

Johnson's good sense, love of justice, and humanity made him censure folly or frivolity in literature, and to unite sound wisdom with literary appreciation. His personal liking for the great metropolis, as the best residence both in winter and summer, did not, however, lead him to much examine or describe its poorer population. He loved the London of literary merit, of intellectual intercourse, and learned conversation; while to Walter Scott, its position in the singular reigns of James I. and Charles II., noticed in 'Nigel' and 'Peveril of the Peak,' gave it a peculiar historic interest. These two kings, their Courts and statesmen, with the manners, customs, and troubles of their times, are described by one uniting the gifts of a novelist with the knowledge of a studious antiquary. Yet he seldom dwells long on descriptions of London, which is perhaps to be regretted. His chief delight is to recall the Scottish civil wars, the Crusades, and romantic stories of former times in Great Britain. His sketches of London are more designed to illustrate the characters of kings, ministers, and historical celebrities than those of its poorer population. The latter in due course, however, found an able, most gifted, and original exponent in Charles Dickens. This most popular writer of fiction since Scott saw little or nothing in history to suit his peculiar literary talents. He devoted them to inventing characters and events, generally in London.

When he began to write Jacobite recollections

had disappeared from Britain. The results of the battle of Waterloo not only restored European peace, but had for some years placed England in the forefront of the powers of Europe. This grand, responsible position she has since maintained more by a prudent, pacific, unaggressive policy than by war. During many years England has rather avoided European warfare while turning her conquering energies chiefly in the direction of Asia and Africa. In these quarters of the world the British steadily extend or confirm their conquests and influence, and hitherto with a success which indicates permanent supremacy. All opposition to the reigning House has vanished. No external danger has for a long period threatened Great Britain, guarded by her admirable fleet, and on friendly terms with the chief European powers. Even the Napoleon family, as shown apparently by its last reigning representative, nourished no national enmity against England which was openly avowed.

A little before the middle of the nineteenth century the emancipation of Roman Catholics and of Jews from civil disabilities was warmly advocated by influential Englishmen, especially in London. Such concessions to subjected fellow countrymen seemed the more safe and reasonable in British opinion when the divided empire, no longer distracted by foreign war or domestic revolt, could fairly study its internal condition. It was thus in a time of profound national peace, and only a few years after

Scott's historical novels had so aided to enlighten British minds, that the first works of Dickens appeared. His 'London' had little to do with historical events, characters, or information. Except in 'Barnaby Rudge,' where the anti-Catholic riots of 1780 are described, the author adheres to fiction alone, though in his subsequent 'Tale of Two Cities' the French Revolution just before Napoleon's time is glanced at, but no historic characters are introduced. In 'Barnaby' Dickens proves himself utterly free from religious prejudice. His fairness, however, may not arise, like that of Scott, from historic impartiality, but from comparative ignorance or indifference about the philosophy of religious fanaticism. His great design, shown in his best works, is to condemn and ridicule religious hypocrisy in every way and in many different forms. His knowledge of modern English life apparently makes him consider this odious or contemptible vice as of greater importance and likely to do more evil than is usually supposed. He associates Lord George Gordon, the real fanatic who nominally headed the riots in 1780, not with bigots or enthusiasts, but with mean, crafty ruffians of his invention, who are utterly devoid of religious principles. To expose hypocrisy, cant, and false pretences is the object of Dickens, while to expose religious fanaticism was that of Scott, and herein lies a most remarkable difference between the two greatest British novelists of the century. This difference is in great measure attributable to the peculiar changes in the political and religious state of Britain during their separate periods.

When Scott wrote, the influence of Napoleon's wars and a renewed national antipathy against the French, of whom Bonaparte had shown himself the popular incarnation, prevailed largely throughout Great Britain. Though no rival prince opposed the reigning British monarch, and all Jacobitism had practically vanished with the death of the Pretender Charles Edward, yet sad remembrances of Jacobite wars and sufferings lingered in parts of Scotland. To complete the national reconciliation was Scott's great object, and was, in fact, accomplished with true patriotic success. His first novel, 'Waverley, or 'Tis Sixty Years Since,' appealed to the immediate descendants of the opposing parties in the last Jacobite rising of 1745. His account of the Scottish Highlanders was perhaps the first ever written that really interested the English people, hitherto either ignorant about them, or inclined to view them in Milton's words as 'thieves and redshanks.' The Jacobite leaders, mostly Highlanders, unlike Irish revolutionists, displayed, and probably possessed, little eloquence to aid their cause. Wolfe Tone, the Emmetts, and other Irish revolutionists in more recent years showed in speeches and writings great command of language and beauty of expression; while the Jacobite leaders, whether Highland chiefs or English gentlemen, showed little of either. They usually with firm emphasis exclaimed at their last moments, 'God save King James!' meaning the old

Pretender, and suffered execution without display of eloquence.

The Jacobites were evidently men of action alone, devoted to their cause, fighting bravely for it, and suffering death or exile with silent fortitude; but the Irish, after the disastrous revolt of 1798, singularly devoid of heroism or noble deeds on either side, yet glorified it with all the charm which eloquence and poetical talent could convey to posterity. The brave fidelity of the Highlanders, their picturesque dress, and romantic country, interested some Englishmen far more than they interested Scottish fellow countrymen, the Lowlanders, of whom many, according to Macaulay, viewed the Highland garb as 'the dress of a thief.'[1] Indeed, he declares that the Highlanders were regarded by more civilised Scottish men much as Red Indians were regarded by European colonists in America; but this statement is probably exaggerated.[2]

In 'Waverley' the Highland chief McIvor and his devoted follower Evan, executed for rebellion in behalf of the Stuart family, surpassed in pathetic

---

[1] *History of England.*

[2] Of these eminent writers, Scott and Macaulay, who differ so much in their views on Scottish history, though each knew it thoroughly, Thackeray observes in a different style from his usual sarcasm:—'Here are two examples of men most differently gifted, each pursuing his calling, each speaking his truth as God bade him, each honest in his life, just and irreproachable in his dealings, dear to his friends, honoured by his country, beloved at his fireside. It has been the fortunate lot of both to give incalculable happiness and delight to the world, which thanks them in return with an immense kindliness, respect, affection.'—*Roundabout Papers*, p. 216.

interest most imaginary persons in contemporary novels. Educated or thoughtful men in Great Britain were effectually induced by Scott to see that, within their civilised dominions sanctioned by existing law, generous, noble fellow countrymen had suffered cruelly for political offences alone. It is possible, perhaps, that some reaction in favour of Jacobitism might have inspired enthusiastic readers; but this result Scott carefully discouraged. His readers, despite their aroused sympathy for Jacobite sufferers, were also shown, as it were, between the lines, that they merited compassion rather than approval or confidence. Their heroism in adversity was indeed admirable; but calm reflection would likely warn readers that in triumph the most dangerous qualities of the Jacobites would soon make them tyrants as implacable as their political predecessors in the reign of the Pretender's father, James II. Macaulay ably describes this king's cruelty to rebels against his authority under his illegitimate nephew the Duke of Monmouth. The severities of James II. at this time may be well compared with those of the opposite party subsequently under the Duke of Cumberland, surnamed the 'Butcher' by his opponents in 1745. In violating the claims of humanity there may not, perhaps, be very much difference between them. But whether it is just for posterity to blame either kings, generals, or judges for enforcing existing laws against ' rebellion ' is a question deserving probably more calm attention and self-control than it has usually received from either historians, politicians, poets, or novelists. 'Treason' against existing rule, no matter how established, was generally believed to deserve death by all opposing parties in Great Britain, and had always been thought to do so from the most remote times of British history. Thus Monmouth and some followers were legally executed as 'rebels taken in arms' against existing authority, which they undoubtedly were.

The same penalty for precisely the same offence was inflicted on vanquished Jacobites in 1715 and 1745. Their own stern example was literally followed, not improved upon, by George I. and George II., who in their turn considered men calling themselves loyal to a banished king as rebels to a reigning one. The laws against 'treason' were evidently not much changed from the reigns of James II. to George II. inclusive. The government of James II. on one side, and the Duke of Cumberland on the other, may none of them have shown or felt humane reluctance in enforcing existing laws against rebels; but they were not enacted by these men, who were usually blamed or execrated for enforcing them according to their legal duty. Historical students may well observe how often kings, statesmen, soldiers, or judges were termed cruel tyrants for obeying existing legislation as if morally responsible for it. In fact, often in British history the legal cruelties inflicted, or rather permitted, by successive rulers, had little or nothing to do with their personal feelings or characters. Men in power found their duties in the form of legal obligations made for them by previous enactments, which were framed in the alleged interests of the nation at large, and which had never been repealed.

In some cases rulers or their subordinates might and did remonstrate against such severity. But they were often overruled by the advice of those around them, as well as by the voice of public opinion, generally apprehending fatal danger to existing rule from the least compassion shown towards those who had attempted to overthrow it. Shakespeare accurately expresses English public opinion upon this subject till recent times:

> Abate the edge of traitors, gracious Lord,
> Let them not live to taste this land's increase,
> That would with treason wound this fair land's peace !
> *Richard III.* act v.

CHAPTER XVIII

The cordiality between England and Scotland increased by Scott's writings—Reception of George IV. in Scotland—Contrast between Scott's and Macaulay's opinions of Scottish Highlanders—British parties united during the wars of Napoleon I.

To judge historical personages by the moral standard of other times is certainly unfair, and has led historians and historical writers to form mistaken conclusions about them.[1] It seems evident that the cruelties inflicted by British opposing parties on each other from long before James II.'s reign till that of George II. were scarcely considered such in the present sense of the term. Each party had in the other's opinion committed the same crime of rebellion against established rule, and alike deserved the same penalty. Legal severities were really thought essential to the safety of the reigning party, while political victims on both sides longed to inflict the same penalty as that to which the fortune of war had condemned themselves. In fact, therefore, the personal feelings of the victors could seldom

[1] 'The men of each age and country must be judged by the ideal of their own age and country, and not by the ideal of ours.'—Lecky's *Political Value of History*, p. 50.

avail those victims whom existing laws sentenced to execution as a public duty. The real disgrace of such judicial cruelty lay among the public generally, both in Britain and on the Continent, over whom a Christian clergy either could exercise no merciful influence or seldom tried to do so. In the Statute Books of most if not all Christian countries considering themselves highly civilised, there remained for centuries laws against religious opinions, as well as against treason, strangely inconsistent with what are now considered Christian principles.

When such severity was legalised even against peaceful individuals for matters of opinion, armed rebellion could expect no clemency in even Christian countries long after the political establishment of the religion of Mercy. It is evident that the last recorded words of British political victims seldom deprecated the cruelty of their victors as a crime. They only regretted that their relative positions were not reversed, when it was sufficiently clear that their conduct would have been the same towards their prisoners. No political party apparently proclaimed mercy towards fallen foes as their future object or as a moral duty.

If, therefore, Lords Derwentwater, Balmerino, and other executed Jacobites, perhaps resembling Scott's McIvor in 'Waverley,' had triumphed, there seems every probability that the severities of their party in James II.'s reign would have been revived. The adherents of the reigning family and of the so-called Pretender alike called and thought each other rebels, and the legal penalty of rebellion in Great Britain and Ireland was certain death. The only question was which of the royal rivals was the Lord's Anointed, as it was thought equally sinful to rebel against either by their respective followers. Though the reigning House of Hanover was upheld by the most intelligent and best educated men in England, political parties were more divided in Scotland.[1]

The chief adherents of the banished Stuarts were evidently Scottish Highlanders, and though a few Englishmen of wealth and influence favoured the same cause, the majority in England and most Scottish Lowlanders considered them enemies, if not uncivilised plunderers. In this last opinion many Scottish Lowlanders induced the English to view fellow Scottishmen with mingled contempt and distrust.[2]

But the English, especially the London public, were induced by Scott to pity his Highland Jacobites, evidently representing the real leaders executed within living memory, and yet to feel

---

[1] 'Jacobitism, in England little more after the reign of George I. than an empty sound, subsisted in Scotland as a vivid emotion of loyalty, a generous promptitude to act or suffer in its cause.'—Hallam's *Constitutional History*, chap. xvii.

[2] 'The enmity between the Highland borderer and the Lowland borderer was the growth of ages. The Highlander was an object of hatred to his Saxon neighbour, and, from his Saxon neighbours, those Saxons who dwelt far from him learned the very little that they cared to know about his habits. When the English condescended to think of him at all, they considered him as a savage, a cut-throat, and a thief.'—Macaulay's *History of England*, vol. iii.

confidence in the ruling party, represented in
'Waverley' and 'Rob Roy' by Colonel Talbot and
Frank Osbaldistone. In 'Waverley' McIvor and
Talbot impressively represent their opposing political
parties. Romantic interest and compassion are
aroused for McIvor, but more esteem and respect are
the due of Colonel Talbot, and thus Scott induces
readers to admire the Jacobites without desiring
their triumph. The most steady adherents of the
House of Hanover and the immediate descendants
of its defeated foes were alike interested, and to
some extent drawn together in recognition of mutual
merit by Scott's calm, judicious fairness expressed
by the delightful power of his literary genius. The
complete and permanent union of England and
Scotland must always interest admirers of British
rule. It could hardly be thought really accomplished till the reign of George III., and was
specially manifested during the visit to Scotland of
his successor, George IV., in 1822.[1]

This event was not only a brilliant spectacle, but
displayed the cordial blending of British religious
and political parties. No rival for the throne remained; the Stuarts were extinct, at least in the
male line. The recollection of Jacobite revolts had

[1] 'The preparations for His Majesty's reception under the
direction of Sir Walter Scott were of the most magnificent
description. The ancient loyalty of the Scotch broke forth with
unexampled ardour; the devoted attachment they had shown
to the Stuarts was now transferred to the reigning family. The
clans from all parts of the Highlands appeared in their
picturesque and varied costumes.'—Alison's *History of Europe*,
vol. ii.

for some years altogether yielded in interest to the tremendous Continental warfare which, ending on the field of Waterloo, beheld English and Scottish united with the chief powers of Europe against the French enemy.

The youthful valour or enterprise of Great Britain had been for some years diverted from all idea of civil war by the attractive martial campaigns of Napoleon, whose very name aroused hostile enthusiasm.

> Perhaps a recruit
> Might chance to shoot
> Great General Bonaparte

was said to be the poetical temptation offered by recruiting sergeants at this time to rustic or ignorant and youthful candidates for military honour. As if to complete the reconciliation of parties in Scotland, from the formerly opposing families of Argyle and Montrose to peasants and artisans, Scott's historic novels had peculiarly enlightened the minds of all thoughtful Scottishmen. Most of his works were given to the British public during the Regency and subsequent reign of George IV. Scott had, though only through the medium of literature, taken the practical lead in checking English prejudices against the Highlanders by enlightening instead of confirming former ignorance about them. Yet even recent Scottish historians take surprisingly different views of the national reconciliation. Alison, agreeing with Scott, favours the Highlanders, while Macaulay, to whom they seem the foes of true freedom if not of civilisation itself, seldom mentions them without contempt and dislike.[1] His allusions to George IV.'s visit to Scotland are a thorough, even an amusing, contrast to those of Alison, and doubtless to those of Scott also. These three eminent Scottishmen differ essentially about their country's history, yet are comparatively free from either political or religious bitterness. Unlike many Irish writers they seem practically free from that implacability which to this day influences or perverts a vast amount of oratorical and literary talent in Ireland. The good-humoured raillery with which Scott treats opinions and men whom he opposes, and the polished contempt of Macaulay for everything he considers barbarous, ignorant, or uncultivated, were clearly never meant to arouse or preserve those popular prejudices which have influenced Irish history even during recent years. Though it might be sincerely hoped that this result was not the wish of either Irish poets, historians, or politicians, many were largely responsible for maintaining it. But

[1] 'The power of the chiefs was destroyed, the people were disarmed, the use of the old national garb interdicted, the old predatory habits were effectually broken, when a strange reflux of public opinion began. Pity succeeded to aversion. As long as the Gaelic dress was worn the Saxons had pronounced it hideous and ridiculous, nay, grossly indecent. Soon after it had been prohibited they discovered that it was the most graceful drapery in Europe. The last British king who held a court in Holyrood thought that he could not give a more striking proof of his respect for the usages which prevailed in Scotland before the Union than by disguising himself in what before the Union was considered by nine men out of ten in Scotland as the dress of a thief.'—*History of England*, chap. xiii.

George IV. in Scotland, surrounded by Highlanders, and himself in Highland dress, apparently completed the national pacification which Scott's literary efforts had tried to promote. On this occasion Sir Walter was in his proper element. Many Jacobites of his fancy and of reality, Balmerino and Derwentwater among the latter, and the Baron of Bradwardine, McIvor, and Redgauntlet among the former, were probably in his historic mind when seeing their descendants or representatives greeting an undisputed monarch and peace among Scottish parties completely restored. Since this gratifying display of Scottish national loyalty no important differences have disturbed the relations of England and Scotland. They have become thoroughly united, and perhaps less prejudice was felt in England against political or religious divisions in Scotland than may have yet lingered in its remote districts owing to local tradition or family feud.

CHAPTER XIX

Great change in European policy towards the Turks since the Greek revolution of 1824—Britain and France unite in favour of the Turks against the Russians in the Crimean war of 1854—Extension of British and Russian influence in Asia.

THE successful revolt of the Greeks against the Turks in 1824 had brought the British, the Russians, and the restored French monarchy into active alliance in establishing a free Greek kingdom. The result of this singular contest greatly increased both British and Russian influence in Asia. In the subsequent Crimean war of 1854 a remarkable change took place in European policy towards the Turks. A comparison between these wars for and against Turkish rule forms a remarkably instructive study in the history of this century. The French under their restored monarchy were allied with British and Russians in 1824 against the Turks, who were at peace with them all, and had certainly broken no faith with any European power. This active alliance, however, of British, French, and Russians in aid of the Greek revolutionists against Turkey, took place some nine or ten years after the battle of Waterloo. But in the Crimean war, 1854-5, these powers were again engaged in war, though with very different objects.

The French reappeared on Russian territory, commanded by the nephew and heir of Napoleon I., firmly allied with the British against the Russians. By their combined efforts the latter were defeated, forced to destroy their fleet in the Black Sea, and Mohammedan rule was thereby preserved by Christian aid over thousands of discontented Christian subjects; yet in both these different wars British influence was indirectly promoted. The French, vanquished at Waterloo, were victorious when allied with the British at Navarino and in the Crimea. The Russians, victorious against the first Napoleon and when aiding the Greeks against the Turks, were now for a time decisively checked in the Crimea. Yet the British, in these three wars against French, Turks, and Russians, were always on the winning side. Most indeed, if not all, the wars of this century left British power or indirect influence stronger than before, while the Russians have steadily extended their conquests, almost entirely by land, till now their vast dominion stretches from the border of Sweden to the north of China. The British, whose wishes or interests were opposed to European and American conquests, have yet extended or consolidated their rule in Asia and Africa, and, despite some slight reverses, with a success which is apparently permanent.[1] India, and parts

[1] 'In nearly the whole of the north American and Australian continents, and in those parts of southern Africa most suitable

of south and of east and west Africa, were the chief scenes of their recent conquests or explorations. Among their varied non-Christian subjects the Mohammedans are politically the most important, representing the faith of the independent countries, Turkey, Persia, Afghanistan, and Morocco. The Hindoo millions in India can hardly be said to have an independent sovereign. The numerous Buddhists in Burma, China, and Ceylon are to a great extent under British power or influence. In Thibet, owing to its remote position, the Buddhists are more independent; but the unaggressive or unwarlike nature of the inhabitants seems hitherto to rather avoid than court intercourse with Europeans. The state of the secluded densely populated empire of China was always most peculiar. On its northern frontier it is more and more overawed by Russian influence, while in the east it has lately been defeated in a short war by the Japanese. This singular people, unlike the Chinamen, admire and cultivate European manners, customs, and alliances with rare intelligence. Their friendship for the British is specially gratifying to all interested in the progress of national civilisation.

The Japanese in every respect seem a pleasing

---

for European races, the English-speaking peoples are in possession. No other peoples have so firmly and permanently established their position. No limits can be set to the expansion they are likely to undergo even in the next century, and it would seem almost inevitable that they must in future exercise a preponderating influence in the world.'—Kidd's *Social Evolution*, chap. ix.

and creditable contrast to their Chinese neighbours in their estimate of Europeans, and particularly of the British.[1] Throughout India and the Cape of Good Hope British power seems not only confirmed, but extending its influence to adjoining lands. Yet the British encounter hostility from the Dutch Boers in South Africa, and no further enmity from native races gives the same trouble to them as the stubborn opposition of Dutch and German colonists, who, successfully defying African natives, now turn the same fearless front towards Europeans as formerly they turned towards the Kaffirs and other tribes. Free from foreign control, and firmly established in the land of their adoption, these colonists seem steadily opposed to British influence if not intercourse, to which, for the sake of their common civilisation, it is to be hoped they may become reconciled.

[1] 'Thy greatness O England, is not thy own making.
'The warm wind, that comes from the West, and the fruitful rains which it brings, are brought to thy shores by a power that is not thine own.
'Thou wast placed in the centre of the land hemisphere, and the whole world turns towards thee.
'Thou art the world's mart, and thy wealth is the world's.
'Thou art the product of ages of human labour from Abraham and Homer downwards.
'The wor'd demands from thee a service which is thy due.
'Thy fleet ought to be employed not merely to protect thy interest, but to right the world's wrong.
'Japan, too, comes to thee, not to beg help of thee, but to claim from thee fellowship of brothers, which is thy honour to give and ours to receive.
'In all our strifes of onward progress great is our need of thy arts, thy laws, thy institutions, thy literature as well.'—A Japanese editor on the greatness of England, London *Times* of May 1, 1897.

In the south of Asia and in the Indian Archipelago it seems that, often where British power does not extend, its influence to some extent prevails. Thus, the independent Japanese are peculiarly friendly to England, while their numerous Chinese neighbours are more and more in fear of the Russians on their northern, and of the British towards their southern, frontier. The Russian progress in the far east of Asia at the close of this century is one of its most remarkable events. Though checked in their advance on Turkey by the Crimean war and jealously watched ever since by the European powers, the Russians seem turning most attention to the eastern portion of their Asiatic dominion, while the British appear destined to oppose them by war or diplomacy in eastern Europe and throughout Asia. The nervous fear of Russia among the Anglo-Indians is of long standing, and it is a serious hindrance to the progress of civilisation that these European powers are continually thwarting each other. Their unfortunate rivalry thus maintains, at present, semi-barbarous rule over subjected thousands, who seem worthy of a better fate. Were England and Russia united or free from mutual distrust, there would probably be no limit to their political supremacy in Asia, as there at present exists no formidable non-Christian government in the world. Undisputed political pre-eminence might now be asserted by Christian powers for the benefit of mankind generally, did not political jealousies check and delay each other's progress. This political rivalry restraining the advance of civilisation is a remarkable contrast to former historical times, especially those of the Crusades. At that period, and long afterwards, Mohammedanism was warlike, aggressive, and enterprising. No other faith since Christianity had spread through Asia and Africa with the same energetic power. Its enthusiastic votaries had first abolished the Arabian paganism, then overcame the Parsees in Persia, the Brahmins in India, and politically triumphed over other religions in Asia and Africa. When Mohammedanism stopped in its victorious career, it found that only Christians could oppose its military power. The defeated millions of Brahmins and Buddhists in central and southern Asia remained most of them unconverted and some politically independent, but comparatively unaggressive, while the scattered Jews, passing entirely under Christian and Mohammedan rule, were usually the oppressed and obedient subjects of both. During many centuries, therefore, Christianity and Mohammedanism rivalled one another in central Asia, in eastern and for a short time in southern Europe, and in northern Africa.

All military genius or success has comparatively abandoned the votaries of every other faith. But the fact of Christian powers warring against each other for the avowed purpose of preserving Mohammedan rule over Christian populations longing for deliverance is altogether new in the world's history. Yet such was the design and result of the Crimean war, and is still the tendency of European policy. It is evident also that British, Russian, and French authority or influence in Asia and Africa is rewarded by this policy in the increased loyalty of Mohammedan subjects. As neither Mohammedan subjects nor neighbours of Russia took advantage of their conqueror's reverses, the defeat of the Russians may perhaps be termed, therefore, merely a temporary check, their progress in Asia having steadily advanced ever since. Persians, Tartars, and Chinese along their vast boundary are more and more influenced or overawed by them, even where their direct rule may not extend.

British progress in India was chiefly made by conquest before, and by consolidation since, the Crimean war. This century, especially its latter part, has seen this peaceful confirmation of British, French, and Russian power over millions of Asiatic and African Mohammedans. In no case, except for a short time in Afghanistan, has Christian advance been repulsed by the latter. This mountainous country, inhabited by a brave, suspicious race, has hitherto preserved independence, and is often the scene of intrigues between the Russians on its northern frontier and the British on its southeast. The former are politically supreme in Khiva and Bokhara, though not their acknowledged rulers; while the British, since their annexation of the Punjaub, hold the frontier town of Peshawur on the Afghan frontier, and can from thence defy attempts at invading India.¹ An Afghan prince has lately visited England and Russia, and his country is on friendly terms with both. The British wars in India, in former and recent times, were on the whole far more serious and sanguinary than any contest of the Russians in their vast Asiatic territories. All these wars finally ended in European triumph, and Afghanistan, though nominally free from English or Russian rule, is yet the scene of their diplomatic intrigues. It has produced some brave chiefs, but none capable of leading martial natives from its mountainous region, to the strength of which its comparative independence is chiefly due.

At the present time all serious opposition to British, French, and Russian supremacy has ceased among non-Christian nations. Though on the Indian frontier some warlike hill tribes occasionally attack the British, and in eastern Africa Europeans are still defied by the Mohammedan Khalifa in the Soudan, their resistance must finally yield to European perseverance and discipline.

---

¹ 'It is in accordance with the principles of our advance hitherto that Afghanistan should form the buffer state between India and Russian Central Asia.'—*Asiatic Quarterly Review*, January 1898.

CHAPTER XX

Increasing loyalty of Mohammedans and other non-Christians to Great Britain, France, and Russia—Friendship of these three powers for the Turks—They discourage the Greeks in warring against Turkey—Indignation of Mr. Gladstone at this policy.

It may seem surprising that while the royal families of Britain and Russia are now connected and more friendly and intimate than ever, yet the political jealousies of the nations they rule still cause rivalry in Asiatic policy. Their political supremacy is no longer threatened by any Asiatic race; the age of Mohammedan champions has apparently vanished. The half-friendly, half-submissive visits of Asiatic princes to the British and Russian capitals recently are impressive signs of increasing Christian authority. Yet, in a religious sense, the political triumph of that faith neither causes nor seems to promote the conversion of subjected or allied non-Christians to any great extent. Though Mohammedans seem to have lost former warlike enterprise or enthusiasm, their religious faith remains firm as ever. Whether under French rule in Algiers, under the Russians in Asia, or under the British in Asia and Africa, the subjected millions show little inclination to join any of the three forms of Christianity professed by their different rulers. The Khalifa in east Africa, still resisting the British, can hardly be called a Mohammedan champion, as his unpopularity among many of his own people and his disavowal by Mohammedan governments force him to remain on the defensive.

In the chief Mohammedan countries the rulers are either friendly to European powers or afraid of them. Britain, Russia, and France remain the only Christian powers ruling large Mohammedan populations. It is remarkable that this century has seen these three nations at war with one another: Britain and Russia allied against France in Napoleon's time, and Britain allied with France against Russia in the Crimean war; yet these wars gave no new territory to independent Mohammedans, and at present soldiers of that faith are freely enlisted in support of Christian rule in Asia and Africa, while Mohammedan princes, either subjects or allies, make friendly visits to European courts. This pacific spectacle has been oftener shown recently than at any former period, and may be thought a significant sign of the times. It seems a practical proof of the popularity as well as strength of European rule; yet though intercourse between nations of all religions is so much increased and usually of a friendly kind, there is little sign of religious conversion except in rare instances, and in some countries no reconciliation between native Christians and Mohammedans. No nation has avowedly changed its religion or its form of the same one for many years, despite frequent political changes. The recent brief war between the Greeks and their former Turkish rulers on behalf of Cretan and Armenian Christian subjects of Turkey ended in the defeat of the former. The European powers, Great Britain and France, showed the same desire to preserve Turkish rule as in the Crimean war, and were joined in this policy by Austria and Germany. The same friendship to Turkey was even shown by Russia, her latest European foe, the Russians apparently desiring the maintenance of Turkish rule as much as the French and the British.

The Germans and Austrians also showed a marked though passive opposition to the Greeks. This remarkable alliance in feeling of the chief Christian powers in favour of the Turks against the Greeks aroused the vehement, perhaps imprudent, ire of the aged statesman, Mr. Gladstone. He especially denounced Russia and Germany as ruled by 'two young despots,' describing the Christian powers and Turkey as six 'Goliaths,' united against the 'young David,' Greece. But his avowed indignation which once might have influenced the British was little heeded, either by opponents or former adherents. The Turks, being in far larger numbers, were victorious in a short contest with their assailants. This result doubtless gratified Mohammedans in every part of the world, yet no other nation of that faith took part in the dispute, which was left entirely for European powers to finally settle. They showed a decided resolve to preserve the unpopular rule of the Turks over Christian subjects in Europe and in Asia, and by alternate advice and occasional threats have often tried to influence the Sultan in governing them. The apparent indifference of other Mohammedan rulers during these remonstrances and complaints may seem surprising under circumstances so trying as those of the Sultan in their estimation, yet he seems to consult none of them, nor to care for their alliance, though bound together by a common faith. Alone ruling an agitated population of Mohammedans, Christians, and Jews, this Mohammedan ruler has long tried by diplomatic intrigue, pretences, or professions to baffle and elude the designs or wishes of Christian allies. His peculiar policy of combined submission and obstinacy, often practically defying the strongest powers in the world by skilfully availing himself of their mutual jealousies, has lasted several years, and to the present time seems rather successful.

His Armenian subjects, when lately attempting to revolt, were most severely punished, and their rebellion or rioting completely quelled. The hasty, ill-advised war of the Greeks in aid of the Cretan insurgents ended in Turkish victory, and the Sultan may perhaps boast that his power in Armenia and other provinces is firmer than before. Not only have Armenians been crushed, the Cretans discouraged, and Greek foes defeated by the Turks, but European ambassadors at Constantinople find the Sultan still inclined to evade or disappoint them, when offering advice with what he may think too much pertinacity. His present position indeed may not be so weak as it was, or has been for a long time represented. Though practically unaided by Mohammedan allies, he preserves the sympathies of millions among co-religionists under Christian rule; and, above all, he reckons confidently on the constant jealousies of the Christian powers. The determined opposition shown to the Greeks by them all, especially by the Germans, during their recent attempt at warfare, together with the slight and unavailing sympathy shown by Europe generally for the oppressed Armenians, prove a thorough change of European feeling or policy towards Turkish rule, from remote times till the Greek revolution of 1824 inclusive. The political weakness or unaggressiveness of Mohammedanism at present decidedly influences the European powers. They have, in fact, begun to dread each other more than they dread any non-Christian nation. The Turks, therefore, neither seek nor require much assistance from Mohammedan allies. While the British, French, and Russians peacefully rule a majority of loyal Mohammedans, they are disposed to view the Turkish Sultan as a useful ally. He has therefore been allowed to quell recent revolts of Christian subjects with great severity, and to defeat the Greeks without interference. Some unheeded protests on behalf of the Armenians were addressed to him by the leading Christian powers, while the successful maintenance of his authority was evidently what they wished to see. With persistent vehemence, perhaps partly arising from his love of everything connected with Greece,

Mr. Gladstone denounced the Sultan, through the London press, as the Great Assassin. This terrible appellation, though firmly pronounced and reiterated by the greatest perhaps of modern English statesmen, was disregarded alike by Christians and Mohammedans. Had he thus spoken when in power it would be hard to guess the result; but indignation, even invective, expressed by this popular statesman when out of office was completely ignored. His views on the important and unsettled Eastern question do not, therefore, seem those of a majority in the chief European countries at the present time.

Meanwhile British, French, and Russian rule over Asiatics and Africans continues very little disturbed, and is apparently increasing in popularity among them. The coronation of the present Russian Emperor, Nicholas II., at Moscow in 1896, and the Jubilee of Queen Victoria in 1897, displayed Mohammedan loyalty and friendship to both sovereigns in a specially pleasing manner. These celebrations were alike remarkable proofs of the success attending British and Russian policy in governing and dealing with Mohammedan nations. The allied, yet partially subjected, Tartar princes of Khiva and Bokhara and the Circassian troops in the Russian army proved the practical ascendency of the Muscovites in either absolute rule or indirect influence.[1]

[1] 'Mother Moscow, as says the caressing Russian phrase, is, indeed, the source of all Muscovite inspiration. From its churches are promulgated the authoritative utterances of the Greek Metropolitan, statues of Russian heroes adorn its open spaces, the edicts of the white Czar thunder over untold millions from its walls.'—Sloane's *Life of Napoleon*, chap. ix.

At the Queen's Jubilee some native princes of India were among the most loyal to their Empress, as they now term the British sovereign. Thus non-Christian loyalty, alike to Great Britain and to Russia, was displayed at these grand celebrations in honour of British and Russian sovereigns in their respective European capitals. These gratifying manifestations, though their importance may be exaggerated, still prove the absence of any non-Christian rivals of importance to European rulers. This was not the case even about the middle of this century, when the gallant Circassian chief, Schamyl Bey, resisted the Russians in the Caucasus; when the equally heroic Abd-el-Kader resisted the French in Algiers; and when British power in India was menaced by the well-armed, warlike Sikhs, and afterwards threatened by the sudden savage revolt of native Sepoy troops in the British service. But during these wars in different parts of the world, the Caucasus, northern Africa, and northern India, European triumph was alike decisive and permanent. Since their cessation far more signs of loyalty to Britain, France, and Russia are shown than were ever displayed before by non-Christian subjects. The French and the Russians have had to contend chiefly with Mohammedans. The Algerian Arabs, with their Moorish neighbours and co-religionists, have for many years ceased opposing the French, who rule the former and overawe the latter.

The Russians, in dealing with allied or submissive Turks and Persians, subjected Circassians, Georgians, and Tartars, and lastly with the timid, exclusive Chinese, have really found no formidable enemies to encounter in battle. The Buddhists throughout central Asia hitherto offer little, if any, opposition to the Russians; while that of Circassians, Persians, and Tartars has virtually ceased.[1]

Britain and Russia now reckon confidently on the loyal obedience, if not attachment, of millions of Mohammedan subjects, and while apprehension may be felt about their future fidelity, they are now of sufficient importance to induce Christian rulers to maintain increased friendship with Mohammedan sovereigns. This policy is a new feature in international history, and is evidently becoming more developed in theory and practice. Subjected non-Christian nations at present produce no liberating hero, nor show any resolute design to reassert independence of European control. Seditious or discontented thoughts are occasionally expressed, perhaps more lately than formerly, by a portion of the press in India against British supremacy, but as yet they have taken no definite shape nor aroused much popular sympathy. The ferocious mutiny of the

[1] 'A treaty was concluded between Persia and Russia in 1827. It gave the Russians entire dominion of the Caucasus, and as thorough command of the entrance into Persia as would be given to France by the acquisition of the whole of Switzerland and Savoy, with the fortresses of Alessandria and Mantua and the harbours of Genoa, for an irruption into Italy.'—Alison's *History of Europe*, chap. xiii.

Since this important treaty Russia has steadily increased her territorial influence in Asia from the Caucasus to the north of China, though her European progress was checked by the Crimean war, and not hitherto resumed.

Sepoys aroused no national rising, and was suppressed, indeed, partly by the aid of other native troops, who practically aided to maintain British supremacy in India.[1]

[1] 'India for the future belongs to Europe; it has its place in the Indo-European world, it has its place in our own history, and in what is the very life of history, the history of the human mind.'—Max Müller's *India: What can it teach us?* lecture i.

CHAPTER XXI

Continued decline in Mohammedan political power, despite the firm retention of that faith under Christian rule—Danger from political conspiracies in Europe—Revival of the warlike spirit in European countries.

DURING a long period Mohammedanism was extended and maintained by brave, devoted warriors, who, though politically ambitious, were chiefly inspired by religious zeal and resolved to spread as far as possible the religion of the Koran. Gradually, however, its military power has declined, despite the undiminished, if not increasing, number of its votaries. Those who might think that the decline of Mohammedanism would accompany the decline of the political power would, therefore, be mistaken. In the number of believers, and in their sincerity amid increasing knowledge of other faiths, Mohammedanism is probably more advocated by well-informed votaries than at any former time, though its warlike prowess shows little sign of revival. The French retention of Algiers, the Russian conquests in the Caucasus and central Asia, and the completion of British supremacy in India, are the most decisive and probably permanent European triumphs of this century.

Though Schamyl Bey and Abd-el-Kader may have somewhat recalled the career of Mohammedan heroes, Timour the Tartar, Saladin, or Mahomet II., these two recent chiefs, unlike former champions, were entirely on the defensive. To preserve the Caucasus and Algiers under Mohammedan rule, without attempting its extension, was all they tried and alike failed to do. Despite their valour, and perhaps some military skill, the French and the Russians severally annexed their countries, which have since peacefully obeyed those nations. The defeated chiefs evidently left no warlike successors of the same ability, and at present both Circassians and Arabs enlist as soldiers in the armies of their European rulers. In fact, Turks, Arabs, Persians, and Moors, the chief Mohammedan nations of the world, are more in dread of Europeans than of any non-Christians. Yet the slow progress of religious conversion among these races is certainly remarkable, and may appear to many a subject of disappointment.

The present state of the religious and political worlds, the one comparatively undisturbed, the other liable to frequent changes, forms a surprising contrast, while the political supremacy of Christianity seems more established and permanent than ever. Its ascendency is no longer dependent on force, but on the increasing concurrence of non-Christian subjects, many of whom apparently have no desire to exchange Christian rule for that of co-religionists.

But changes in religious belief are hitherto unimportant, at least in a national sense. Subjected Asiatics or Africans, while adopting more and more the dress, habits, and sometimes the language of European rulers, in religious thought seem less changed than at one time would have been thought possible, considering their increased intercourse with Christians.

It would seem from this century's history, especially, that everything connected with or conducive to the progress of mankind is advancing, more or less, from the vast influence of international intercourse, except religion. It alone remains unaffected in position, knowledge, or explanation by all the changes of recent times. Its influence, so distinct from every other feeling of which men are capable, still divides and engrosses the human race, without the smallest enlightenment from either invention or discovery. Thoughtful readers may perceive in historical facts, from the earliest times to the present, that some faiths have totally vanished, others equally ancient survive, and others again unite ancient and newer doctrines in the same creed. The religious toleration now prevailing in most Christian and in some non-Christian lands has no tendency to cause unanimity in religious belief. The position of avowed atheism from the earliest times among a small minority of learned men makes no acknowledged progress in recent years. This secret influence may or may not be increasing, yet, though enjoying perfect immunity,

P

it wins no external triumph and is not avowed by any nation or government. With the masses atheism was never popular in any country. From its disappointing, depressing nature, it can attract and arouse no enthusiasm, and would seem to many persons the sad result of despondency. All countries with any claim to civilisation steadily profess some religious faith, though with less enthusiasm, or devoted fervour in its behalf, than in former days.

In their place, however, there appears a general spirit of political justice allied with religious toleration, the natural result, it may be hoped, of a universal and increasing international communication, with its attendant lessons of intellectual enlightenment and social charity.[1] Nations no longer form their ideas of others from prejudiced report or misrepresentation. Personal or national experiences every year bring different nations and religions into closer contact. There is now, instead of exclusive ignorant fanaticism, a calm recognition of various religious beliefs, which, though giving no sign of agreement, establishes more than ever a spirit of justice between men in distinctions of religious thought.

The history of this peculiarly eventful century is eminently favourable to religious toleration on a more extensive scale and in a more comprehensive

---

[1] 'The history of the modern world we have observed to be simply the history of the process of development that is now tending to bring, for the first time in the history of the race, all the members of the community into the rivalry of life on a footing of equality of opportunity.'—Kidd's *Social Evolution* chap. x.

degree than apparently was contemplated at any time, and it has evidently increased human prosperity as well as security in most parts of the world. In this respect the hopes of the most learned philanthropists in former times are to a great extent fulfilled. Yet there exists another source of social danger which hardly belongs to any particular period, but which, during this age of increasing knowledge and enlightenment, seems all the more surprising and revolting. During the last half of this century the crime of political assassination has been either attempted or committed in the capitals of the most civilised countries. It is usually the work of extensive confederacies, and has no reference to religious bigotry or to national enmity. Those powerful motives for daring enterprise or self-sacrifice, as shown by historical records, have nothing to do with recent political murders, or attempts at murder. The perpetrators try to destroy, without personal motive, the most influential persons, whether sovereigns, statesmen, or prominent members of the ruling classes.[1] In such outrages it is but too evident that the vast growth of civilisation throughout Europe has enlightened some people, without either improving their morality or softening their hearts. Secret, extensive, murderous conspiracies, often

[1] The author heard a man read to a public meeting in Hyde Park the following cheap receipt for a somewhat comprehensive undertaking:—'The way to smash up kings, queens, princes, priests, and policemen, only a penny.' Such language, however ridiculous, can hardly excite mirth when preceded, accompanied, or followed by what it suggests in the form of political assassination.

attributed to the effects of gross ill-usage, have, in many cases, been formed by men who themselves suffer nothing of the kind. Though the leaders in this century have signally failed in obtaining personal authority by their attempts, and have usually incurred ruin or disaster, they have apparently found coadjutors or sympathisers in many different countries owing to the cosmopolitan nature of their designs. These concealed partisans, who are never brought to trial, sometimes vindicate in speeches or newspaper articles the crime of political assassination as being totally different from ordinary murder, which ought to be condoned, if not admired, as a proof of zealous though imprudent patriotism, or comprehensive love for mankind.

During the last few years the frequency and occasional success of murderous plots in European capitals were sufficiently serious to need all the energy of the detective force—a comparatively recent organisation, and certainly the practical guardian of existing civilisation. There probably never was a time when its wonderful skill, vigilance, and acuteness were so required or triumphantly proved as during the last half of this century. The resources of civilisation in forming this force, and the perverted ingenuity by which it is opposed, alike show the progress of a mingled energy and skill, deliberately devoted to the preservation or destruction of human life and property, which are more developed in recent times as if accompanying the chequered history of civilisation. Men dealing with each other in distant countries now possess educational advantages hitherto unknown. The present unprecedented advances in knowledge, learning, and every sort of mental acquisition often tempt optimists to think that men so enlightened must therefore become more moral, humane, averse to strife, and ready to do their duty to each other through the supposed softening influences of intellectual gifts or enlightenment. This fond belief, though contradicted even in Roman history, where intellectual refinement was often found allied with vice and cruelty in the same men, yet strongly actuated some intelligent, learned Englishmen about the time of the great exhibition in London in 1851. This grand, peaceful assemblage of representatives from most nations naturally encouraged the hope that they would return home so pleased with each other as to render future wars between them very unlikely.[1] Yet within a few years after this truly pacific demonstration most of the chief European nations were at war with each other, besides strife being continued of British, French,

---

[1] 'One of the most confident predictions of Buckle was that the military spirit had had its day; that all the force of public opinion in the civilised world would be against it. The American civil war, the war of France and Italy against Austria, the war of Prussia against Denmark, the war of Prussia and Italy against Austria, the great Franco-German war of 1870 speedily followed, and Europe in time of peace has become a gigantic camp.

'Another very remarkable fact has been the growing feeling in the most civilised parts of Europe in favour of universal military service. Not many years ago it would scarcely have found a conspicuous defender. It has now struck a deep root in the habits of Continental life.'—Lecky's *Democracy and Liberty*, vol. i.

and Russians with native tribes in or bordering on their colonial possessions. Instead, therefore, of the permanent triumph of peaceful industry dispelling the attractions or need of warfare among Christian nations, it is evident that vast improvements in the art of war, in artillery and in the management of troops, have increased in public favour throughout Europe to an almost unexampled extent.

Most princes of the different European royal families enter the army. Europe is now maintaining an enormous number of armed men fully equipped with all the munitions of war, constantly engaged in military study, training, and reviews, under the personal command or patronage of the chief people in the country. Thus, at the present moment of Continental peace, the European powers are thoroughly armed, and seem prepared for immediate warfare on the most extensive scale.[1]

[1] 'A military trait runs through the whole world; the great wars and conquests of the last few decades and present international relations which compel most European states to keep their weapons always ready; all this has called forth a military strain of character or necessity for defence based upon guardianship and compulsory organisation.'—Zenker's *Anarchism*, chap. ix.

CHAPTER XXII

Spread of secret societies for political assassination in Europe—Value and efficiency of the detective force more developed—Increasing popularity of the military profession among influential classes, especially on the Continent.

THE enterprising, inventive spirit of this century, which some men hoped would be devoted to the fine arts and to the encouragement of peace, has lately tended rather to training, instructing, and diffusing the military spirit throughout Europe. Notwithstanding the friendly intercourse between British and foreign nations, and among the latter themselves, the least political dispute, distrust, or rivalry might at any time incline them to war, and turn all their military knowledge and improvements to purposes of mutual destruction. In peaceful enlightened lands none in public life dares rely from the lessons of the past upon apparent civilisation as any security from political assassination.

This crime has been lately attempted, or committed, not only by the ignorant or desperate, but, as legally proved, by numerous confederates, sometimes of different nations, including men of education, intelligence, and considerable international knowledge. The efforts of detective police, especially in large cities, have recently been often directed against very different offenders from ignorant local ruffians, yet who are infinitely more dangerous to civilised society. Plots to commit murder of influential persons have recently brought together unscrupulous and desperate men, of many nations united for a common object, in which envy, political fanaticism, and personal love of notoriety are usually the chief incentives. Shakespeare's words, describing 'needy beggars starving for a time of pell-mell havoc and confusion,' scarcely portray some murderous conspirators of recent times. Though doubtless those he describes are among them, some are often guided or influenced by men of education, actuated by perverted or one-sided historical teaching. Their common hatred to men in power of any religion and in any country rivals in ferocious intensity the religious bigotry of the Middle Ages, without the latter's partly redeeming quality of disinterestedness. The mingled cunning, ingenuity, and brutality shown by some Anarchists or Nihilists in civilised European cities during the middle and end of this century present a warning accompaniment to its increased enlightenment from higher education and extended foreign intercourse.[1]

[1] 'In April, 1881, a preliminary [Anarchist] Congress had been held in Paris. The Congress following took place in London on July 14 to 19, 1881. The following resolutions were passed: "To attain the proposed end, the annihilation of all rulers, ministers of State, nobility, the clergy, the most prominent capitalists, and other exploiters, any means are permissible, and therefore great attention should be given specially to the study of chemistry and the preparation of explosives, as

It would appear that the resources and results of advancing civilisation are at times alike perverted to effect its own hindrance or destruction and to recall ancient barbarism. In the midst of the highest mental culture in civilised enlightened cities the most ferocious crimes are attempted, sometimes deliberately committed and authorised by numerous confederates in many countries, some of whom are neither poor, ignorant, nor irritated by real or alleged personal wrong. These criminals are rarely described by novelists, poets, or dramatists. There is in truth little that is poetical, attractive, or dramatic about them. The records of modern police courts best describe these offenders, who hitherto seem either to elude or not to attract the searching notice of able writers in poetry and prose fiction. Neither ignorance, poverty, nor ill-usage can be pleaded for many atrocious criminals among them, yet their outrages, either committed or attempted, reveal a cruelty as indiscriminate and relentless as could be found among actual savages. In their reckless plots against political victims modern Anarchists often show utter disregard about the safety of those to whom they have no animosity. Their supreme object is to

being the most important weapons." The executive committee sought to carry out every point of the proposed programme, but especially to utilise for purposes of demonstration and for feverish agitation every revolutionary movement of whatever origin or tendency it might be, whether proceeding from Russian Nihilism or Irish Fenianism. The London Congress operated as a signal; scarcely had it uttered its terrible concluding words, when it found in all parts of Europe an echo multiplied a thousandfold.'—Zenker's *Anarchism*, chap. viii.

destroy influential men representing or upholding order or government, and in the dynamite explosions so frequent in this century they care nothing for the safety of other people when there is a chance of destroying political foes.

A thoughtful observer of European history may perceive under the appearance of political tranquillity, peace, and civilisation the spirit of warfare not only preserved but encouraged in Great Britain and especially on the Continent. The young princes in most civilised countries, and many young men of distinction, are either educated for the army or induced to view that profession with special admiration and personal interest. Accompanied by the attractions of becoming uniforms, splendid military reviews, the participation of royal personages, the enthusiasm of applauding fellow countrymen, and the admiration of distinguished foreign visitors, it is natural enough that the enterprising youth of Britain and the Continent should glory in the military profession. Perhaps the apparently increasing popularity of brilliant military demonstrations and evolutions was never so general in Europe as during the end of this century. The improvements also in artillery, firearms, and other weapons seem still developing, while martial displays illustrating their efficiency and progressive superiority are admired and favoured by the ruling classes throughout Europe.[1]

[1] 'To the thoughtful student of modern questions, there is no phenomenon so disheartening as the settled conviction which

It is undeniable that the temptation of splendid uniforms, though it may seem cynical to say so, always has great influence in maintaining the popularity of the army. A plain, unbecoming dress would be no small discouragement to some eager recruits. Every attraction, therefore, with which the military profession can be invested is freely, even lavishly, devoted to it throughout Great Britain, and perhaps yet more on the European Continent. The inspiring effect of martial music, the glittering beauty of military uniforms, the favour of the most influential classes and the eager admiration of the lowest, unite to render the modern soldier's life as attractive as Shakespeare expresses in the words of a brave general regretting its abandonment :

> Farewell the plumed troops, and the big wars,
> That make ambition virtue ! O, farewell !
> Farewell the royal banner, and all quality,
> Pride, pomp, and circumstance of glorious war !
> And O you mortal engines, whose rude throats
> The immortal Jove's dread clamours counterfeit,
> Farewell !
>
> Othello, act iii.

In his immortal verses the wars that morally dignify ambition may mean those proving the self-denying

---

seems to prevail that war is an unavoidable evil. The nations that rank first in the march of progress in most cases remove the male part of the population from industry for several years to give them a splendid training, and all this in preparation for mutual destruction. Each feeble device in the mechanism of slaughter remains but a short time in the hands of the nation that buys it of the discoverer, and no great Power dare face the risk of allowing its armaments to become obsolete.'—*Civilisation of our Day*, part ii.

heroism of obedient soldiers in whatever service they may be engaged. The roaring of cannon, so grandly described, may perhaps lose some of its charm or attraction when the results fill either the grave or the hospital, shortening men's lives, or maiming them for life. The hard facts of the soldier's career, its duties, dangers, objects, and frequent results, must ever remain unchanged throughout all time. The deliberate organised destruction of human life by shortening the brief span allowed it by natural laws is the real inevitable result of military ambition, enterprise, and education. Many greatly admire exciting pictures of battles, directed and fought by men in splendid uniforms, bringing to the last test the newest improvements in the inventive machinery of 'glorious war.' Yet those who admire such representations would likely have no delight in pictures of half-naked savages destroying each other with spears, tomahawks, or the scalping knife. But despite the attractions of spirited martial music, gorgeous uniforms, and handsome weapons in what is called civilised warfare, there must be precisely the same desire to cause human destruction as could animate mere savages. A street riot or tumult which often disgusts civilised spectators involves, indeed, a trifling amount of suffering compared with those so-called glorious campaigns on fields of honour, which the majority of Christian youths on the Continent and many in Britain are taught and trained to admire. Yet since the rise of Christianity no century has probably beheld so much warfare between Christian nations as the present one.

At its commencement the wars of Napoleon I. caused unspeakable misery throughout civilised Europe. His final defeat and capture secured complete pacification between those countries, lately the scenes of his campaigns, but only for a brief period. Since his time most of them have declared war with each other: Austria against France and Italy, Britain and France against Russia, Prussia against Austria, and France against Prussia, while domestic revolutions have occurred in Italy, Spain, and France. The intermittent warfare of Great Britain, Russia, and France against native races in Asia and Africa may cause little surprise, being often inevitable, considering European interests in those parts of the world, and usually cause comparatively less loss of life than war between European nations. But the enormous destruction of life and property caused by the strife of civilised nations with each other in this century, though attended by many heroic deeds, is not a cheering or reassuring record for philanthropists to consider. The undisputed supremacy of Christianity, the 'religion of peace,' among these warring nations, has had apparently little effect in inducing them to prefer its real blessings to the attractions or temptations of ambition and political power.

CHAPTER XXIII

Loyalty of non-Christian subjects to Christian rulers specially displayed in recent years—Discouragement of the Christian subjects in Turkey by the European powers in their aspirations for independence.

It is remarkable that European wars, except between Greece and Turkey, during this century have been almost entirely political. Their objects, causes, and results had little connection with the religious element, and the extension or replacement of particular faiths was apparently neither contemplated nor accomplished. The victors and vanquished, except in Greece, whose revolution in 1824 raised it from a Turkish province to a Christian kingdom, remained unchanged in religious opinions by the result of war.

The national desolation caused by warfare in the very midst of civilisation was naturally deplored by consistent philanthropists. Yet despite its terrible consequences, the present popular feeling throughout Europe shows more admiration for its attractions than dread or abhorrence of its results. The horrors of war often seem practically forgotten after their immediate effects on men's minds have passed away. The great and increasing popularity of the military profession is openly encouraged, shared, and promoted by nearly all the European powers. Not only was the memory of Napoleon, 'the mighty murderer' as a philanthropist minority called him, almost adored by the French people, but up to the present time the rewards, honours, and distinctions conferred on victorious soldiers in every civilised land prove the high estimation and the strong prevalence of the martial spirit.[1]

The late imposing celebrations of 1896 and 1897 in honour of the young sovereign of Russia and of the aged sovereign of Great Britain in their respective capitals, alike showed much of the spirit of a military triumph. Each was attended by Asiatic subjects as allies of these European powers. In all history there was never probably so great a display of Mohammedan loyalty to Christian rulers as on these occasions, both in Moscow and in London. These memorable demonstrations of British and Russian power or influence somewhat resembled one another. They were alike in honour of Christian sovereigns who had never commanded in battle, nor headed an invasion of any country. Yet these celebrations, though peacefully carried out, proved in themselves not only the signs, but the proofs, of a vast military triumph. While friendly Christian powers sent congratulating representatives to these

---

[1] 'The pursuit of war tends to become attractive, apart from the ends to which it is directed, as soon as it rises to the rank of a profession, and the highest honours are still conferred upon warriors.'—*Civilisation of our Day*, part ii.

splendid scenes, the allied and subjected millions of Asiatic Mohammedans to some extent followed their example. Besides, the Turkish and Persian ambassadors, Indian princes or their representatives, and Tartar chiefs, by their presence testified the friendship or submission of Mohammedan nations to Britain or to Russia. While these great powers were ruling so many Mohammedans and more loyally obeyed by them than ever before, it was a peculiarly unlucky time for the Greek and Cretan Christians to declare war against Turkey. Yet they ventured to do so during the interval between these remarkable celebrations of Mohammedan loyalty and friendship to the chief powers of the Christian world. But the ill-advised Greeks, believing or wishing to believe, that in a second war with the Turks their former champions would again aid them, rashly plunged into the unequal struggle, and being not only unassisted, but even disavowed, were soon defeated by the far larger forces of the Sultan. In this short disastrous conflict the Greeks and Cretans had the two political lessons before them: the war of Independence in 1824, which, though sympathised with by the Cretan Christians, did not secure their freedom; and the Crimean war of 1854.

They apparently expected to receive the rescuing sympathy of the former; but they experienced the disapproval which might have been expected from the results of the latter. Neither Britain, France, nor even Russia were inclined to repeat their Christian championship of 1824, and in a political sense had some justification for their change of feeling. Since that time the numbers, importance, and proved loyalty of Mohammedan subjects to these three powers had greatly increased in India, central Asia, and Algiers, and the British and Russian rulers now employ Mohammedans among their personal retinue. These three powers at present reckon with confidence on the fidelity of Mohammedan subjects, and with every hope of its being permanent.

They therefore no longer evince indifference to the feelings or wishes of Mohammedan subjects, who were usually in former times considered merely subdued enemies. Great Britain, France, and Russia showed complete opposition to any war intended to arouse revolution in the Turkish Empire, and in this policy were joined by Austria and by Germany, all of whom desired the maintenance of Turkish supremacy over European provinces. The Germans, though ruling few, if any, Mohammedans, eagerly joined other European powers in discouraging the enterprising Greeks longing to liberate their fellow Christians both in Europe and Asia. The Greeks found to their cost that no emancipation of Armenians, or even Cretans, was desired, or at least intended, by the European Governments, to whom they are certainly indebted for their own freedom. It was thus evident that Christian powers during recent years, ruling an increasing number of Mohammedans, are by no means disposed to substitute a Christian power for a Mohammedan, provided the latter is under their control or in strict alliance with

Q

them. This decided preference of political to religious interests seems rather a new policy in European history. It is becoming more general, and was never so openly avowed or practically enforced as during the last few years.

During Napoleon's wars, when Egypt and Syria were the temporary battlefields of Christian powers without interference from Mohammedans, the political decline of the latter was evident enough, and since that time they have certainly been yielding to Christian influence. None of the disastrous wars and revolutions in Christian lands during this century has extended or increased Mohammedan conquest over new dominions. Unlike what is found in Christian history, where often glory, profit, and conquest have been acquired through the alliance of co-religionists, this policy seldom appears in Mohammedan history. Nations professing that faith seem fated to rarely form alliances, even when the destructive wars between Christian countries offer every temptation for a confederation against them.

This century's history, especially of late, proves the steady and confirmed supremacy of Europeans over non-Christian subjects, despite the many wars of the former among themselves. Yet this triumph is almost entirely political, as victorious Christianity and defeated Mohammedanism have neither gained nor lost many votaries by the fortune of war.

Though non-Christian subjects have more opportunity or temptation to become Christians than at any former period, as change of faith would no longer involve danger under Christian rule, they yet usually preserve their ancestral religions.

In this respect alone European supremacy, even when supported by popularity, has hitherto had little effect. European laws, manners, languages, even dress, are becoming rapidly diffused among subjected or friendly non-Christians. But in religious faith the triumphs of Europe comparatively cease. On this great question the opinions of remote centuries continue or reappear in the passive form of peaceful religious distinctions.

The increasing number of Jews now spread among most, if not all, Christian and Mohammedan lands proves this fact as decisively as subjected Mohammedans, Brahmins, Buddhists, and the reviving Parsees in western India. The lessons of history show Christianity in the present age in the position which many of its ardent champions, preachers, and martyrs have prayed to behold, as politically paramount in power or indirect influence over the world. This long-desired result surely proves decided superiority in the legislation afforded, and in the protection extended to its varied subjects.

The beneficial effects of Christian rule are declared by practical, observant travellers to attend not only British, but French and Russian, power and influence over non-Christians. Yet this national amelioration is not the result, or the direct result, of eloquent preaching or religious enthusiasm. It is mainly caused by the political justice and the tolerant views of influential laymen. In some churches even yet intolerant principles are maintained among differing Christians and among some Mohammedans. But they are no longer, as formerly, spread or sanctioned by existing Governments, except in rare cases. In the practical results among nations under Christian rule the moral spirit of that faith is evidently becoming more and more recognised. Yet at the present time its moral success is distinct from doctrinal extension. Some Christian preachers may continue, perhaps with well-meaning sincerity, to admire or sanction the exclusive feelings of the Middle Ages, and to apprehend nothing but religious apathy from their disappearance. But the principles animating Europeans when justly ruling foreign nations surely represent the Christianity of its wisest votaries when enlightened by increasing knowledge of men in all their varied forms, different circumstances, and peculiar history,

CHAPTER XXIV

Increasing secularisation of politics—Reliance of European rulers on non-Christian subjects—Disavowal of atheism by all Governments—Different opinions among the modern Jews about their national destination.

HISTORIANS have sometimes confounded or classed religious influences with religious prejudices, while devout and sceptical men have viewed the secular spirit of recent times with nervous dread or eager exultation. When the apparent decline of clerical influence throughout Christian countries is compared with historical evidence of nations roused to mutual warfare by its power alone, these feelings are natural enough. But closer examination of the differences between mediæval and modern history may greatly modify them. The principles enjoined, though not exclusively, by Christianity, even when not eagerly avowed or proclaimed as formerly, yet nevertheless mainly influence modern European legislation, and in most instances its policy. The Christian faith, considering the extending powers of European races, must spread every year more and more throughout the world, though it seems chiefly confined to them, is very slowly diffused among others, and often hardly known to those refusing to adopt it. It may be owing to the present comparative absence of religious persecution that atheism, which always existed among a learned minority, and had a brief triumph in modern France, is repudiated by every existing government and nation. The most ancient faiths of Judaism and Parseeism, of equal if not greater antiquity than any others, are now maintained by their votaries in complete freedom, and have each sent members to the British Parliament.

Believers in these old religions have, indeed, during recent years made more influential progress than avowed atheists have done. While the political power of the clergy, except in Ireland, was perhaps never so little shown as now, even in countries where it was once supreme the practical influence of Christian teaching, at least in the duties of government, was probably never so widely diffused or so generally acknowledged as in this century. All the religions that have survived the trials, tests, and misfortunes of time are now brought freely together in the increasing amicable intercourse of their respective votaries in every part of the world. Among them none in political subjection retains so extraordinary and so interesting a position as the Jews. They are now almost all under Christian or Mohammedan rule, and perhaps the British nation may justly claim to be the most favourable to their rights and liberties. To a religious mind their historical position under the rule of the votaries of the Gospel and of the Koran is one of peculiar interest. Their feelings towards Jesus and

Mohammed, the religious guides, instructors, and law-givers of their political rulers, present an impressive resemblance. As they became better treated their ideas of the two prophets no longer expressed or indicated complaint or hostility, though confidence in their divine missions is yet steadily withheld.[1]

In the history of nations, as in that of individuals, the most desired objects or aspirations frequently lose much of their charm when attained. Throughout suffering centuries the scattered race had longed, prayed, and hoped for restoration to its ancestral country, which has scarcely been within the range of practical politics till the present century. At present, however, it seems in its power to obtain it by purchase from the Turks, whose pecuniary interests would favour, and their religious prejudices scarcely oppose, an advantageous offer. Yet there never was a time when civilised European Jews were less inclined, or perhaps less fitted, to practically realise their ancestral dream. On the contrary, some of them, called the Reformed Jews, begin to view the United States of America with more interest than any part of the old world. Without showing any wish to

[1] 'Mohammedans and Christians tried by all means in their power to convince the Jews that the Anointed, whose advent was prophesied by the Prophets, had already appeared, the former pointing to Mohammed, the latter to Jesus, as the person realising those predictions. In refuting arguments brought by Christians and Mohammedans against Jews and Judaism and rejecting the Messianic claims of Jesus and Mohammed, Jews are ready to acknowledge the good work done by the religions founded by these men, Christians and Mohammedans, in combating idolatry and spreading civilisation.'—Friedländer's *Jewish Religion.*

live under a Jewish ruler, and evidently well satisfied with the rule of some European nations, many intelligent Jews of the present time seem disposed to adopt this enterprising part of the new world as their future home, where, secure of religious freedom, they may peacefully compete with the civilising progress of the age. Except about their ancient faith, to which they steadily adhere, some modern Jews appear less attached to classical or historical associations than many Christians and Mohammedans.[1]

They eagerly welcome and cultivate modern changes and improvements. Many are among the most wealthy, luxurious, and latterly influential of Europeans. In some Christian lands they are becoming more closely involved with their political, social, and financial conditions, while their religion is as free as that of their rulers. Yet prejudices against them linger in some Christian and Mohammedan countries; and it is said that in the latter the Jews irritate Mohammedan rulers against Christian fellow subjects.[2] The race, however,

[1] 'Reformed Judaism contends that the Jews are a religious community only; that the national existence ceased when the Romans set the temple aflame and destroyed Jerusalem. The career in Palestine was but a preparation. As the early home of the faith, as the land where the prophets uttered their world-subduing thoughts, and the psalmists sang their world-enchanting hymns, Palestine is a precious memory of the past, but it is not a hope of the future. With the dispersion of the Jews all over the world the universal mission of Judaism began. The Jews are citizens and faithful sons of the lands of their adoption. This doctrine has become a vital element in modern Jewish thought.'—*Jewish Quarterly Review*, October 1897, p. 53.

[2] Curzon's *Persia*.

continues as much scattered as ever, and thriving under the most varied conditions. Yet, for the first time probably in their subjected history, a remarkable difference now exists among them respecting future hopes and plans. While the Reformed Jews abandon the long cherished idea of resettling in Judæa, and prefer the new world of North America, another section of them preserving historical aspirations, called Zionites, maintain their ancestral expectation of returning to Palestine.[1] These differences among this vast, yet scattered, nation have hitherto caused no very important change in their actual faith, and seem a political disagreement owing to the unforeseen historical changes of time. Judæa is no longer the land flowing with milk and honey and rightfully owned by the Jews. It has long been comparatively barren, ruled and chiefly inhabited by Mohammedan Arabs and Turks, who, in moments of religious excitement, might perhaps view the Jews with feelings like those of their ancient Philistine neighbours. The Koran of Mohammed proves his dislike to their national pride

[1] 'The Holy Land alone is the country to satisfy legitimate hopes. The settlement there will bring the much needed political and economic relief to the Jews, and will at the same time open a new chapter in the history of Asia. The emigration of the Jews from the eastern parts of Europe is a necessity which grows stronger every day. If only a small percentage of the accumulated intellectual wealth of the Jews from the Continent is transplanted to Palestine, this would at once become one of the finest centres of learning in the highest sense of the word. Modern science shall there find a home, as well as all the results of modern civilisation.'—*Asiatic Quarterly Review* October 1897.

even as Jesus expresses in the gospel. When mentioning Jews relatively, the words of the Christian and Mohammedan prophets bear some resemblance. And yet the fate of the Jews is now, and for a long period has been, to live entirely under the dominion of the followers of both. While, therefore, Syria offers a rather doubtful prospect of happiness to civilised Jews from Europe, exchanging its comfort and enlightenment for the dangerous neighbourhood of Arab tribes and Turkish soldiers, the United States of America tempt them to turn over a new leaf in their wonderful history, to cherish if they like their partly glorious, partly disastrous, past, but to devote their education and knowledge of the world to peaceful competition with civilised nations, without desiring national independence. They seem at present divided about their ultimate course of action; but evidently some are no longer animated by the local partialities of their ancient race, but anxious to be friendly to all just rulers, and in this respect Britain stands in the foremost rank. In religious variety the British Empire seems to represent the religious world in miniature, and the present popularity of its rule seems a practical rebuke to the governing policy of Christian nations in former times, its own included. Its non-Christian neighbours have become friendly and loyal by slow degrees, while its European territories have lately received no addition, the acquisition of Cyprus being more than counterbalanced by the previous cession of the Ionian Islands to the Greeks.

In America the British, while retaining Canada and some islands, attempt no conquests. In Africa British power or influence in the south is opposed and thwarted by the Dutch Boers, and no longer by the original natives. In the east British indirect control still prevails over Egypt, and it seems that Great Britain emulates the French, Italians, Germans, and other Europeans in their singular enterprise in what is called a European scramble for Africa, especially its eastern portion. Great differences of opinion are expressed by Europeans on this subject, some saying that the suppression of the slave trade and the advance of civilisation might be the sure results of their triumph. Others, again, rather compassionate the African natives, whose resistance is entirely defensive.[1]

There may be truth in both views; but as the success of Europeans must always favour civilisation more or less, it may be expected that these African expeditions will prove no exception to what history has proved a general rule in every part of the world. In Asia British dominion is less extensive but of greater importance, comprising more subjects, and is perhaps more endangered from revolts than that of Russia. The rule of the latter,

[1] 'Among the most active aggressors are Great Britain, France, Germany, Italy, and Belgium. What is the moral of this discreditable game of grab which the three great nations of Europe, France, Germany, and Great Britain, have been playing at the expense of the unhappy Africans? Deception and diplomacy have been the machinery. Lust of land and gold have been the motive power.'—*Asiatic Quarterly Review*, October 1897.

when established in Asia, has been generally less disturbed by either rebellious subjects or hostile neighbours. Asia presents a vast, interesting, almost inexhaustible field for European conquest, exploration, and intrigue. In these physical and mental efforts the British in Asia, except in the extreme north, are pre-eminent over other nations. While their control or influence throughout India, Burmah, and China overawe or conciliate native opposition, they are rivalled in the north-west of India and on the northern frontier of China by the intrigues and advance of Russia.

Though British rule in India has not for years been disturbed by serious revolt, some signs of popular disaffection towards it have lately appeared in a new and remarkable manner. The Indian press, a thoroughly British introduction, has in a few cases recently turned its influence against English authority. As yet no important results have ensued, but an opposition so new and so totally different in its nature from any previous native enmity, inevitably arouses some apprehension. The Russians in Asia hitherto seem undisturbed by any similar opposition from their Mohammedan subjects.

These European powers, ruling or controlling the greater part of Asia, are still separated by intervening countries, Afghanistan, Mongolia, and Thibet. Tartary is falling so much under Russian influence that the intermediate Afghan mountains, held by an independent race, may be considered the present barrier between British dominion and that of Russia on the north-west frontier of India. The predominance of Christian authority now represented by Britain, Russia, and France can hardly be thought endangered either in Asia or Africa. In the vast American continent native races no longer preserve an independent country. Europeans, or their descendants, rule it without any sign of serious opposition from the partially vanished aborigines. Yet British power seems neither to increase nor diminish in this quarter of the world, which now, chiefly divided among separate republics, appears rather excluded from European intercourse, except in financial affairs.

The energetic, prosperous people of the United States, mostly of British descent, seem remarkably unaggressive in foreign policy. Though far more influential and intelligent than any other population in America, they yet rather resemble them in abstaining from the intrigues and strife of European, African, and Asiatic politics.

In recent years public attention seems more directed to the historic lands of the old world than to any part of the new. Though the chief European and Asiatic nations are at present at peace with one another, the martial spirit aroused by rival military resources, and the ceaseless continuance of political intrigues, seem increasing throughout the most civilised countries which philanthropists might hope would specially value and preserve the blessings of national peace.

One of the lessons of history taught as much by that of Christian nations as by any other, is the undeniable attraction of warfare. After its cessation thanks are usually offered, and sincere gratitude felt for the restoration of peace. The grief of losing friends or relatives, the sight of maimed sufferers for life, and of crowded hospitals, together with the heavy expenses it entails, render warfare sad indeed to all who see or feel its inevitable consequences. Yet in succeeding generations, after a few years, sometimes directly its terrible recollections lose their vividness, its peculiar attraction for mankind, despite religious warning or injunction, resumes its sway in almost every nation. Napoleon the First's career showed the exciting, yet in a philanthropic sense, the degrading sight of nearly all European Christian nations waging destructive war with each other for political objects alone. When he was finally captured, some people laying the desolation of Europe entirely to his charge, fondly imagined that with his fall warfare would almost disappear at least from Christian Europe. Yet since his time most of the nations once at war with Napoleon have been at war with one another. The peaceful inspiration of a universally professed Christianity has failed altogether to discourage the practice or even the love of warfare among the most influential of its votaries, though it may be reasonably hoped it has introduced a more merciful spirit in the treatment of vanquished foes. This though only of late years it seems to have really done, and it is a consolation philanthropists well need, considering the persistent maintenance, even the encouragement of the warlike spirit by nearly every Christian nation.

CHAPTER XXV

Danger to monarchs, statesmen, and influential persons from political assassination in civilised European countries—Efforts and efficiency of the detective force—Difference between political assassins and other criminals.

THE prevalence in different countries of plots to commit murder for political objects has in the last half of this century assumed a significance of a new, peculiar kind. In former times similar crimes were often planned or committed by political rivals or by isolated individuals made reckless and desperate by personal misery, like Shakespeare's description of two murderers hired by the usurping king Macbeth:

> *First Murderer.* I am one, my liege,
> Whom the vile blows and buffets of the world
> Have so incens'd, that I am reckless what I do
> To spite the world.
> *Second Murderer.* And I another,
> So weary with disaster, tugg'd with fortune,
> That I would set my life on any chance
> To mend it, or be rid on't.
> *Macbeth*, act iii.

They were also often perpetrated by men infuriated by real or supposed personal wrong, or who imagined they were denied some favour and advantage in the power of their victims to grant. During many recent years, however, these crimes have apparently assumed a more deliberate or unimpassioned character. They are the work of large confederacies in distant countries professing different religions; some, if not most, of these plotters are men of education, firmly united in a common resolve to destroy people in power, whether sovereigns, statesmen, or members of the ruling classes. This is their indiscriminate design, which they often pursue in a cool, practical, business-like way—if such a term may be used—very different from the fiery excitement, deep passion, or desperate enthusiasm historically associated with murderous plots. It is to baffle and detect such outrages that the increasing vigilance and prompt dexterity of the comparatively modern detective police are so specially needed.[1]

These detectives seem, indeed, the peculiar social antidote for a somewhat new form of a widespread social disease. These extensive murder conspiracies are almost entirely for political objects, and attempt or accomplish their designs in different

---

[1] 'The detective force is so well chosen and trained, proceeds so systematically and quietly, does its business in such a workman-like manner, and is always so calmly and steadily engaged in the service of the public, that the public really do not know enough of it to know a tithe of its usefulness.'—Dickens's Rep inted Pieces.

Since Dickens wrote this the force, then newly organised, has had to encounter criminals of a different kind from those described by the great novelist. In hardened atrocity they may resemble both Shakespeare's murderers in 'Macbeth,' and some of Dickens's ruffians; but in education, general knowledge, and acquaintance with foreign countries the Anarchists, dynamitards, or Irish Invincibles of this century differ from most, if not from all, criminals hitherto described in poetry or in prose fiction.

lands quite irrespective of national or religious distinctions. Their objects, and methods, therefore, in various countries and under different circumstances present a general resemblance. Whether called Nihilists, Anarchists, or Invincibles, on the Continent, in England and in Ireland, their resemblance in cool yet ferocious determination is sufficiently evident when their members are brought to public trial. When tried these men rarely complain of personal injury or offence. They are not united by religious or national preferences, and have usually no private enmity to intended victims. Their extraordinary coolness and utter unscrupulousness distinguish them from most other assassins. Moreover, these modern criminals appear singularly reckless whether people to whom they are indifferent suffer or not with their intended victims. This hateful peculiarity has been noticed by statesmen and newspapers, and cannot fail to have the useful effect of preventing popular sympathy with indiscriminate foes to life and property.

When convicted, these men usually show neither enthusiasm, remorse, nor fear. Cool, dogged, and resolute they seldom care to arouse sympathy by eloquent speeches or moving appeals. They seem firmly devoted to their secret society, and to care nothing for either the safety or the opinions of those outside it. Few, if any, of the villains described by Shakespeare, Scott, or Dickens, seem to resemble these criminals. Utter callousness about the sufferings of victims, or of the danger of those to whom they are indifferent, is a prominent characteristic of these confederated assassins.

Many inventions of recent civilisation are sometimes utilised by them, while foreign communication and the increased facilities for travelling are freely turned to account by these men, whose designs equal the worst crimes of which mankind is capable. In poetry or prose fiction murder is usually associated with personal resentment, extreme poverty, or the influences of political and religious prejudices; but in the criminal records of this century the police have reason to know that many of these political assassins were uninfluenced by such causes. Some of the most determined were men who knew the world, had often travelled, possessed no small amount of general information, had no personal knowledge of their victims, and felt neither the bitterness of poverty nor the exasperation of personal injury. In some respects they appeared as civilised as the most harmless among their fellow-countrymen. In fact, their frequent ingenuity, knowledge of languages or of different lands, and other educational advantages, had to be reckoned with in their detection and subsequent fate.

Wholly uninfluenced by religious fanaticism, they usually allege political aspirations or injustice as their motive or justification. The common saying that in the midst of life we are in death may be paraphrased respecting Christian capitals, that in the midst of their civilisation there remains an element of moral barbarism, when men of education commit, or aid the commission of, crimes as reckless and cruel as could be perpetrated in heathen lands. Yet it is a consoling reflection that in every country hitherto these murderous attempts, successful or not, always failed in their ultimate objects. Even when assassins slay victims and escape, their success has never placed them or their associates in political power.

They never replace those they destroy in any position of pre-eminence. Public condemnation is usually aroused in all classes; the ruling powers may be for a time in dismay, yet they continue to govern as before. A murdered sovereign is usually succeeded by the legal heir, and a statesman by the ablest representative of his party. The murderers if captured usually suffer death, or endure life-long penal servitude; and if they escape may remain concealed among sympathisers, but they never aspire to public influence.

Recent history shows that murderous attempts on public men, successful or not, bring no results except the legal punishment or future concealment of the criminals. Yet, amid the perils and sorrows accompanying the attractions of political power, these assassins constantly remind civilised society that all the gifts of education, genius, and ingenuity can be devoted to crimes as disgraceful to human nature as those of ignorant savages.

CHAPTER XXVI

Scott and Dickens on religious fanaticism and on religious hypocrisy—Dickens generally avoids historical allusions—Lever and Lover rather avoid Irish politics.

In the time of Walter Scott all danger from religious or political persecution had disappeared from Great Britain, but vivid interest in its recent history still remained. In the subsequent days of Charles Dickens even this interest had in great measure ceased among the English public. Dickens evidently thought that deceit, hypocrisy, and heartless cruelty to children and to paupers were among the chief social evils in England during national peace, when his first works appeared. His novels, like those of Scott, immediately attracting attention, produced a marvellous effect in the peaceful amelioration of the most unfortunate classes among his fellow-countrymen. Perhaps of all novelists none has done more to enlighten the British people generally than Dickens by inducing the richer classes to interest themselves more in the poorer than was ever known, or at least manifested, before.

In different ways, Scott and Dickens more than any previous novelists contributed to instruct as well as amuse fellow-countrymen, whom, in many classes and religious divisions, they induced to aid the cause of suffering or deceived humanity. In the cause of practical philanthropy to reconcile, from a social standpoint, different classes of fellow-countrymen was the moral object which thoughtful readers must perceive in these writers. Their works may be too often more admired for their romantic or sensational interest than for the moral and social principles which inspire them.

While Great Britain may be considered specially enlightened as well as interested by her literary men, Ireland owes far less to the same influence. Irish writers about their country are usually devoted to 'party' interests, religious or political, with little regard for the rights or merits of opponents. The merry novels of Lever, Lover, and other writers rarely mention Ireland's history. It is a subject chiefly left to interested politicians or prejudiced theologians, and the result is that, despite the remarkable wit and eloquence of the Irish, these gifts are usually devoted to 'party' glorification or censure. 'To give up to party what was meant for mankind' was the half-playful, half-reproachful charge of Goldsmith against his great Irish political contemporary, Edmund Burke, in the last century.[1]

Since their time Ireland, amid the vast improving changes throughout Europe and notwithstanding its own large amount of national talent, yet remained

---

[1] Goldsmith's *Retaliation*.

in sympathies, ideas, and feelings closely inclined to those of the Middle Ages. The religious hypocrisy Dickens denounces so keenly among Englishmen of his own time he would have found replaced in Ireland by a deep-rooted fanaticism, of which his best works show little knowledge or experience. To men wishing to know Ireland and the Irish, therefore, Scott's novels are more instructive than those of Dickens, though neither wrote about Ireland.

While the hypocrisy Dickens describes in the Reverend Stiggins, the Reverend Chadband, Pecksniff, Uriah Heep, Gashford, &c., could never injure society except in narrow limits, the fanaticism Scott portrays has greatly influenced legislation in almost every Christian country.

Dickens nearly always avoids politics and history; neither apparently attracts him. But the lessons taught by Scott's historical novels instruct politicians to the present day. Other able British writers, less popular than Dickens, have since Scott's time enlightened the British public by historical and social works referring to ancient, mediæval, and recent times.

Of these, perhaps the most influential, pleasing, and popular are the historian Macaulay and the novelists Bulwer Lytton and Thackeray. Unlike Scott, Macaulay finds little or nothing attractive in the Middle Ages or in the feudal times. His favourite subjects are the classic literature of Greece and Rome, together with the educational and social development of modern England. His scholastic taste delights in connecting the departed glories of classic days, their intellectual appreciation and results, with the Great Britain of his own times. The intervening centuries, so interesting to theologians, poets, and romance writers, he usually mentions with dislike or comparative indifference. British development in every way—educational, political, and social—is his favourite subject, which his 'Essays' and subsequent 'History of England' have alike done much to promote. His rare power of making real history nearly as attractive as fiction may be compared with that of Dickens in rendering the lowest phases of London life peculiarly interesting to general readers. Historical narration and details of low life in London were seldom thought attractive, though highly important to those whose profession or duty it was to study either. Dickens and Macaulay, however, succeeded in investing these subjects with an interest which few readers before their time believed them capable of inspiring. The real characters Macaulay describes become no longer the dull, almost inanimate, personages represented by many historians. They are portrayed with the full power, force, and vividness of a man personally acquainted with them.[1]

Though debarred by modern historical rule from inventing conversations or soliloquies like Shakespeare

---

[1] 'History, as I understand it, should know how to catch men and peoples as they would appear in the midst of their epoch.'—Napoleon's words to Wieland, Sloane's *Life of Napoleon*, chap. xiii.

in 'Richard III.' especially, yet Macaulay possesses the power of investing historical characters with a vivid, life-like interest, second only to that of a gifted novelist or dramatist. His hero-worship, or enthusiastic, unreasoning admiration for certain persons, a feeling viewed by Carlyle as a noble sentiment, is Macaulay's chief weakness. Though in Carlyle's case this tendency arouses generous sentiments, it may be hardly consistent with an historian's duty of representing fallible men without fear or favour. This weakness in Macaulay may be exaggerated by opponents, wishing his works to be more distrusted than they deserve. In fact, a historian making real persons as interesting as in a romance was a surprising novelty in British literature, and even induced Carlyle to term Macaulay's history a 'novel.' On the other hand, avowed romance writers when writing biographies do not always succeed, as proved by Walter Scott's rather dull 'Life of Napoleon.' In this work the great novelist, carefully restraining romantic fancy, presents a dry, uninteresting history of a man whom in a novel he would likely have described with intense interest. Macaulay, at the outset of his career, indicates a wish to render history as interesting as fiction,[1] and in this attempt he finally succeeded beyond any other modern historian.

The instructive as well as pleasing influences of British literary men of this century were more diffused throughout the Empire and the Continent

[1] Essay on History.

than those of their predecessors.[1] The latter interested or influenced a small learned minority on the Continent among studious men, who were probably little known to most of their fellow-countrymen. British writers in this century, specially favoured by the increasing international communication of the time, address not only a majority in their own country, but a great variety of intellectual persons in every civilised land. This vast literary intercourse or diffusion was never equalled in former times, and seems still on the increase. The rich and the poor, the educated and the comparatively ignorant—in fact, most people who speak English in foreign countries—are more or less acquainted with the works of some British writers of this century.

Not only the attractive talents, but the reasoning and thoughts of such men delight the vast masses of the British community. Even when unaccompanied by eager eloquence, or by the excitement of political argument, the silent yet powerful influence of literary genius remains apparently permanent among the British public. Scott, in his capacity as a national writer, was in himself a literary union of England and Scotland. All his works describing their civil wars, or rebellions, their religious or political triumphs and defeats, taught a valuable lesson to a divided population in encourag-

[1] 'Of all our great poets since Milton, Byron and Scott are at once the most recognised by foreign nations, and yet owe the least to foreign poets. If the French now study Shakespeare, it is because Scott and Byron allured them to study English.'—Bulwer Lytton's *Caxtoniana*.

ing reconciliation among descendants of former foes. Dickens subsequently performed a rather similar philanthropic duty to his nation through a literary medium. In his time the British people needed enlightenment of a more immediate and domestic kind. Foreign wars and domestic revolts for religious or political triumph had become matters of history; while in Scott's time their apprehension or remembrance still aroused an interest, which, when Dickens wrote, had quite passed away. Great Britain, enjoying not only domestic peace, but increased and steady Continental ascendency, had become better educated, and in some of its classes more luxurious. Yet, despite these advantages, there remained social evils, which, if not worse than before, appeared more glaring and inexcusable amid increased enlightenment and prosperity. The neglect or cruelty endured by children and paupers, both in and about London or in remote parts of England, were among the first subjects to which Dickens drew public attention.

These descriptions involved no 'party' interest and aroused neither political nor religious excitement. They were eager, keen, soul-stirring appeals to the sense and humanity of the British nation at large, without reference to politics or history. They were practically earnest suggestions for home improvement among the English poor, based on facts, yet illustrated by fiction, without reference to other subjects. The works of Dickens were peculiarly adapted to his own time. They appeared during the invention and first use of railways and telegraphs, when international intercourse was established not only beyond precedent, but beyond previous ideas of possibility. Accordingly, his accounts of the London streets, characters, and peculiarities were quickly spread throughout Britain, the Continent, and foreign and colonial capitals wherever the English language was known.

His ideal persons, chiefly London people, soon became well known in all parts of the world inhabited or ruled by Englishmen, and London, the most business-like and practical of cities, became by the genius of Dickens invested with the attractive interest of a sensational novel. Without trying, like Shakespeare and Scott, to describe its kings, statesmen, warriors, or distinguished persons, with comparatively slight allusion to its aristocracy or fashion, Dickens associated its lowest classes and oddities with an interest previously unknown in literary history.

The scenes of nearly all his works are laid in England, chiefly in the London of his own period. Political and religious disputes, hitherto subjects of absorbing interest, he avoids. Persons and scenes in London low life, previously thought only interesting to lawyers, or to clergy for professional purposes, or from a sense of religious duty, Dickens makes really attractive. He presented degraded and eccentric characters and ways of living to the educated world with a power, a truth, and a new strange interest which captivated the most refined or fastidious members of English society. In his preface to

'Oliver Twist,' he rather deprecates the possibility of making real thieves interesting like Captain Macheath and other dashing smartly dressed highwaymen described in novels, poems, and plays. Yet in this very work he invests Fagin the thief-trainer and Sikes the housebreaker with a vivid interest, which no bandits or thieves in former fiction ever surpassed. Scott's robbers and highwaymen in the 'Waverley Novels' resemble, perhaps, most of all those of Dickens. But they are usually portrayed in a few powerful, graphic sketches, and soon give place to kings, statesmen, brave chiefs, and beautiful heroines, while Dickens traverses modern London with the skill of a detective, combined with the heart, motive, and penetration of a Christian philanthropist.

CHAPTER XXVII

Contrast between Macaulay's and Bulwer Lytton's love of classic literature and Thackeray's dislike or indifference to it—Macaulay's power of making history attractive—Different influences of these writers on the British reading public.

THE novels of Dickens's literary contemporaries, Bulwer Lytton and Thackeray, show the minds of two gifted Englishmen, each possessing great knowledge of their times and fellow-countrymen, yet who take an amusingly different view of their classical education. The former loves the classic days, thoughts, genius, and character of ancient Greece and Rome, in which admiration he almost equals his historical contemporary Macaulay. Throughout his beautiful novel, 'The Last Days of Pompeii,' Bulwer's love of classic times and associations rather resembles Scott's vivid interest in the chivalrous, almost mediæval, days of Europe.[1] Classic study had produced in Bulwer Lytton much the same animating and lively effect. Like Macaulay,

[1] 'The date of my story is that of the short reign of Titus, when Rome was at its proudest and most gigantic eminence of luxury and power. What could afford such materials for description, or such a field for the variety of display as that gorgeous city of the world whose grandeur could lend so bright an inspiration to fancy, so favourable and so solemn a dignity to research?'—Preface to *The Last Days of Pompeii.*

he for some time took little part in his country's politics, but finally did so with success and distinction. He united in himself the novelist, the classical student, and in his latter days the statesman. While, however, as a novelist, he delighted the British public by his peculiar beauty of expression and profound learning, he showed little power of rendering his fictitious characters interesting or natural; and none became favourites with the public like those of Scott, Dickens, or Thackeray, nor were his historical descriptions equal to those of Scott. Though a most sentimental novelist, he could also give practical and political advice to the public of his enlightened times.

Bulwer Lytton when older showed a rare and remarkable combination of talents seldom seen in one man and often thought hardly compatible with each other. A writer who could be both sentimental, fanciful, and practical alternately, who could amuse the public and himself by his variety of mental gifts, was eminently shown in him, especially during the end of his literary career. Though his parliamentary life was brief, he became Colonial Secretary, and his speeches, though marred by too vehement delivery and gesticulation, were usually admirably expressed and formed very instructive reading. Macaulay, in addition to great historical knowledge, classic learning, and marvellous memory, was an intense lover of England's history during the development of its political freedom and social enlightenment. Its remote records or traditions had little interest for him. His special delight was to compare or connect the classic glories of Greece and Rome with the brilliant triumphs of modern Britain. He felt so strong an interest in the characters and events of his favourite historical periods that, before writing his great History, he eloquently regretted that previous histories had usually been given to the public in a dull, uninteresting form.[1]

Impressed with a desire to rival the charm of fiction in historical narration, Macaulay, many years after his 'Essays,' wrote a 'History of England' which, though comprising a very limited period, was never surpassed by a British historian for mingled interest, learning, and graphic power. His 'hero-worship,' which some novelists are able to restrain, tempts this historian to make heroes or villains out of real men whose genius or success, either for good or evil, sometimes weakens his judgment by exciting his feelings beyond calm reason. Thus Cromwell and William III., their policy, actions, and adherents, are alike glorified with the zeal of an enthusiastic novelist for his own creations. In his mind they are the friends, champions, and benefactors of their race as well as country, whose occasional faults it is hardly necessary to mention, while their foes should

---

[1] 'The effect of historical reading is analogous in many respects to that produced by foreign travel. The student, like the tourist, is transported into a new state of society. The perfect historian is he in whose work the character and spirit of an age is exhibited in miniature. By judicious selection, rejection, and arrangement he gives to truth those attractions which have been usurped by fiction.'—*Essay on History*, written in 1828.

be described as little deserving of respect or sympathy; yet his philanthropic mind forces him to mildly censure some acts of historic favourites with the reluctant brevity of a conscientious though enthusiastic admirer. The sale of Charles I. by a Scottish faction to an English one, warmly justified by Buckle,[1] he briefly owns 'did not much exalt the national character' of the former.[2] Yet he devotes no eloquence in condemning men with whose politics he rather sympathises, whereas similar conduct in opponents would probably have invoked his indignant censure. Other instances of his partiality occur in allusions to the conjugal infidelities of James II. and William III., the villain and the hero of his eloquent 'History.'

They prove that Macaulay, though only occasionally, shows the spirit of a novelist in describing real men, and thus tempts detractors to exaggerate this hero-worship, and therefore to underrate the value of his admirable 'History.' Despite its faults, and the efforts of unfair opponents to make the most of them, his great work exercised considerable influence over the British public. It consistently raised British character, genius, philanthropy, legislation, and improved social state in the opinions of intelligent foreign or colonial readers, while his taste and feelings were greatly influenced by the literary models of antiquity.

He delights in all connected with education, and seems what he probably was—the pet pupil of intel-

[1] *History of Civilisation.*   [2] *History of England.*

ligent industrious teachers. The mental education, which many call the drudgery of learning, was to Macaulay the cordial and welcome reception by his inquiring mind of the transmitted wisdom of the past. These studies he eagerly connects with the increasing enlightenment and prosperity of the British Empire, to whose intellectual interests at home and abroad his own sympathies are evidently devoted. Bulwer Lytton shares Macaulay's love of classic times, but they incline his genius in another direction. Instead of making historical or literary comparisons between ancient and modern celebrities he portrays classic scenes and customs, though not historic characters, in sentimental rather than sensational novels. Classic ideas and manners in ancient Italy, its scenery and artistic splendour, revive around him a land of enchantment. Both he and Macaulay wrote early in life, each subsequently expressing in notes or prefaces some changes that time had impressed on their minds.

The latter says of his beautiful essay on Milton that it contained scarcely a paragraph of which his matured judgment approved. Bulwer Lytton, in his spirited novel 'Paul Clifford,' where the young highwayman hero denounces legal oppression, entreats readers to remember that Mr. Clifford's sentiments are not his own. Yet Clifford's words as well as character were likely enough to find sympathy among some readers.

The strong influences of classic taste and learning are evident in the writings of these eminent men even when they may not make direct allusion to them. The delightful impression which classic lore made on their minds was exactly what earnest, intelligent teachers would have desired to produce. Yet perhaps Bulwer Lytton and Macaulay were bright exceptions to, rather than illustrious specimens of, classical education in Britain. The contrast in its appreciation between some of the chief novelists and historical writers of this century is interesting to examine. Scott admires classic times, occasionally alluding to them in his works, as when mentioning historical representations in 'Kenilworth,' but never makes them the subject of a novel. Bulwer Lytton tries to endow them with the sentimental, vivid, picturesque interest of modern days; while Macaulay, in prose and verse, glorifies all connected with them in his most eloquent, instructive style. He is in this respect like the prize-boy of the British school system of his time, and all connected with school recollections he views with an affectionate and, some would think, an extremely rare interest.[1]

His great English literary contemporaries, Dickens and Thackeray, take different views from Macaulay about the charming impression left by classic studies upon youthful minds. Dickens terms

[1] 'The celebrity of the great classical writers is confined within no limits except those which separate the civilised from savage man. In the minds of the educated classes throughout Europe, their names are indissolubly associated with the endearing recollections of childhood—the old schoolroom—the dog-eared grammar—the first prize—the tears so often shed and so quickly dried.'—Essay on the Athenian orators, *Miscellaneous Works*, vol. i.

the Romans a 'terrible people,' the 'implacable enemies' of English schoolboys.[1] Thackeray evidently feels much the same, and openly avows utter dislike to all connected with or reminding him of a classical education. So embittered was he by remembrance of school life that it greatly diminished his enjoying a visit to those classic lands whose literary associations delighted Bulwer Lytton and Macaulay throughout their busy lives. A large majority of British youths during last and in the beginning of this century probably shared Thackeray's ideas of classical education. He much regrets his dislike to it, especially while visiting some chief scenes of classic interest. In his peculiar, humorous style the author of 'Vanity Fair,' who so deeply revealed English character of his own time, owns that school recollections really prevented his enjoying those classic memories which to some other Englishmen render Greece and Italy specially interesting. In taste and feeling Thackeray was a thorough Englishman of his own period. He seldom alludes to ancient times or to foreigners, while showing a profound knowledge of his fellow-countrymen which has hardly been surpassed, if equalled, by any novelist. He also possessed the somewhat rare good

[1] 'Dr. Blimber's establishment was a great hot-house in which there was a forcing apparatus incessantly at work. All the boys blew before their time. Mental green peas were produced at Christmastime, and intellectual asparagus all the year round. Every description of Greek and Latin vegetable was got off the driest twigs of boys under the frostiest circumstances.'—*Dombey and Son*, chap. xi.

sense of knowing exactly where his chief powers lay.
He therefore openly, though amusingly, shrinks
from describing those scenes of antiquity which he
evidently did not appreciate.[1]

Thus Bulwer Lytton, Macaulay, Dickens, and
Thackeray viewed classic learning with nearly
opposite feelings of enthusiastic delight or gloomy
remembrance. The two former invest it with the
charm of sublime wisdom and romantic interest;
the latter, abandoning it as a melancholy remembrance, chiefly devoted their vast powers of observation to describing the modern English world of life
and character as they found it existing around
them.

[1] 'If papa and mama (honour be to them) had not followed
the faith of their fathers, and thought proper to send away
their only beloved son (afterwards to be celebrated under the
name of Titmarsh) into ten years' banishment of infernal
misery, tyranny, and annoyance, to give over the fresh feelings
of the heart of the little Michael Angelo to the discipline of vulgar
bullies, who, in order to lead tender young children to the
temple of learning, drive them in with clenched fists and low
abuse; if they fainted, revived them with a thump or assailed
them with a curse; if they were miserable, consoled them with
a brutal jeer—if, I say, my dear parents, instead of giving me
the inestimable benefit of a ten years' classical education, had
kept me at home, it is probable I should have liked this country
of Attica, in sight of the blue shores of which the present
pathetic letter is written. To make a long story short, I am
anxious to apologise for a want of enthusiasm in the classical line,
and to excuse an ignorance which is of the most undeniable
sort.'—Thackeray's *Journey from Cornhill to Cairo*.

CHAPTER XXVIII

Literary pursuits of Messrs. Gladstone and Disraeli—The former's denunciation of the Turks and partiality for the Greeks—Remarkable views of Disraeli respecting the modern Jews.

THE two great political contemporaries of Macaulay, Bulwer Lytton, Dickens, and Thackeray, and who alternately ruled Britain during the greater part of their time, were the rival Premiers Gladstone and Disraeli. They also visited classic countries with remarkably different feelings. Both were by choice rather than necessity literary men, devoting brief relaxations from political work to publish their written thoughts to the British nation. Literary pursuits were evidently a relief to each from the harassing cares and duties of political life. Mr. Gladstone found his chief pleasure in recalling and examining the ancient Greek poets, Homer especially. Though resembling Macaulay in this predilection, he seems to be more interested in them than in Roman writers, who interest Macaulay almost equally. But neither the Middle Ages nor the feudal times that delight Walter Scott have much attraction for them. The comparison or connection of classic times with the

Europe of their century seems of supreme interest to both Gladstone and Macaulay.

The former found a peculiar attraction in subjects often thought only interesting to professional teachers. He seemed by taste and choice to unite two characters often thought rather incompatible. An intense liking for profound or abstruse study almost worthy of Scott's Dominie Sampson was in Mr. Gladstone mingled with the keen vigilance, ready wit, and clear penetration worthy of a man holding the highest political position in the most civilised of modern empires. Classic studies, religious thoughts, and social questions of deepest import were in his comprehensive mind allied with the promptitude, vigour, and acuteness of an active, practical man of the world. While knowing or dealing with the ablest politicians or men of genius of his time, it was to him a pleasing recreation to study the heroes and sages of antiquity. As prudence enjoined his treating contemporaries, either partisans, opponents, or mere acquaintances, with more or less caution, owing to the responsibilities of his position, he evidently found it a real relief to study and examine the thoughts of men long passed away, from whose wisdom he might derive instructive entertainment, without restraint or apprehension.

Thoughts and times difficult or unknown to most men were to his powerful intellect a pure and safe enjoyment. Studies usually found perplexing and wearisome were to him interesting relaxations from the cares of political life. His classic taste clearly influenced his political conduct when sympathising with the Greeks in their last disastrous war against the Turks. The eager interest he expressed in them, and his openly terming the Sultan 'the Great Assassin,' indicate the enthusiasm of a classic scholar as well as philanthropist overcoming the caution of a calm politician. Such language against a sovereign at peace with his country, expressed by an aged statesman out of office, may have rather embarrassed responsible British ministers, but had no effect upon their policy. Yet his peculiar influence over the British public in many ways was always evident.

There perhaps never was an English statesman uniting classic taste and appreciation with such accurate knowledge of the men, circumstances, and thoughts of his own times. Like Macaulay, he seemed to take far more interest in the ancient and modern worlds than in the mediæval. His peculiar delight was to vary studying the Greek poets with the literature and politics of his own enlightened period, of which he was certainly one of the highest intellectual representatives. In Mr. Gladstone's and Macaulay's works classic and modern tastes are remarkably blended. It is often said that deep, profound interest in abstruse studies, or in the literature of the remote past, expressed in dead languages, renders men unsuited for their times by making them absent in mind, dreamy, and fanciful. This idea, however, whether sometimes true or not, was singularly reversed or falsified in these two eminent instances. Their mental influence in different ways throughout Great Britain was not only vast and profound, but seems of a permanent nature. British opinions which they so ably expressed were, during their lives, diffused to an uncommon extent owing to their period being hitherto unrivalled in facilities for extending literary knowledge throughout the civilised world.

A remarkable contrast to this literary statesman and political historian appeared in a contemporary, who might be fairly termed their political, and to some extent literary, rival, Benjamin Disraeli. He also combined the gifts of a politician and literary man in his remarkable instance. During the political influence of Messrs. Gladstone and Disraeli, the most attractive writers in English prose fiction since Walter Scott appeared in Dickens and Thackeray. Their works were probably more appreciated than any former English fictitious literature, owing to the vast increase of readers in Britain, the Continent, and throughout the Colonies. Dickens and Thackeray were the delight of all classes among the British public at home and abroad; and their popular works spread through countries where few, if any, English books had ever been known before. The literary efforts of Gladstone and Disraeli, though proceeding from men of far more influence than Dickens or Thackeray, were much less read and never possessed anything like the same national interest. Gladstone, in the 'Juventus Mundi,' 'Homer and the Homeric Age,' and other works, showed his delight in recalling the glories of ancient

Greece, which evidently relieved his mind when wearied with the cares of politics. Disraeli, in 'Tancred,' 'Coningsby,' and other novels, describes the beauties of Asiatic scenery and modern English life, besides often making political allusions. Yet neither he nor Mr. Gladstone, despite their genius, literary taste, and proved knowledge of human nature, ever invented a single interesting character.

Though politically encountering the wisest men of their times at home and abroad, these literary statesmen apparently could achieve no success in describing imaginary persons. Yet during their public career they must have known far more distinguished and interesting characters than were ever personally known to comparatively retired men like Dickens and Thackeray. But these writers, in the observant experience of their private lives, examined and revealed what neither Gladstone nor Disraeli could do when delineating the passions of human nature. Neither of these statesmen could describe imaginary characters with anything like the genius with which they certainly understood those in real life. Mr. Gladstone evidently enjoyed recalling the Greek and Trojan heroes of Homer, and it seemed really as if his study of those classic characters aided him in extending or confirming his vast influence over the men of his own time. Disraeli, though writing many novels describing English life, chiefly among the aristocracy, constantly intersperses them with allusions to the politics of his own period in which his chief powers evidently lay. This extraordinary statesman, of Jewish descent though Christian faith, was during a long, important period Mr. Gladstone's chief political rival. In their positions of alternately Premier or Leader of the Opposition they ably headed British political parties. It was Disraeli's remarkable fate, however, to finally lead the Tory or Conservative party, comprising a majority of the British and Irish aristocracy and landed gentry. He owed little or no advantage to ancestral or family influence. All his power was acquired in the reign of the present Queen; yet he gradually became the trusted political leader of a class sometimes accused, justly or unjustly, of wishing to restrict the chief power within the social limits of their own party, and to discourage the talents of those in lower station. But Disraeli ultimately managed to obtain their complete confidence, and when out of office amused his leisure, like Mr. Gladstone, in literary work of his own choice. Instead, however, of turning like the latter from one mental labour to another, from political to classical or theological studies, Disraeli devoted his leisure to novel writing. In some of his fictions he deals with English public life, dwelling on political discussions with peculiar interest. He shows, however, more the spirit or taste of a statesman than of a romance writer. None of his imaginary persons attract much notice; they are not lifelike, and have little of the interest often found in novels written by inferior men.[1] In his

[1] 'Wherever there is any true genius, there will be some peculiar lesson which even the humblest will teach us more

remarkable biography of his political friend, Lord George Bentinck, he has one singular chapter (XXIV.) different from the rest of the work. It rather resembles a distinct historical essay of great ability, yet brought somewhat abruptly to a close. His chief object in it is apparently to raise the Jews throughout history in modern Christian estimation by attributing to that wonderful race the chief credit for European civilisation and accomplishments. As a man of Jewish family, yet Premier in a Christian country, his views on this subject doubtless aided, if aid were needed, to elevate Jewish subjects yet more in the British empire, where they have long occupied a position of security, and latterly of influence, unknown formerly under Christian rule.[1]

Disraeli, in this remarkable chapter, regrets that modern Jews still accept only 'part of their religion,' and evidently tries to reconcile them to Christianity by calling the Christian Prophet the hero of their race, and wishing to identify Christian triumph of

sweetly and perfectly than those far above them in prouder attributes of mind.'—Ruskin's *Modern Painters*, vol. i.

[1] 'There is no race at the present that so much delights and fascinates, elevates and ennobles Europe as the Jewish. Were it not for music, we might in these days say that the beautiful is dead. When the Russian, the Frenchman, and the Anglo-Saxon, amid applauding theatres or the choral voices of solemn temples, yield themselves to the full spell of a Mozart or a Mendelssohn, it seems difficult to comprehend how these races can reconcile it to their hearts to persecute a Jew.'

Yet since this was written Russian and German Governments, despite such soothing influences, are said to have persecuted Jewish subjects, or treated them with great harshness. Whether this severity was justifiable or not remains, on the Continent at least, a matter of opinion.

mediæval and modern times with those of the ancient Jews, owing to the Christian Founder belonging to their nation.[1]

This extraordinary appeal, though written by so distinguished a man, and published among the most influential of the British people, Christian and non-Christian, produced little, if any, apparent effect even on English Jews. It caused no special reply, and did not seem to arouse assent or provoke contradiction. Doubtless the genius and political success of Disraeli gratified all Jews, especially in Britain, and probably tended to elevate yet more their social position. His remarkable appearance was also a favourite subject for caricatures in comic newspapers, both with adherents and opponents; but his success as a novelist yielded altogether to Dickens and Thackeray. The characters invented by those two great observers of modern English nature still remain household words among the British literary public. They are hardly inferior in truth, though they are in importance, to those of Shakespeare and Scott, whose graphic descriptions extended far beyond their own times, often including people who had lived in remote countries. Yet all were delineated by the genius of men of whom

[1] 'The pupil of Moses may ask himself whether all the princes of the house of David have done so much for the Jews as the prince who was crucified on Calvary? Has not He vindicated all their wrongs? Has not He avenged the victory of Titus and conquered the Cæsars? What successes did they anticipate from their Messiah? The wildest dreams of their rabbis have been far exceeded. Has not Jesus conquered Europe and changed its name to Christendom?'

one at least wrote 'not for an age, but for all time.'

Neither Bulwer Lytton nor his political ally Disraeli, despite parliamentary experience and position, were successful in inventing or describing original characters.[1] Their picturesque descriptions of scenery, command of language, appreciation of classic times, and personal knowledge of modern politics were their strong points. Dickens and Thackeray, whenever they allude to these subjects, are not in their proper element. They apparently knew this, by usually adhering to their inimitable descriptions of modern English people, in which they are still unsurpassed in interest and real merit.

But Shakespeare and Scott to some extent combined the gifts of all these writers with their own. Their profound knowledge of human nature in almost every stage of its civilised history has never been equalled. Their descriptions of historical and imaginary persons are never limited by the bounds of personal experience or contemporary history, but, in Shakespeare's case, especially seem inspired by some power above the natural range of human genius or ability.[2]

---

[1] 'Both were successful in the double career they adopted. But the highest success of one was in politics, and that of the other was in literature. With my father the passion for letters preponderated. And whereas literature was but an appendage to the political career of Disraeli, politics were only the appendage to the literary labours of his friend.'—*Life of the First Lord Lytton*, by his Son, vol. ii.

[2] 'He seems to have been sent essentially to take universal and equal grasp of the *human* nature, and to have been

All these great writers have tended in different ways to pre-eminently enlighten the British nation and to inspire a love of justice and high principle among them, which, in domestic legislation, and foreign influence, seems practically rewarded by a long domestic peace and by a vast increase of colonial loyalty.

removed therefore from all influences which could in the least warp or bias his thoughts.'—Ruskin's *Modern Painters*, vol. iv.

CHAPTER XXIX

The literary efforts of Dickens and Thackeray chiefly devoted to describing modern London and modern English character—Their works, while delighting and enlightening the British public, had comparatively little effect in Ireland.

THE motives, ideas, and opinions which Shakespeare and Scott ascribe to historical persons are usually much in conformity with their descriptions by professed historians. Many among the British public understand the characters of men in former times far more clearly from the sketches of the immortal dramatist and of the great novelist than they could receive from mere historical records. In England, during the last century, some benevolent people evidently felt more pity for imaginary persons in pathetic romances than for the political victims of their own times. When the triumph of armed opponents is probable, or even possible, and a constant source of apprehension, it is not easy for an alarmed or endangered public to do justice to their motives, or to view them with any indulgence. Thus irritation caused by alarm generally prevailed throughout the British civil wars and rebellions from or before the wars of the Roses till the battle of Culloden inclusive. In such contests there is usually a comparative absence of noble qualities which warfare with distant or foreign nations often arouses. When fellow-countrymen are engaged in deadly strife, it causes an amount of mutual suspicion and implacable hatred between relatives and former friends from which foreign wars are exempted.

The results of civil wars or rebellions often rankle in the minds of the defeated, preserving through generations an inheritance of vindictiveness or sense of injury. Shakespeare's plays and Scott's novels, describing those periods with a fairness rare among historians, possessed an enduring moral value in enlightening British minds, to which the subsequent peaceful strength of the empire is greatly, though indirectly, due. The usefulness of Dickens and Thackeray among their countrymen, compared with that of Shakespeare and Scott, in this respect can be well understood when the difference of their respective periods is examined. Shakespeare wrote when the recollections of civil wars, state executions, plots, and rumours of plots animated many around him in the world of London. He might safely describe the amorous intrigues of Cleopatra, the imperious conduct of Julius Cæsar, or the crimes of King John and of Richard III. But the recent love intrigues of Elizabeth and Mary Stuart with Essex, Bothwell, and Norfolk, together with the despotic violence of Henry VIII., though splendid subjects for a dramatist, were by Shakespeare carefully, perhaps loyally, avoided.

Scott wrote most of his historical novels soon after the final triumph of the European alliance against Napoleon. At this time the British were well prepared to hear and believe impartial truth about their own former civil wars and rebellions. The fall of Napoleon and the national rejoicing when free from danger of French invasion inclined the British people all the more to hear ancestral wars described with fairness. Religious and political parties in Great Britain were united, perhaps without exception, in feelings of national triumph at the victory of Waterloo. Napoleon neither had, nor tried to have, allies in Britain; no religious nor political party in it wished him success more than another. He was the avowed foe to the British of every class. They, therefore, were better disposed than ever to calmly examine the history of their civil and religious disputes. The historic volumes of the 'Waverley Novels' irritated no party and offended no religious sect when portraying their past contentions with an impartiality of which few historians proved themselves capable. Later in this century the long domestic peace enjoyed by England, the vast accumulation of wealth, the increasing size, interest, and world-wide importance of London and the chief English towns were specially suited to the peculiar descriptive and inventive powers of Dickens and Thackeray. Religious bigotry, once so strong an element in British history, had well-nigh disappeared from public, though perhaps not altogether from private, life. All religious denominations were pro-

T

posed as eligible for Parliament and for taking a responsible part in ruling the empire. The admission of Jews and other non-Christians to Parliament followed that of Roman Catholics, and finally men avowing atheism were likewise admitted.[1]

This complete enfranchisement of men in matters of opinion was both the cause and effect of vast changes in the British public mind. Religious bigotry and persecution, if not sectarian enthusiasm, had gradually lost their hold or influence in Great Britain. The historical prejudices against Jews and Mohammedans had likewise yielded to their increasing political or financial intercourse with the established Christian divisions of Europe. Among these Britain stood foremost as the chief practical advocate of religious toleration throughout the wide and varied bounds of her foreign dominions. In London the votaries of all religions could now meet not only in safety, but entitled to equal protection with those of the established faith.

Dickens, who well represented the spirit of his time in ' Barnaby Rudge ' and ' A Tale of Two Cities,' makes only brief, contemptuous allusions to religious intolerance. His one historical character, Lord George Gordon, he describes nearly as like an idiot

[1] 'In civilised nations whose intellectual culture has its peculiar characteristics, the Jews of the country share the same views as the mass of the nation. The German Jew takes an essentially German view of all questions of intellectual and social life, which a century ago was not the case. It is not otherwise with the British and French Jew; he thinks and feels in common with the great nation in the midst of which he lives.'—Löllinger's *Studies in European History.*

as Barnaby himself. Had Scott written about the periods of these stories he would likely have introduced some religious fanatics in the former and sketches of the chief French revolutionists in the latter, yet Dickens avoids all such allusions. None can describe hypocrites and rogues full of false pretences better than he; but religious or political prejudices he either does not understand, or from some other reason refrains from describing. He generally avoids even mentioning historical personages. He is indeed a rare, brilliant specimen of the English intellect in this century, but his sympathies are more with the future than with the present, and more with the present than with the past. The enlightened improvements due to modern civilisation interest and gratify him much as they do Macaulay. The accomplished historian delights in classing or connecting recent educational progress with the ancient days and classic works of antiquity. Dickens rarely, if ever, makes classic allusions, except when associating classical education with extreme dulness and mental depression. Unlike Scott, he rarely mentions or quotes from Shakespeare, Milton, or other famous authors of his own or any foreign country. It might be said that he was a man of far more literary genius than literary taste or appreciation.

He is the brilliant and most original philanthropic novelist of his own period, despising as much as detesting religious or political prejudices. He takes little interest in examining their causes, or the various and interesting motives which for ages have induced some of the noblest minds to obey their influence. In this historical or retrospective examination Walter Scott specially excels, but Dickens has, or indicates, no idea of it. In his 'American Notes,' for instance, he briefly alludes to the Trappist monks as if that gloomy religious order of devotees were really insane, and immediately leaves the subject. Scott would probably have examined with romantic interest the causes which may lead men to abandon the pleasures of this world through a rigid yet self-denying sense of religious duty. But no religious enthusiasts have the least interest for Dickens. Even in 'Barnaby Rudge,' describing the London anti-Catholic riots of 1780, he introduces hypocrites and ruffians most skilfully, but not a single religious enthusiast or sincere fanatic, except Gordon, who is a historical character. In fact, neither Dickens nor Thackeray describes nor seems to appreciate the true nature of either religious or political intolerance.

This historical influence Scott examined with peculiar penetration yet with a thoroughly calm judgment. No man could be more free from it than he, while his mingled wisdom and good feeling made him study its nature, history, and results with really exhaustive power. The chief excellence of Dickens and of Thackeray is their skill in exposing almost every variety of social deceit, roguery, meanness and false pretence. These vices, perhaps more common or more mischievous in large rich cities than elsewhere, these London authors pursue with well-merited keen censure. No political or religious object, no wish to promote or check a particular policy or to further the cause of any particular sect or party, actuates their thoughts. They avoid showing political or sectarian bias so completely that men of all opinions read their works without either triumph or irritation. The hypocrites and rogues whom Dickens exposes so keenly, whether clergy or laymen, are never classed among a particular denomination. He scrupulously avoids arousing dislike to any special sect or party. His general popularity in England, irrespective of either, proved how well he knew or represented English, perhaps Scottish, but certainly not Irish, public opinion in this respect. The fact of his describing utter rogues in 'Reverend' gentlemen, such as Stiggins, Chadband, &c., would shock some Irish readers, who might think any censure or ridicule of clergymen either wrong or unbecoming in a novelist, unless, indeed, he had zealously written in the interests of some opposing religious sect. British opinion on this subject was totally different. Even estimable clergymen as a rule in Great Britain had no objection to see unworthy members of their profession so censured, but this calm judgment would, even now, not be general in Ireland. Some Irish readers would be more inclined to ask what particular sect the author meant to censure in these instances, whereas Dickens had no idea of condemning any in particular, but to expose or ridicule the unworthy in all.

In former times this sectarian impartiality or indifference would have been distrusted even in Great Britain, and Dickens probably urged to state his religious opinions in self-defence, or to prevent misconstruction. He was, fortunately for himself, peculiarly suited to his own period in England, and especially in the intelligent, appreciating world of London. He evidently represented and shared the general feelings of a nation which, emerging from a long period of religious or political intolerance, was able and willing to encourage mental freedom among its various divisions. Great Britain, resting in triumphant repose after the Waterloo victory, gradually learned the wisdom of maintaining friendship with nations of different religions as a sure means of consolidating her rule over distant dominions. It was about, or soon after, this time when British power was apparently more respected on the Continent than ever, that Scott had successfully reminded British readers of the crimes and follies of not very remote ancestors in their treatment of each other during civil wars or rebellions. A few years more elapsed, and the gifted young London novelist Dickens could likewise describe without offence, yet with keen ridicule, the hypocrisy and avarice which in his time had, as it were, replaced the political cruelty or religious fanaticism of former days. In London, if not throughout most of England, sectarian zeal or bitterness had greatly lost influence when Dickens began to write. He could therefore denounce the Reverend Stiggins, the

Reverend Chadband, Messrs. Pecksniff, Uriah Heep, Gashford and Honeythunder, all pretending to be religious men, without offending any sect among British readers.

Thackeray also concealed, or did not cherish, either religious or political partialities. Nearly all his chief characters, like those of Dickens, are English, and mostly Londoners. But the religious professions or opinions of either the good or the bad, of Lord Steyne, Colonel Newcome, or Colonel Dobbin, are withheld. Those of the younger Sir Pitt Crawley are sarcastically mentioned, but he is thoroughly worldly, and clearly not meant to represent any particular sect. Old Miss Honeyman has a horror of Catholic priests, for which she is neither praised nor censured, but slightly ridiculed. The indifference of Dickens and Thackeray to religious prejudices, if not to religious distinctions, would have once been in Great Britain, and may yet be in Ireland, greatly misconstrued, yet was correctly understood in the England of their days. A comparatively enlightened public easily saw that both authors were promoting social improvement in principle, habit and character, with no special reference to political or sectarian interests. Their British popularity, therefore, was restricted to no particular class or sect. They were equally acceptable to nearly all their fellow-countrymen, and, indeed, to most intelligent English-speaking people in every part of the world. They neither made nor tried to make changes in religious or political views,

and were, therefore, precisely the novelists best
adapted to the English public of their period. They
were also pleasing and really instructive to intelligent foreigners in their descriptions of modern
English character, and Dickens, when reading aloud
his works to a French audience, told the author
of this work that they guessed his purpose when
indicating the elopement in 'David Copperfield'
sooner than English audiences did. Most of his
and Thackeray's works exclusively describe English
people in a spirit so free from national prejudice
as to render them almost cosmopolitan in general
attractiveness. Their effect in favouring or advocating the pacific enlightenment of Great Britain
apparently confirmed or completed Scott's previous
efforts in the historic and social philosophy of the
'Waverley Novels.' Religious and political bigotry,
so keenly yet so temperately censured in the latter,
is by Dickens and Thackeray treated almost as a
thing of the past, an odious remembrance of national
or social barbarism.[1] They seemed to consider it
one of the vanished evils of a bygone time which
educational progress would never permit to revive;
but the history of the three kingdoms during recent

[1] The author once told Mr. Dickens that sincere religious
bigotry, free from the hypocrisy of Messrs. Stiggins, Pecksniff,
&c., was still a strong influence among all parties in Ireland.
The great exponent of cant and hypocrisy seemed surprised at
what he called 'the old, stupid thing' being still popular in that
country. Had he lived there he would have found it not only
among the old, or the stupid, but often guiding great talents,
inspiring profound conviction, and animating enthusiastic
eloquence.

years hardly justifies this pleasing belief. The best works of these writers were composed in the lifetime of the late Prince Consort. This Prince seemed the incarnation of the civilised spirit of his century, and as time passed his popularity steadily, though perhaps slowly, increased throughout Britain. He became in many respects, as named in the Queen's diary, 'the patron of Art and promoter of Peace.'[1] It was probably not till after his death that his real merits and the superiority of his philanthropic character were fully acknowledged by educated Englishmen.

To see Britain heading modern civilisation, to encourage intellectual emulation rather than martial ambition or territorial covetousness, was the Prince's earnest desire, and his influence in Britain, if not throughout civilised Europe, seemed to be generally increasing, till he was summoned to another world.[2] It was, a short time before, an expectation as well as a hope among many in Britain that religious toleration amid universal peace would for the future

[1] *Life of the Prince Consort*, vol. iv.
[2] '"England's mission, duty, and interest," he had written to Lord John Russell on September 5, 1847, "is to put herself at the head of the diffusion of civilisation and the attainment of liberty." The same energy, the same intellectual activity which had put her in the van of nations, the Prince believed would enable her to hold her place under any alteration of circumstances. He understood her people too well to doubt that they would see with pleasure the spread throughout the world of the blessings which they had conquered for themselves, and be content to run even considerable risks in accelerating that better understanding of each other, without which the unity of mankind is impossible.'—Sir Theodore Martin's *Life of the Prince Consort*, vol. ii. chap. 36.

prevail in civilised European countries. Some worthy philanthropists actually suggested the comparative disarmament of Britain, in the fond hope that Christian nations had become too civilised, peaceful, and reasonable to revive the horrors of war. This idea was probably encouraged by the pacific spectacle of the Industrial Exhibition in London of 1851.

Though, probably, neither Macaulay, Bulwer Lytton, Dickens, nor Thackeray entertained this belief, they yet apparently took a more hopeful view of future European peace and prosperity than subsequent years have justified. They usually mention national prejudices as well as religious bigotry with contemptuous aversion, instead of examining those deep-rooted, dangerous feelings with the calm discrimination of Walter Scott. Students of Ireland's history to the present time will derive more instruction from Scott in understanding Irish religious prejudices since the Reformation, though they never refer directly to Ireland, than could, perhaps, be derived from subsequent novelists, or from most historians. Macaulay declares that amid British enlightenment the thick darkness of the Middle Ages still rested upon Ireland. It is certain that many theological and political ideas or prejudices of former times, described by Scott, yet almost ignored by subsequent British writers, remain in Ireland as popular as ever. Macaulay, however, may mislead readers by calling the unchangeableness of the Irish in political or religious prejudices 'thick darkness.'

It yet inspires some men as able, if not as well educated, as himself, and is revealed in eloquent speeches at popular meetings in Ireland, and latterly more than ever in those of Irish representatives in the British Parliament.

The hostility of modern Ireland to Britain is one of the most perplexing questions of this century. In some respects it is of a contradictory nature, as brave Irish soldiers and sailors, learned able lawyers, and trusty police devote themselves as firmly to British interests as either English or Scottish could do. Yet the most popular men in the greater part of the island, whether in Parliament or not, are those who are loudest or most sincere in condemning British authority in every possible way. Irish enmity to England no longer seeks aid from France, nor takes its stand under a native chief. It may have a vague connection with the United States, but this connection has no very definite form. Yet Ireland's energy, eloquence, and money are often devoted to anti-English demonstrations, and it cannot be denied that they represent the feelings of a majority. This singular alienation among a population whose minority are most faithful to Britain, seems chiefly caused by the exasperating effect of one-sided historical teaching. A firm belief is transmitted from generation to generation in Ireland that they are the hereditary victims of a tyrannical neighbouring nation. Yet this belief does not prevent their enlisting in their tyrant's service, in which they are eminently distinguished by a rare, courageous fidelity. But the bravest Irish soldiers, the most just and firm of Irish judges under the British Crown, have the constant mortification of hearing their Government eloquently and fiercely denounced by the most popular men in the country, to enthusiastic, credulous audiences, as Ireland's historical foe and oppressor.

CHAPTER XXX

Difficulties of British statesmen in dealing with Ireland—Its exceptional position amid European changes and enlightenment.

MACAULAY, in common with many eminent British writers, reveals a disappointment about Ireland and the Irish surprising in a man of his great attainments.[1] Modern British historians have generally attended more to the Continent and to distant parts of the world than to that perplexing, troublesome island so near to them. Even British statesmen have shown, and like the late Chief Secretary, Mr. Forster, indicated, that they understood little about Ireland till they came to know it personally. In reality the many intellectual changes so influential in Britain during the present century have not had the same effect in that country. This fact, if calmly examined, may cause surprise, but scarcely justifies the irritation indicated by Macaulay. Enlightened British writers, perhaps acquainted with many other

[1] ' " I do not mean to take the white sheet," Macaulay is reported to have said, " for I acted honestly and conscientiously, but I now see that all we did for the Catholics has turned out badly." " In Ireland, as on the Continent, the question of priestly influence in politics is one of the most pressing of our time." '—Lecky's *Democracy and Liberty*, vol. ii. chap. 6.

countries, often imagine that ignorance alone keeps Ireland little changed in religious and political prejudices, and also in hereditary enmity to British rule. They incline to attribute these feelings to this cause, which may chiefly preserve them in distant parts of the British dominions. In this belief some British writers and statesmen find themselves mistaken, as Ireland's history, even in recent years, clearly shows that feelings and opinions long believed in Great Britain hardly compatible with good sense or knowledge of the world remain popular among many able, intellectual Irishmen.

It has constantly surprised British statesmen to hear in Ireland all connected with English rule ridiculed or denounced with the utmost power of that language. Ireland's singular discontent induces the able historian, Mr. Lecky, to call attention to the memorable fact, that while Britain rules her vast Eastern Empire of two hundred million subjects, she has failed in governing Ireland, containing at most about three million disaffected subjects.[1] He also says, 'The chief key to the enigma is to be found in the fact that Irish affairs have been in the very vortex of English party politics, while India has hitherto lain outside their sphere and has been governed by competent administrators, who looked only to the well-being of the country.' Whether these assertions be admitted or not, Irish parliamentary elections steadily arouse the sometimes dormant, but never extinct, spirit of animosity against fellow-

[1] *History of Ireland*, chap. 13.

countrymen, and sometimes against England as the main support of the few against the many Irishmen who desire national independence. This state of feeling among a divided people immediately recalls to historical students the ideas or hopes of the Middle Ages. Among a people imbued with hereditary enmity, no amount of education can overcome the ancestral influences of inherited animosities. Thoughtful observers will in Ireland be more often reminded of the feelings expressed in Scott's historical novels than of those in the works of Lever, Lover, or Carleton. These writers usually glance lightly at Irish character, without much historical allusion. Their favourite subjects are comic sketches of Irish military or peasant life, while most other Irish writers devote their talents more to political or theological advocacy than to the philosophy of general history.

The politics of their own country, as a rule, interest and engross Irishmen beyond any other subject, save those which professional interests require. Yet usually they are discussed more in the style of special pleading than in that of calm or free reasoning. This is inevitable when Ireland's history is examined without sufficient reference to Continental nations, with whom, since the Reformation, Irish interests, hopes, and apprehensions were closely and peculiarly involved. An extreme instance of Irish political bitterness occurs in a late history by the exiled conspirator, Tynan, when denouncing Mr. Parnell for disavowing in Parliament the murderers of Lord Frederick Cavendish and Mr. Burke in Dublin during 1882. He writes with a power of expression and eager eloquence far more usual among Irish than among British revolutionists. He makes even classic allusions to dignify, or extenuate, a deed which every civilised country would pronounce criminal in the last degree.[1]

Most Irish historians, with few exceptions, yield to partiality, and become more or less partisans. Macaulay reveals this influence when extolling Cromwell's Irish career, while admitting its undeniable cruelty. Few writers on Ireland's history seem to admire real impartiality, and accordingly British colonists and Irish natives are represented either as the friends or the foes of their common race. To record noble acts of opponents or crimes of partisans hardly seems to these writers a moral historical duty to the public. Their object resembles that of able advocates in a law-suit, of which the reading public is the historical judge, and to admit guilt in partisans, or merit in opponents, seems almost treason to writers yielding to political

---

[1] 'When Charles Stewart Parnell arose to take part in this hideous debate, and when the burning, blistering, slanderous words came hissing from his lips in the senate of his country's foe—when he, standing in the presence of Ireland's enemies, stigmatised the men who died for Ireland as assassins, then an agonised thrill of horror went pulsing through the nation's frame, as she stood bleeding beneath the blows dealt her by her moral assassins in that chamber; and Ireland, seeing the uplifted steel of Charles Stewart Parnell, covered her face with her robe, and, falling prostrate at the base of Liberty's statue, cried out like the dying Cæsar, " Et tu, Brute ? " '—*History of the Irish Invincibles*, p. 532.

or religious prejudices. The advance of time, the spread of education, and the increase of foreign intercourse, produce less effect among the home-staying Irish, Protestants as well as Catholics, than would seem credible to those unacquainted with them. During a time of national and local peace they may conceal their feelings, but during parliamentary elections or political celebrations, the mutual hostility of Ireland's divided population is up to the present day revealed to a surprised British public. The history even of the last half century shows little material difference in this respect from that of former times, though the increased efficiency of repressive forces is more competent to suppress outrage. But the mutual alienation of the divided people, without personal quarrel, the resolute, dogged enmity with which they arm themselves with deadly weapons at public meetings and processions, and the bitter language of their leaders and newspapers in denouncing each other, reveal the dangerous inheritance of former civil wars or rebellions. On such occasions it is often shown that Irishmen in this century are as ready to destroy one another with improved or newly invented revolvers, as their ancestors were with pikes and skeans. The dangers of Irish parliamentary elections and those of former times are in some places much the same. Their results are now diffused by wire, watched by vigilant police, and reported in an increasing variety of newspapers. Yet in the fury of opposing parties, in the real danger to life and limb to which even Mr. Parnell was exposed when popular favour turned against him, there appears little abatement in the ferocious nature of Irish political excitement. But for the aid of police or soldiers, and the assistance they derive from railways and telegraphs, there is reason to believe, from Irish election history of the last twenty years, that outrages as savage and dangerous as ever would have occurred in parts of the island.

This vindictive bitterness in Irish elections presents a gloomy contrast to what Dickens humorously describes in 'Pickwick.' In that most amusing of English fictions, rival newspaper editors vainly try to rouse party spirit for the sake of their own private interest or vanity. The comic disappointment of Messrs. Pott and Slurk, whose readers take less interest in local politics than they do, would be almost unknown in Ireland. In that excitable country newspaper writers have regretted with reason the serious consequences produced among an inflammable people by the irritating effect of their articles. Though Ireland, at least formerly, was often called a cheerful, merry country compared with the graver population of England and Scotland, it has for some years lost something of this character. National history or politics which in Great Britain engage calm discussion are usually enlivened by comic caricatures or good-humoured, witty topical songs, which among the Irish would likely cause dangerous irritation. Among the three kingdoms, England and Scotland, always credited with possessing shrewd, self-controlled inhabitants, now take a far more cheerful or comic view of political life than Ireland, which often resounds in speeches and newspapers with denunciations of differing parties. The exasperation of political enmity, sometimes causing fatal results, among Irishmen without personal quarrel, seems almost unknown in Great Britain. The same spirit may not have been known there for a long period, as there seems no account of hereditary injuries and reprisals among the North British peasantry after the Jacobite wars. The sufferings of those times were caused and chiefly felt by leading men, and had comparatively slight effect on peasants or artisans. These classes, after the cessation of warfare, relapsed into perfect peace; the State trials being principally those of chiefs and influential men.

Macaulay describes the same result after the Wars of the Roses in England, which were caused by the higher classes, on whom the penalties of defeat fell almost exclusively. In Ireland, public feeling, often concealed, has little changed among the mass of the peasantry since the war of James II. against William III. That contest, virtually ending in the Boyne battle, and connected in sectarian interests with the previous wars of Cromwell in Ireland, left an impression on the Irish which was never effaced, nor in some places much weakened. The subsequent revolts of 1798, and, in this century, the Fenian movement and the land agitation headed by Mr. Parnell, never replaced these former historical recollections in the Irish popular mind. The rebellions of 1798 and '48, the first headed by Tone,

Fitzgerald and the Emmets, the second by Messrs. Smith O'Brien, Mitchel and Meagher, never fairly represented the popular will, though their different leaders had a brief, disastrous influence. The 1798 leaders avowedly wished Ireland to imitate the existing French Republic, which the Irish masses would never have admired.

The '48 leaders, though influential till actual revolt was attempted, were then easily arrested, tried, and sentenced to banishment without eliciting much popular sympathy. The previous peaceful agitation organised by Daniel O'Connell was far more popular with the Irish majority, of whom he was no unfit representative. He never encouraged armed revolution, but on the contrary always discouraged it, steadily professing loyalty to the British monarchy. With O'Connell's remarkable exception, who was a devout Catholic, the chief Irish political agitations from 1798 inclusive were headed by Protestants, who, though mainly supported by Roman Catholics, were strongly disavowed by most of their co-religionists. Tone, O'Brien, and Mr. Parnell, in their different periods, found this to be the case, and alike finally experienced, Parnell especially, a practical repudiation by Irish Catholic adherents at the close of their career. This unexpected disavowal was due in every instance to the influence of the Irish Catholic clergy. This body, formed by professional training, duties and interests, to both arouse and restrain enthusiasm, were peculiarly fitted to discriminate between what they thought a right objection to

Protestant rule and the alternative of democratic revolution, which on the Continent was always hostile to the Papacy.

While, therefore, eloquent leaders, Protestant or Catholic, denounced British authority, advocating Irish independence as a general principle, the priesthood could conscientiously encourage them. But when these leaders, allied either openly or in secret with foreign political partisans, proposed an Irish Republic, or advocated separation from England by actual revolt, then, and often not before, the Irish Catholic clergy warned their people to no longer follow the guidance even of friendly sympathisers beyond a certain point known to themselves. This limit often allowed any amount of peaceful complaint against Great Britain, and of eager eloquence in behalf of alleged national rights, but cautiously discouraged all idea of armed rebellion, or active alliance with foreign republicans against the British monarchy.

CHAPTER XXXI

Enduring power of clerical influence in Ireland—Its diminution on the Continent in political questions—O'Connell's popularity in Ireland compared with that of Mr. Parnell.

THE indignation revealed by Wolfe Tone in his Diary, by Mitchel in '48, and lately by Parnell's followers against the Irish Catholic clergy, though in such different men, was aroused by similar causes. They could not, or professed not to, understand why the priests should tolerate, if not sanction, bitter denunciation of British rule, and yet oppose actual attempts to subvert it. A few priests, indeed, had openly joined the '98 revolt, but were disavowed by their spiritual superiors, and ever since, when some inclined to favour revolution, they were usually induced, or compelled, to obey their clerical chiefs and refuse complicity with open rebellion, or with direct incitements to it. Enthusiastic Protestant revolutionists, and some eager or reckless Catholics, loudly denounced what they thought meanness or treachery in this conduct, and tried by passionate appeals to the Irish masses to shake their confidence in the priests as political guides. In these denunciations some loyal Protestants joined, from distrust of the Catholic clergy, who they tried to prove were always abettors of the popular dislike to England since the Reformation. Historical evidence comprising that of the Continent as well as of Great Britain and Ireland, if calmly examined, may explain the policy of the Irish Catholic clergy more clearly than either friends or foes have often done. The interests of their unchangeable Church, menaced during the last few centuries by Christian opponents, who, though divided among themselves, were as united against her as she was indiscriminate against them, were always their primary object, above national claims, desires, or preferences. While eager laymen of all religions may advocate political freedom, legislative improvement, or national rights and distinctions, the Catholic clergy must first decide how any contemplated political change may affect the interests of that form of Christianity which they are bound to diffuse, guard, and maintain above every other consideration.

Whether they apparently sanction revolutionary conduct in some countries, or despotism in others, their first object must be to place religious interests before either political or national ambition. In one sense Catholic priests are the most cons'stently loyal of all clergy, but their loyalty must first be devoted to the Church, which requires steady adherence to whatever rulers among co-religionists are most likely to promote, or among non-Catholics least likely to injure its true cause. A moral, yet practical, policy of this nature has often disappointed the hopes or eluded the power of eager revolutionists, unscrupulous despots, or ambitious princes. None of these has ever been able to alter or perhaps fully understand it. Shakespeare in 'King John' clearly illustrates this clerical policy, though only directed against an obstinate Catholic monarch. When the French are invited by the Papacy through Cardinal Pandulph to invade England, owing to the King's quarrel with the Pope about an ecclesiastical appointment, John, finding his subjects against him, submits to the Papacy, and the Cardinal then, knowing the Pope's mind, induces the French to leave England. The French prince Lewis indignantly remonstrates, as he anticipated a glorious conquest, but Pandulph, representing his Church, listens to the fiery youth, without entering into much discussion, and in one short expressive sentence indicating the Papal policy calmly closes it.[1]

[1] *Cardinal.*   Hail, noble prince of France!
    The next is this,—king John hath reconcil'd
    Himself to Rome ; his spirit is come in,
    That so stood out against the holy church.
    Therefore thy threat'ning colours now wind up,
    And tame the savage spirit of wild war.
Prince Lewis.   What is that peace to me ?
    Am I Rome's slave ? What penny hath Rome borne,
    What men provided, what munition sent,
    To underprop this action ?
    Have I not here the best cards for the game,
    To win this easy match play'd for a crown ?
    And shall I now give o'er the yielded set ?
    No, on my soul, it never shall be said.
Cardinal.   You look but on the outside of this work.
    King John, act v.

This policy, exclusively ecclesiastical and founded on religious history, has often provoked or puzzled warriors and politicians at different times and in different countries. Napoleon I. was deeply offended with the Papacy for morally resisting his usurping the French crown. Vigilant or suspicious Protestant rulers, as well as disavowed Catholic rebels, have made similar charges against a Power which alone amid all others has always studied spiritual interests before national prosperity, influence, or temptation. Throughout all countries the aims of the Catholic clergy can never vary, despite apparent contradiction owing to national differences. Thus in Ireland they seem democratic, opposing rulers or landowners, while on the Continent they are considered by foreign republicans as warm advocates of monarchy and of proprietary rights. Some of them in Ireland, especially when drawn from the peasant class, have favoured revolutionary ideas and unwillingly obeyed clerical superiors in abstaining from their vehement advocacy. But the ultimate practical supremacy of Catholic prelates over Ireland's majority has always survived the enthusiastic, brief excitement of a period, or the temporary winning influence of popular leaders. A consistent policy, historically devoted to the cause of one special form of Christianity, may alternately astonish, favour, or oppose many political parties, nor can it be expected to do otherwise among men whose views, thoughts, and hopes are, as a rule, personal or worldly. While arbitrary rulers or eager revolutionists have alike denounced this peculiar influence, for sometimes aiding or not opposing sedition, and at other times advocating or not censuring despotism, it has really been more morally and inevitably consistent than either. It represents a spiritual power independent of national distinction, and from its historically sacred position essentially proof against popular enthusiasm or worldly ambition. All personal, local, and patriotic hopes or perils it completely subordinates to the interests of the Church, with no special preference for race or country, being enjoined to bring mankind indiscriminately under its spiritual authority and moral control.

In Ireland Daniel O'Connell was peculiarly devoted to the views of the priesthood. Many political successors aspiring to lead the Irish have blamed this patriotic leader with singular bitterness, and partly for his extreme respect for the clergy. The most recent Irish leader of note, Mr. Parnell, despite his Protestantism, powerfully influenced a majority of Catholic fellow-countrymen, including some of their clergy. Yet, directly the Catholic prelates withdrew confidence from him, he lost theirs also, and was transformed into an object of popular abuse, and even menace. His utter disavowal by the Irish Catholic majority by the advice of their clergy was a most signal proof of clerical power over Irish minds. This power has remained little changed among the same population since the civil war between James II. and William III., as Irish priestly influence among the majority has ever since usually prevailed in all contests decided by numerical superiority.

Nor is this fact very surprising when Ireland's peculiar history is fairly examined. The landed gentry and wealthier classes in Ireland represent only a small minority. Until recent years few Irish Roman Catholics except their clergy had much education. The latter, maintaining frequent sympathetic intercourse with France, Spain, and Italy, always preserved some knowledge of European politics, while their comparative, perhaps wilful, ignorance of Protestant countries or literature often made them misunderstand, and misunderstood by, British statesmen. Their enduring influence over an Irish majority has practically experienced little change from remote times to the present. Occasionally energetic Catholics, as well as Protestants, may deprecate or ridicule this sacerdotal power. Eloquent denunciations of it may succeed for a time in obtaining applause from many Protestants and from reckless or excitable Catholics, yet hitherto, whenever the secret proof of popular feeling is revealed during parliamentary elections or other public occasions, the nominees of the priests have generally secured large majorities even in cases where little was personally known of the men recommended to public confidence. It is sufficiently evident that to the present time the Irish priests represent the political views of a large majority in their country. Among co-religionists abroad this clerical influence appears less felt, and would in some Catholic countries, France especially, be altogether repudiated.[1]

The reason for this difference, perhaps, may be thus partly explained. The interference of French priests in politics would necessarily be in behalf, directly or indirectly, of the deposed monarchy. No Protestant influence in France can oppose Roman Catholicism as in Ireland, where the Protestants have for centuries been devoted adherents to British authority. In France they are so few and uninfluential that the cause of Christianity itself, against an energetic spirit of atheism in Paris, is almost entirely involved with its Roman Catholic form. In France the priests who interfere in politics would likely be viewed with suspicion by a ruling Republic, owing to the steady devotion of the banished princes to the Catholic faith. But in Ireland priestly influence morally represents the feelings of a vast majority, and it may be owned by candid non-Catholics that it merits more confidence from Irish people generally than the temptations of most political leaders who have hitherto aspired to lead them. The Irish majority may practically consider that preference for their clergy even as political guides to such men as Wolfe Tone, Mitchel,

---

[1] 'The stringency of the French laws against priestly interference with politics is very great, and no disposition has hitherto been shown to relax it. The proceedings which are of almost daily occurrence in Ireland would not be tolerated for an hour by the French Government.'—Lecky's *Democracy and Liberty*, vol. ii. chap. 6.

and Parnell might be justified in Shakespeare's famous lines :

> The friends thou hast, and their adoption tried,
> Grapple them to thy soul with hooks of steel;
> But do not dull thy palm with entertainment
> Of each new-hatch'd, unfledg'd comrade.

CHAPTER XXXII

Failure of Protestant political leaders in Ireland—Final success of the priesthood in opposing Mr. Parnell—They still politically represent the Irish majority.

THE career and fall of Mr. Parnell may always be considered an important lesson in Irish politics. In Ireland, in Britain, on the Continent, in America, and in the Colonies, wherever Irishmen dwelt, his popularity was probably wider than that of any previous Irish leader. This extension was naturally owing to this century's affording an amount of international intercourse previously unknown. His speeches, addresses, and public letters were diffused among admiring Irishmen in almost every part of the world. He nominated whom he chose to represent Ireland in the British Parliament, and these were generally returned without opposition, or by large majorities. His popularity was for some time sanctioned by the Catholic clergy, till the result of a divorce suit, in which he was co-respondent, and made no defence, induced them to advise and exhort their people to withdraw from their favourite leader further support or confidence. The large majority of their hearers immediately obeyed, and the man who before this disavowal was almost the popular idol in the greater part of Ireland became viewed as a disgrace to his party.

On one occasion he was seriously injured by former admirers, pelted, abused, and narrowly escaped with his life from a violent mob. A courageous minority, consisting mostly of Catholics, still adhered to him and warmly denounced what they termed priestly tyranny in politics. Yet though this small party showed great intelligence, zeal, and energy for the disowned leader, the Catholic majority firmly obeyed their clergy with steady consistency. During their contest and mutual recrimination, most Irish Protestants kept aloof from either party. Though Mr. Parnell was an avowed Protestant, he had no influence over most of his co-religionists maintaining British rule in Ireland, which he desired to abolish, though by peaceful means, and the whole account, especially the end of his career, forms an instructive illustration of Irish history and character.

All the aids of modern improvement in publication, travelling, and international communication, Mr. Parnell utilised to their full extent. He was completely a man of his time; there was nothing dreamy or fanciful about him, he was always ready-witted, bold and practical. His words were flashed by telegraph throughout every part of the world where Irishmen could be found. He had often travelled and spared no exertion in seeking Irish support or approval in every town and country. In this appeal, he was for a time, perhaps, as successful as he could have desired. His political position for some years was most singular, and apparently successful. He steadily professed Protestantism and was of British descent. None could term him a Celt, or find any connection between him and Irish chiefs of former times. In birth, religion, and personal qualities he decidedly belonged to the Irish Protestant minority, yet among that minority he had few followers, as nearly all opposed or distrusted him from first to last. His strength, like that of other Irish popular leaders, lay in his extraordinary influence over the Catholic majority. In this respect he rather resembled his revolutionary predecessor, Wolfe Tone, in 1798. Yet, while Tone was a professed republican, and a self-made French subject, relying rather on France than on America for revolutionary aid, Mr. Parnell was more cosmopolitan in his views and feelings. In many ways he represented and utilised the advantages of his enlightened progressive period. He addressed not only Irishmen in every country, but also appealed to both the British people and to foreigners. No historical tradition, sectarian limit, or social preference had any influence with him.

He discouraged open revolt against Britain, while firmly advocating Ireland for the Irish by ardent yet peaceful agitation. He rarely invoked either poetry or eloquence in favour of his views. There was, in fact, nothing romantic, sentimental, fanciful, or poetical about him. Had Charles Lever or Moore written in his time they could hardly have made him a hero. Cool, practical, and courageous, Mr. Parnell was emphatically a thorough, resolute man of business, yet strangely involved with an excitable, devout population.

He seldom mentioned religious questions, and seemed to rather avoid the subject. While avowing Protestantism amid eager Catholic followers, and distrusted by most of his co-religionists, he made, or rather tried to make, his agitation entirely secular. He avoided much allusion to former days in Irish traditions, eminently proving himself a practical politician with thoughts and energies devoted to his own times. Amid a population hitherto thought peculiarly devout and poetical, this calm, determined, matter-of-fact leader might seem out of his element, yet was politically supreme over a large majority of Irishmen for some years.

Wolfe Tone and he were alike thought by their respective admirers to well understand the difficult problem of Irish character, and probably both thought so themselves. To each leader, applause, money and political support were eagerly devoted by many ardent Irish Roman Catholics. There seemed for a time, indeed, to be a thorough confidence between them and their Irish followers, but, like the old saying of a man reckoning without his host, each leader, despite the difference of their times, had overlooked or despised the chief principle which has always ruled Ireland's majority. This principle was not merely religious veneration, but the special influence of Roman Catholicism. Its almost indescribable power over the Irish masses in their own country was secretly despised or defied by Wolfe Tone, as proved in his private diary. This singular revelation, not published till after his death, displayed a scornful hatred of the Papacy which, had Tone ever obtained real power over the Irish, would have soon lost him their support altogether.

Mr. Parnell, likewise, despite his great gifts, advantages, and practical sense in using them, either ignored or underrated the enduring power of clerical influence over the Irish majority. He had perhaps some excuse for his grand mistake in this respect. His perseverance and energy had not only induced a large Irish majority to follow him, but had gradually made a favourable impression on some British hearers to whom former Irish popular leaders had seldom thought of appealing. His ascendancy over Irishmen at home, in Britain, America, throughout the Continent and in the Colonies, was unprecedented, and may have tempted him to overlook, and thus be unprepared for, the tremendous change among the Irish majority in their conduct towards him, as hitherto his influence, sanctioned or not opposed by their priesthood, had been almost supreme. The priests had indeed been indirectly warned by the Papacy not to favour Mr. Parnell so eagerly, but this counsel they had little regarded, trusting him as an able, sincere advocate of the rights or interests of their fellow-countrymen. Their sudden repudiation of his leadership brought no influential priest into the political field as Mr. Parnell's rival or successor.

There was no fervent denunciation of him by any religious enthusiasts. He was, as it were, by the clergy pronounced morally, and therefore politically, unworthy to lead their people, who by a large majority at once obeyed their priests.

This disavowal was published immediately after Mr. Gladstone's rather similar repudiation of the Irish leader, with whom the veteran English statesman had been previously friendly to some extent. Each disavowal was owing ostensibly to the result of the divorce trial, but the Irish Catholic clergy found themselves in a perplexing position, when suddenly believing it right to withdraw confidence from a man whom before they had trusted and indirectly caused others to trust.

Mr. Parnell and his remaining adherents felt the conduct of the clergy most keenly, and its effect seemed to really shorten as well as embitter his life. He soon after died, protesting, without mentioning the divorce case, that he had always deserved and never forfeited the political confidence of his revolted followers. But these protests were now vain; even his appearance, worn, agitated, and distressed, could arouse no compassionate reaction in his favour among the Irish majority deeming it their duty to repudiate him. His utter abandonment by so many eager vehement admirers seemed like a triumph of the spirit of the Middle Ages over that of the nineteenth century.

No rival popular orator replaced him, or refuted his charges of ingratitude. No political partisans could supplant him in the extraordinary ascendancy he had exercised over his followers. He was solemnly as well as suddenly declared, and generally believed, no longer worthy of Irish Catholic confidence by the unanimous voice of the hierarchy. Against their firm decision no popular appeal was made, no national remonstrance offered. In Irish opinion, by clerical command, the hitherto popular chief was immediately transformed from a respected leader into a condemned man. Enthusiastic greeting was with amazing rapidity changed to denunciation, mingled with threats of violence, from the Irish majority.

Though an energetic minority adhered to him, his popular influence with the majority was over, and in subsequent parliamentary elections the influence of the priesthood was usually supreme. They now saw their mistake in favouring a leader whose private character had proved inconsistent with those principles it was their duty to support. Ever since their repudiation of Mr. Parnell, their practical influence resumed sole supremacy over Ireland's majority. Popular opinion in Ireland still chiefly trusts, as it has always done, the national priesthood as political as well as religious guides in any emergency.[1]

---

[1] 'In modern times the devout Catholic is very apt to look upon the Church as his true and his higher country, and he accordingly subordinates all his political actions to the furtherance of its interests. There are many signs that Catholicism will in the future tend more and more to an alliance with democracy. It has in most countries lost the dignities and privileges on which its former power largely depended. The powers with which it was once closely allied no longer govern

As might be expected, the Irish Catholic majority were warmly reproached, by some co-religionists and by many non-Catholics, for their sudden change of attitude towards their favourite leader. But, as in all historical instances, clerical pre-eminence in Ireland remained unmoved by eloquence, complaints, or enmity.

Mr. Parnell's death certainly removed from Ireland one of the most determined, if not dangerous, foes to British rule which it has yet produced. Without trying to ally himself with foreign nations, or intriguing like Tone to obtain foreign intervention, he endeavoured, with success, not only to confirm Irish dislike to British rule, but to persuade the English and Scotch to consider their authority over Ireland as unjust and disastrous. There never was, perhaps, before a Protestant leader of British descent who did, and tried to do, more harm to British ascendancy in Ireland. His political extinction was neither caused nor hastened by opponents. He had resisted British influence for years and apparently with increasing success, when his sudden disavowal by his own party effected all that his foes had failed to accomplish, and since his time British rule in no country has met with so energetic a foe. In their foreign dominions the British are still troubled with occasional petty wars or outbreaks, chiefly on the frontiers, but their authority in no part of the world

the world, and it has always sought to connect itself with what is strongest among mankind.'—Lecky's *Democracy and Liberty* vol. ii.

seems now seriously endangered by either foreign enemies or rebellious subjects. In Asia rivalry with the Russians continues and may increase, especially in the direction of China. Yet it may be hoped that such jealousy, delaying the spread of European civilisation, will soon cease, perhaps through the mutual friendship of the British and Russian royal families, whose worst enemies now appear among Nihilists and Anarchists, in the very heart of their European dominions.

CHAPTER XXXIII

Friendly feelings between opposing political parties in Britain—
In Ireland party spirit retains its former bitterness.

THE friendly sentiments existing between the British public and their rulers, irrespective of political or religious differences, is a pleasant contrast to former times and to some foreign countries even at present. Thus rival statesmen, alternately serving the most popular of British sovereigns, have long been praised, blamed, admired, or ridiculed and made subjects for caricatures or 'topical' songs in London before crowded, good-humoured audiences. Yet as a general rule these allusions are singularly free from malice or hostility. During many years British statesmen of differing politics have been in England and Scotland rather the favourites of the public, and considered men of whose talents they may be nationally proud, however their opinions may differ.

This pacific reasonable state of popular feeling is a happy change from former times in both countries, and it may be regretted that hitherto it hardly extends to Ireland. Among many of the Irish, men in power, or aspiring to it, are viewed with feelings more like those of the Middle Ages, and which still appear in contests between rival presidents in the republics of South America. In those countries the difference between political opponents and mortal foes seems little recognised during times of political excitement, when rival leaders and their followers often destroy each other with ruthless ferocity.

In Ireland, likewise, it seems not easy for its excitable people to discriminate between peaceful opponents, with every legal and moral right to be so, and dangerous enemies, as recent Irish parliamentary elections clearly testify. On some of these occasions, even within the last few years, soldiers and police found it difficult to save opposing parties from dangerous outrage. Such violence is often not deliberate, but when excited men armed with revolvers discuss Ireland's history or politics the danger is often serious. Irish history during the last twenty years surely justifies this assertion; when not only are avowed opponents irreconcilable in matters of religion or politics, but leaders once popular, praised and flattered, are endangered from offended partisans as much as from consistent opponents.

Politics, often the favourite subject for jokes, wit and merriment in Britain, especially in London, are literally no joke in Ireland, but become revelations of hereditary hatred, class jealousy, and religious prejudice. These causes of irritation influence many Irish minds about political questions affecting their divided country. The calm, good-humoured steadiness with which British statesmen oppose, thwart, or supplant each other without personal quarrel, owing to their common respect for legal rights and privileges, is among the surest evidences of British civilisation. It proves that ambitious rivals recognise their best policy, as well as moral duty, never to let political opposition degrade itself into personal spite or quarrel.

It shows that opposing statesmen realise the fact that if they allow private feelings to overcome professed principles it would only lower them in the opinion of the public whom they wish to influence, and who in their turn are thus able to influence them. This example prevails also in some, but not in all, Continental countries, for duels between rival statesmen or public men are still common in France, Italy, and Germany. Yet such personal quarrels do not seem to cause enmity among their respective political partisans.

In Europe neither rival claimants to a crown nor opposing statesmen have much reason to dread one another, unless indeed they may yield to their own ambition unsupported by public opinion. Their real dangers in the perils of modern political rule, however, are serious enough, chiefly arising from the reckless malignity of Anarchist foes to civilised society. These men openly avow the doctrine that political murder is no crime, but an act of patriotism in retributive justice.[1]

[1] 'A public opinion is very morbid which looks on these things as venial. It is the custom in England to assert that

This common danger to men in power, in every country, probably aids to maintain that widespread national peace which now prevails, even among nations preserving large standing armies. Nothing is said to unite people closer together in mutual sympathy than constant danger from a common and malignant foe. The same feeling may well actuate nations which is known to inspire individuals. During the last half century some British and foreign rulers and statesmen were deliberately murdered from no personal or national enmity, but from that indiscriminate hatred to men in authority which is at once the most extraordinary and disheartening accompaniment of the civilisation of this age.

It is like a sudden revival of barbarism in the midst of the highest enlightenment, amid apparent peace and general tranquillity. Congratulations or condolence now often pass between endangered rulers, or their friends in distant lands, inevitably inspired by the earnest sympathy of a common apprehension. This international fellow-feeling of ruling classes in distant countries, united by common danger, despite national rivalry or religious difference,

such crimes as the murders in the Phœnix Park, or the massacre, or attempted massacre, by an Anarchist bomb of a number of innocent persons, are not political. It does not appear to me reasonable to deny this character to acts which were inspired by no motive of private gain or malice, and were directly and exclusively intended to produce political ends. But the fact that they are political does not attenuate their atrocity, nor ought it to mitigate the punishment of the criminal,'— Lecky's *Democracy and Liberty*, vol. i. p. 192.

is a comparatively new feature in civilised history. During late years, the increasing international communication which has so enlightened Europe has been strangely perverted into forming confederations among people of different lands for the common purpose of assassinating political rulers.

In Ireland, so famed for eloquence and poetry, these gifts are sometimes devoted to exonerate, even glorify, men convicted of political murder. Though rebellious speeches and writings always found able advocates in that country, yet the vindication by educated men of deliberate murder is perhaps more evident lately than ever. The term rebellion, as thoughtful historical readers will discover, was always capable of very different constructions, especially in civilised lands. In political contests each party must oppose rebellion against itself, and when rebel leaders become rulers they usually make their own example penal to the last degree. Each party in the Jacobite revolts, for instance, called the other rebels, as what was thought loyalty by one was thought treason by the other. One party adhered to a German prince, the other to the heir of a deposed king, styled by the existing Government as a 'Pretender' to his ancestral rights.

In previous times the Commonwealth, with Cromwell and Milton for champion and advocate, likewise denounced imitation of its revolutionary example as a penal offence involving moral guilt. During that extraordinary contest in Great Britain and Ireland, each party declared it a sin to rebel against established power, whether wielded by a weak monarch or by an energetic soldier.

During the Jacobite risings, unlike Irish revolts, the aid of eloquence was little invoked on either side. People were urged to recall a deposed or maintain a reigning royal family, by solemn appeals to the claim of Divine Right, or by a firm repudiation of the banished House of Stuart. But neither British statesmen nor Jacobite chiefs often resorted to eloquence in advocating their views. A few battles, brief state trials, and speedy executions distinguished the Jacobite revolts with an implacability little consistent with the religious faith professed by both parties.

In the subsequent European wars of Napoleon I. most civilised nations were called to arms in the tremendous conflict by brief practical orders and proclamations. But in Irish revolts and seditions, at least from 1798 inclusive, eloquence in speeches and writing was a most remarkable feature, yet almost exclusively directed against existing government. A party in power, indeed, is rarely eloquent in advocating its own maintenance, or in persuading the discontented to obey it. Rulers or statesmen and their paid subordinates, eagerly advocating preservation of their own authority and the consequent retention of honours and salaries, would have little effect on an excited or discontented public. But the appeals of eager, often needy, revolutionists are likely to be more impressive. Eloquence and poetry are soon enlisted in their favour, expressing the feelings of men who personally, as well as politically, for private as well as for public reasons, long for a change in the government with an enthusiasm the sincerity of which cannot be doubted. This has been eminently the case in Irish history. The power of persuasion is usually, therefore, employed by revolutionary leaders. In justifying rebellion, especially in Ireland, this power has always been resorted to, and generally with great effect among an impressionable and ardent rather than a reasoning people.

The Irish revolutionary attempts against Britain in 1848 were marked, and to some extent dignified, by the enthusiastic eloquence or powerful writings of the revolutionists Meagher and Mitchel. In later years Irish sedition became, without perhaps the will of its leaders, more allied with the dangerous secret societies in other countries.

The eloquent, poetic fervour displayed by many Irish rebels through successive generations, from the days of Edmund Spenser till after the middle of this century, has become recently less perceptible, and is often replaced by a more practical or covetous spirit.

The gay, lively style of Irish literature also has lately been changed to one of a more serious, if not morose, cast. The bright, cheerful works of Lever and Lover, full of merriment, wit and jocularity, which in the early or middle part of this century delighted the British as well as the Irish public, yield in popular attraction to historic or political works, usually opposing British authority, without actually preferring any foreign rule, but often indirectly advocating republicanism. These views, especially since the death of O'Connell, who always supported the British monarchy, seem to increase in popularity among Irishmen at home and in America. Irish speeches and writings not only oppose British connection with Ireland, but are often hostile to British interests and policy throughout the world, and many popular leaders take no pride in Burke, Wellington, or other celebrated Irishmen who were devoted to Britain.

Among Irish writers who firmly support British rule, and identify themselves with British interests, Mr. Lecky is among the most influential. In his rather uncommon instance, like those of Gladstone, Disraeli, and Bulwer Lytton, literary genius and a taste or capacity for political work appear to some extent united. When men combine historical knowledge with calm judgment of cotemporary events and characters, their views are likely to be more free from party vehemence, enthusiasm, or prejudice, influences which many able statesmen are sometimes unable to control. Men studying the lessons of time through the medium of impartial history might be thought specially fitted for the duties of government; yet often historians and other writers find it a very different thing to fairly describe the great men of former times, and to deal calmly with perhaps similar characters when in personal contact with them. Neither Gibbon, Hume, Alison, Scott, or Macaulay was distinguished in political history, despite their talents and success in describing that of former periods. Yet eager politicians, hastily raised to power for ably advocating some special measure, sometimes prove unable to deal with the peculiar, weighty troubles or responsibilities of ruling the vast mass of different nations now comprised within the British empire. The value of historical knowledge when controlled by impartiality, in calming the mind and enlightening the judgment, is practically inestimable in legislating for the welfare of a civilised nation.[1]

[1] 'History is never more valuable than when it enables us, standing as on a height, to look beyond the smoke and turmoil of our petty quarrels, and to detect in the slow development of the past the great permanent forces that are ever steadily bearing nations onwards to improvement or decay.'—Lecky's *Political Value of History.*

CHAPTER XXXIV

Consolidation of British and of Russian power over colonies and non-Christian nations—China gradually attracts more European interference—Increasing importance of the colonies publicly acknowledged by British statesmen.

MACAULAY emphatically pronounces English literature among the 'many glories of England,' to which his essays and history were alike instructive and interesting additions. His accomplished mind apparently embraced civilised or intellectual history from the most remote period to his own. He is a thorough historian of mental culture, genius, and enlightenment. He loved to associate the great minds of Greece and Rome with modern illustrious Europeans. The records of barbaric or even feudal times had little interest for him. It is in the steady progress of the human mind, from its earliest dawn in the development of its knowledge, that Macaulay takes special delight, and of which his descriptions so charmed and enlightened the British intellect of his own century.

The lessons of history, with the additional confirmation of learned travellers, in the present enlightened period, have pre-eminently fitted the

British nation for its grand mission as a ruling empire. This really glorious and beneficent position it maintains with a success never previously equalled except by the Romans. The noble capacity for governing millions of subjects differing in race, religion, and habits is as triumphantly proved by the British at the present as it was by the Romans in former times.

Among modern nations, the Russians alone rival the British in this respect. No other Christian or Mohammedan power displays such peculiar qualifications for ruling distant and varied races of mankind. In this grand achievement of human superiority, the Romans bequeathed to Europe a legacy of enlightened wisdom and practical justice. Yet their former power was very limited compared to that of Russia and Britain. Southern and central Europe, northern Africa, and parts of the south-west of Asia constituted nearly all the dominion that the Romans could explore, or rule for any length of time.[1]

The present period sees European races not only supreme in America, but replacing its ancient inhabitants. In Africa all the portion ever ruled by the Romans is under either European direct rule or influence. Its eastern parts are at present subjected to European invasion of a political rather than a

[1] 'The attainment of universal sway by the Romans certainly emanated from the greatness of the national character. A rich treasure of ideas was accumulated as a consequence of experience and numerous observations. National intercourse was animated by the Roman dominion and the Latin tongue spread over the whole West, and over a portion of Northern Africa.'—Humboldt's *Cosmos*, vol. ii.

religious nature, undertaken by many European powers, in mutual agreement apparently not to obstruct each other, though without formal alliance. Its western and southern parts are likewise greatly under European rule or indirect control, and thus most of Africa seems now more or less subject to European conquest as well as exploration and discovery, its native races being either subdued, or on the defensive against European discipline and perseverance.

Asia, the most ancient of lands, the birthplace of all religions, is yielding more every year to European power or influence. Its countries, which are most independent, are also the least progressive or the least improving. The large empire of China, full of inhabitants who seem singularly helpless, or unwarlike, is now attracting what some would call the covetous interest of Russia and, more latterly, of Germany. The former on its northern frontier seems opposing British influence, to which the enterprising Japanese are more friendly than to that of the Russians, who seem acquiring increased ascendancy over the unwarlike Chinese.

The present times show a remarkable desire among European powers to oppose or rival each other in distant parts of Asia and Africa, and to have no wish, at least for the present, to arouse warfare in Europe. The most intelligent Asiatic and African races are more or less acquainted with Europeans, and while their majority either obey them, or acknowledge their political influence, they also understand more about their habits and religion than ever. In India especially, many of its natives begin to rival Christian rulers in education, knowledge and general civilisation. The British and the Russians, despite mutual jealousies, cannot fail to diffuse some European enlightenment wherever they prevail, though in different ways. Yet hitherto European improvements among Asiatics, though vast and increasing, are usually not promoted by any alliance of Europeans in the cause of humanity.

Political and commercial interests, in distant parts of the world, seem among Europeans to replace in importance the religious enthusiasm of former times. Unlike the period when Christian powers were united by religious sympathy in foreign wars, the modern triumph of the British and of the Russians throughout different parts of Asia is anything but a subject of congratulation to each other, as in a moral, philanthropic sense it should be. Yet at the present time two remarkable circumstances, unknown in former history, should cause more friendship between these ruling empires, though political jealousies seem to prevent its acknowledgment. Their reigning families, each without a rival, are closely connected by marriage, while the common danger from Anarchist plots against both necessarily inclines them and their chief ministers to personal sympathetic friendship, in precautions against so insidious and dangerous a foe.[1]

[1] 'The Anarchist party placed all its hope in armed insurrection, and, until that insurrection could be effected,

The lessons of this century prove the permanence and extension of European power in every part of the world. It may remain a question of national comparison, too often influenced by patriotic partiality, whether British or Russians should be most proud of the moral results of their increasing power over subjected races. This supremacy in importance and responsibility is now becoming more than ever noticed by British statesmen, perhaps by Russian also. Their foreign subjects, far distant by geographical necessity, are now practically close at hand, owing to the vast recent facilities for increased communication.

Loyal subjects of Britain and Russia, whether of European race or not, show a fidelity to their rulers no longer caused by fear alone. They seem generally flourishing, contented, and prosperous, with no desire of following the example of America in emancipating themselves from European control. Colonies and distant dominions, peopled either by European or native races, are steadily becoming like one vast federation, little separated by distance, and resolved to obey the British monarchy.[1]

advocated dynamite assassination and all other means of destroying a capitalist society.'—Lecky's *Democracy and Liberty*, vol. ii.

[1] 'The special mission of the United Kingdom has been clearly marked out by her insular position, and by the qualities of her people—by their love of adventure, their powers of organisation, and by their commercial instincts. It is to be seen persistently colouring all her later history, through which the steady expansion of the empire has proceeded, and during which she has, sometimes unconsciously, sometimes even unwillingly, been building up and consolidating that great edifice

It may be hoped that this result is chiefly due to their general preference for British laws and institutions, as well as habits and customs. In ancient history, modern nations have only the example of the Romans in foreign and colonial rule, successful indeed, yet on a far smaller scale owing to the immense discoveries of distant and unknown countries since their time. In the noble combination of heroic conquest and beneficent rule, the Romans were not only unequalled, but scarcely resembled, by any nation in former times. Their splendid victories, instead of being disgraced by the usual results of plunder and ruin of subjected foes, usually ended in promoting their enlightened improvement and practical welfare. As a general rule, to which there were some serious exceptions, where the Romans prevailed they introduced all the civilisation of which their age was capable, and their laws remain the foundation of British legislation.[1]

In religious legislation it appears certain that while heresy—or opposition against Judaism, Christianity, and Mohammedanism — were often made capital offences by their respective votaries in historical course, the faith of Jupiter was seldom enforced or maintained by the same penalties among

of Imperial dominion which is now as much a necessity of our national existence as it is a legitimate source of national pride.'—Extract from Mr. Chamberlain's speech in Glasgow, November 1897.

[1] 'The mercantile law is deducible in great part from the Imperial code of Rome. It is chiefly conversant with personal property, the laws regulating which are to be looked for in that of Rome.'—Blackstone's *Commentaries*, chap. 52.

Roman subjects. In this respect, as perhaps in others, the colonial or foreign government exercised by modern Europeans reverts more to the Roman model than to that of mediæval Christianity or of Mohammedanism.

Historical students may perceive in the descriptions of pagan Rome, poetically alluded to by Milton,[1] a certain resemblance in its former rule over distant and varied subjects, to what is now exercised in London, Paris, and St. Petersburg. During the Middle Ages, few Asiatics or Africans found their way to European capitals. After the fall of the Roman Empire, European nations were for a long time preoccupied by their own dissensions, by the discovery of America, and by its wonderful colonisation, while Asia and Africa remained comparatively unexamined by them. Recent history, however, especially that of the last few years, shows the revival of that European rule over Asiatics and Africans once exercised by the Romans, and now transferred on a far more extended scale to the British, to the French, and to the Russians.

The inferiority of most colonies to their mother countries in art and literature seems remarkable amid the enlightenment of the present period.[2] The immense increase in general information during this century induces many European scholars, especially English, French and Germans, to examine and

---

[1] *Paradise Regained.*

[2] 'In the realm of knowledge and art no great achievements on the part of our colonies are to be recorded.'—Caldecott's *English Colonisation*, chap. 12.

republish works of former times, as well as to explore ancient lands, illustrating or explaining them with all the resources of modern information. They reveal principally to fellow-Europeans ancient Asiatic and African history, with a combined classic knowledge and amount of investigation hitherto never in the power of man to unite to the same extent. Yet their thoughts and discoveries are chiefly addressed to European readers, and are far more appreciated by them than by the descendants of those races whose ancient fame they elucidate and proclaim. The present time sees most of the learning, information, and enterprise of the age transferred to Europe, and chiefly to its western division. It is here that the highest existing power and intellect are to be found. The natives of Assyria, Palestine, and Egypt do little to recall the past wonders of their ancestral countries. It is western Europe, whose own remote history is comparatively unknown or undistinguished, which now specially revives and appreciates the glories or the wonders of antiquity. The elucidation of Asiatic and of Egyptian history, as well as the appreciation of the more recent Greek and Roman times, are in this century almost exclusively due to the learning, genius, and enterprise of western European nations. It is they whose mingled political influence and educational information enable them to illuminate alike the ancient and the modern world, by uniting the study of the former with experience of the latter. Wherever they prevail they carry with them the highest classic knowledge hitherto attainable, while exercising the chief military power of the present age.

The influences of the two chief capitals in western Europe, London and Paris, on their respective countries are remarkable contrasts to each other. London seems always to have represented English feelings, as well as progress in every way. It is, and always has been, the literary exponent as well as the legislative and political ruler of the country. It combines the most sincere national patriotism with a knowledge of and intercourse with other lands, not in the power of any county or provincial town. It represents, in fact, the historical record, the political authority, and the intellectual position of England. Its pre-eminence in wealth and knowledge, instead of alienating it from the country at large, seems to specially qualify it to be England's guide, instructor, and guardian. Paris, on the other hand, has, at least for many years, often misrepresented the feelings, the wishes, and the opinions of the French people throughout the country districts.[1] The energetic denunciation of all clerical influence, and the revolutionary sympathy with anti-monarchists in other countries, so often shown by Parisian orators before applauding audiences, would find little support in many of the French provinces. While the French people generally cannot help being proud of their gay and brilliant capital, abounding with every sort of artistic

[1] See Lecky's *Democracy and Liberty*, vol. ii.

and picturesque attraction, Paris cannot be said to fairly represent French national feelings or desires. But London is, as it were, all England in miniature, representing in their highest forms the intelligence, the world-wide knowledge, and, above all, the calm, orderly, yet courageous wisdom of the English nation.

CHAPTER XXXV

European supremacy apparently firm and permanent over foreign conquests and colonies—Continued danger to European rulers from assassination—Efficiency of modern police in protecting life and property.

THE colonial success of Britain is one of the most important facts of the present time. Countries once thought remote or uncivilised are now in friendly enlightened intercourse with the home Government. It is remarkable that Gibbon and Macaulay alike predict, though perhaps in jest, the rise of New Zealand in intellectual greatness. Gibbon, in mentioning that 'the literary and commercial town of Glasgow' was once said to contain a cannibal population, introduces New Zealand as a land likely to produce rival literary merit.[1]

Though as yet no sign appears of Macaulay's famous foreboding being realised of a New Zealand traveller sketching the ruins of London, the anticipation of Gibbon is much more likely than when he

---

[1] 'We may contemplate in the period of the Scottish history the opposite extremes of savage and civilised life. Such reflections tend to enlarge the circle of our ideas, and to encourage the pleasing hope that New Zealand may produce in some future age the Hume of the southern hemisphere.'— *Decline and Fall*, chap. 25.

wrote. The increasing intelligence or education of British colonists, and natives under British rule, is a remarkable sign of the times, and is now more acknowledged than ever by British statesmen earnestly, and hitherto successfully, trying to increase their loyalty to the British Empire. The complete religious toleration now extended by Britain throughout all her distant colonies has evidently been rewarded on the whole by their preference for her authority. When British colonies were first established, the restraints or disabilities imposed on English dissenters at home induced them all the more to settle in distant lands, which, though under British rule, were free from anything of the kind.[1] The revolt of the Americans when they threw off the British yoke was chiefly of a political nature. No form of Christianity gained or lost by the independence of the United States, while throughout the rest of America the divided forms of western Christianity, Roman Catholicism and Protestantism reappeared in all their hereditary distinctions, and in their profession remain unaltered to the present time.

The freedom of religious thought and utterance is established and seems increasing in countries ruled by Christian powers. They now sanction a toleration to non-Christians which formerly they would not have extended to differing versions of their own faith.[2] The result, in preserving endless

[1] Hume's *History of England*, chap. 71.
[2] 'What were called heathen religions are now treated as phases in the historical development of religious ideas, and

differences in religious opinion, may disappoint zealous enthusiasts, and would have been thought unlikely formerly when religious unanimity was both desired and expected. Many religions, or sects, whose votaries once thought political supremacy almost essential to their safety, now flourish peacefully under British rule.

The State religion, that of the royal family, and of the English majority, apparently neither gains nor loses in number by political pre-eminence. It is, in fact, the political ruler and the religious fellow-subject of other forms of religious belief, without either special privileges or legal pre-eminence.

The present position of Great Britain and her colonies is remarkable for social peace and religious freedom. While Spain and Portugal have lost nearly all their colonies by successful revolts, the British, the Russians, and to some extent the French, now derive support and assistance rather than incur opposition from their foreign dominions. The foreign subjects as well as the colonists under Britain are apparently obtaining more and more the full reliance of their European rulers, and this reliance is evidently the result of a mutual confidence between the home government and the distant subjects, which has never been equalled, or perhaps resembled, since the fall of the Roman Empire. The political principles of that empire seem reviving in

instead of looking for what is strange, grotesque, and offensive in them, students are far more bent on discovering what is reasonable, useful, and true in these newly-opened mines of ancient thought.'—Max Müller in *Civilisation of our Day*.

many ways at the present time. Roman statesmen in the reign of Augustus might recognise more resemblance between modern British rule and their own over foreign nations, than between their system and that of either Christians or Mohammedans during the intervening Middle Ages. The chief danger to social security—common to the rulers of all civilised states or empires—seems now to arise from within rather than from without their own territories. Enlightenment, law, and order, represented and maintained by wise, influential rulers, are more endangered by murderous plots among fellow-countrymen than by foreign foes. Civilisation is apparently at war with itself, when enlightened rulers and statesmen are struck down by murderous conspirators, who in education and intelligence cannot be termed uncivilised, despite the barbarity of their deeds. In opposing such men, who seem to pervert the arts or inventions of civilised life to effect its destruction, the detective police have lately been more useful and more employed in European cities than the regular army. They seem in their increasing efficiency, acuteness, and vigilance to be the special antidote for this widespread and insidious danger. Even when they cannot prevent the immediate success of political assassins, they usually succeed in effecting their subsequent detection.

When Dickens, about the middle of this century, described this force, it was newly organised. At first their efforts were mostly devoted to tracing and arresting criminals in Britain, usually about London.

Since Dickens wrote about them British detectives have greatly increased in energetic usefulness, as the range of their duties became wider. They are now virtually connected with detectives abroad to an extent probably neither contemplated nor needed at their first formation, and, like other public men, they have to carefully observe the progress or changes of national history.

The inventions, discoveries, and political events of the last half-century inevitably draw civilised lands into a closer and less exclusively national alliance than was either necessary or thought possible before.[1]

Yet a common danger, distinct from religious antagonism or political rivalry, threatens civilised society in every country alike. Unscrupulous, discontented men inhabiting civilised countries are often induced by hardship, envy, or love of notoriety, to pervert the inventions of modern enlightenment against their maintainers and promoters. Societies of men, sometimes called Socialists, in different civilised countries, show a remarkable sympathy with one another, independent of religious or national affinity. To them the interests of sectarianism or of national patriotism are literally nothing, being abandoned in a comprehensive union of the discontented or unfor-

---

[1] 'Only one hundred years ago nations and communities were as distant from each other in time as they were at the Christian era. Since then the ends of the world have been drawn together, and civilised society is becoming one vast, highly-organised, and interdependent whole.'—Kidd's *Social Evolution*, chap. 1.

tunate in the most civilised countries of the modern world.[1]

British detectives, therefore, are no longer restricted to deal with local criminals or offenders. The most dangerous objects of their unremitting vigilance may belong to any civilised country. The success of the detective force has hitherto been, perhaps, greater than is generally known or acknowledged, as, unlike some other forces, it is more useful than ornamental. No becoming uniform, brilliant reviews, or popular applause reward the efforts of these most useful public servants. Their recompense, like their work, is no subject for joyous manifestation, but lies simply in the public confidence and in the secret consciousness of arduous duty ably performed. Yet all their foresight, skill, and prompt courage are sometimes unable to save valuable lives from the meanest assassins.

The success of such criminals in destroying illustrious men may recall Shakespeare's warning about the danger of triumphant power from apparent weakness :

> A falcon, tow'ring in her pride of place,
> Was by a mousing owl hawk'd at, and kill'd.
> *Macbeth.*

The peaceful security of the British Empire at home and in distant countries is proved to need all

---

[1] 'The denationalising influence of Socialism probably goes deeper. Its very essence is to substitute a class division for the division of nationalities, and to unite the workmen of all countries for the overthrow of the owners of property. Mr. Bax has expressed the feeling of the genuine Socialist:—"The

the devoted, courageous vigilance of this valuable force to preserve rulers and legislators from a foe perhaps less numerous, but far more cruel and reckless, than any national opponents.

The results of recent history in Europe seem to justify the policy pursued by its chief powers in uniting against Napoleon I. The chivalrous French nation, so distinguished during the Crusades against the Mohammedan conquerors of Syria, and considered by the Papacy as the historic champion of Christianity, was thoroughly captivated by the genius of Napoleon. He had made war upon nearly every Christian nation in Europe, solely for political purposes. The religious element had no part in his designs. The calamities of warfare had been eloquently described to the French people, by one of their most pious writers, many years before the genius of Napoleon had turned all their energies in its fatal direction.[1] Since the formation of

foreign policy of the great internationalist Socialist party must be to break up these hideous race monopolies called empires, beginning in each case at home. Hence anything that makes for the disruption and disintegration of the empire to which he belongs must be welcomed by the Socialist as an ally." '— Lecky's *Democracy and Liberty*, vol. ii.

[1] ' War never fails to exhaust the State. Nor can a nation that should be always victorious prosper; it would destroy itself by destroying others, the country would be depopulated, the soil untilled, the trade interrupted, and what is worse, the best laws would lose their force, the troops, conscious of their own importance, will indulge themselves in the most pernicious licentiousness with impunity. A prince who in the acquisition of glory would sacrifice the lives of half his subjects and the happiness of the rest is unworthy of the glory he might acquire.'
—Fénelon's *Telemachus*, book 14. Hawkesworth's translation.

Christendom its nations were never so involved in war with each other as they were by Napoleon. That wonderful man apparently desired the complete conquest of Europe, and had at one time nearly succeeded. Since his fall the chief European powers, though sometimes at war with each other, have never effected, or tried to effect, the other's extinction. Their wars are now chiefly directed against the natives of Asia and Africa, and in these wide, rich fields for conquest, trade, and exploration, European triumph is decisive and seems increasing every year.

While, however, European habits, laws, dress, and languages are extending more and more, theologians may be surprised that Christianity by no means accompanies the political extension or success of Christian nations. The present time sees not only Jews, but Brahmins, Buddhists, Parsees and Mohammedans, studying European literature and speaking English, while adhering firmly to their ancient faiths. The revival, indeed, of ancient religions, which even in mediæval history were thought declining, is a remarkable sign of the present times. Jews, Mohammedans and Parsees, while availing themselves of the laws and improvements in Christian lands, yet seldom abandon their faiths. The hereditary influence of ancestral religions still animates them under every worldly change in this age of progress.

The position of atheism also deserves peculiar consideration at this time. It existed in the earliest

z

periods, and remains among perhaps similar minds though in different countries and under altered circumstances. In many lands it has now every freedom, like other opinions, in appealing to human reason, and is no longer crushed or persecuted by zealous theologians. It now has, in fact, all the advantages that its advocates once desired for it. Yet it makes little, if any, apparent progress among acknowledged opinions. It has also the additional mortification of seeing the most ancient forms of religion reviving amid the intellectual progress and mental freedom once thought incompatible with them.

The desire or belief in the moral obligation to persecute religious opinions for the sake of maintaining the only one supposed to be true has almost disappeared from modern legislation. It never reappears in new forms of legal enactment, though it may yet linger among some ignorant or enthusiastic minds. The present time sees the religion of Jesus in more political power than any other, and either absolutely ruling or indirectly influencing the votaries of almost every existing faith. Yet in the midst of its peaceful and increasing supremacy there is apparently less zeal or enthusiasm shown or expressed about Christianity than at any previous period of its checkered history.

Its success as a ruling or legislating system was certainly never so extended as at the present time. The votaries of its historical predecessor, Judaism, and those of its historical successor, Mohammedanism, are alike its political subjects, or under its power indirectly in nearly every country, while the votaries of all other religions remain quiescent, doctrinally unchanged, or independent, yet politically subservient, more or less, to its external influence. This influence, however, is general, not denominational, and among Christians some surprise may be felt at the survival of nearly every sect into which their faith was divided. During and since the establishment of Protestantism some writers foretold the speedy downfall of Roman Catholicism, as a pagan interpretation of their own religion. Yet it continues the faith of most enlightened European nations, while Protestantism in differing forms still rivals it in the estimation of the highest Christian intellects.

The religious and political feelings as well as position of most civilised lands at the end of this century show a surprising contrast to those of former times. Many objects and desires which their wisest men longed to attain or accomplish, are now within the easy reach of their posterity, who apparently care little or nothing about them. During centuries the cherished hope or secret prayer of the scattered and persecuted Jews was to regain Judæa, even while enduring Christian and Mohammedan rule over them. This oppressed and humbled race are now in many countries rich, influential, and respected; they adhere to their ancient faith, and their ancestral land is now governed by weak Mohammedans under the political protection of Christian powers, who have actually lost men and money to maintain Turkish rule. In fact the Jewish country and the Christian holy land is now under Turkish authority by the exertions as well as by the desire of the European Christian powers. That it could be purchased from the Turks by the rich Jews of western Europe seems not unlikely, but the wish to resettle in Judæa appears to no longer animate all the Jews, some of whom have declared that they would prefer settling in America. The historic dream of Christian Crusaders was to establish free or triumphant Christianity over Mohammedanism. This enterprise they vainly tried to achieve when their foes were led by brave chiefs and able warriors, who not only retained Syria, but pushed their conquests into Christian Europe. At present no Mohammedans attempt invasion of Christian lands. The Turks, the only Mohammedans ruling in Europe, or who have many Christian subjects, owe retention of political authority entirely to the active assistance of Christian allies. Thus in the cases of both Jews and Christians their historic aspirations seem now within their reach at the very time when their commercial and political interests alike oppose their gratification. In the divisions of the Christian world a similar change in feeling and position seems also perceptible. When Protestants first disputed with Roman Catholics, it was the belief of each that political authority was almost essential to the permanent success of either. In this belief the most earnest or zealous of both strove through the medium of actual warfare, of legal enactments and relentless persecution, to extinguish what they thought a superstition or a heresy. The present time proves the mistaken nature of their former policy. Enthusiasts of former times might perhaps think their co-religionists now resembled the creations of a dream, in passive indifference to the important interests and fearful perils around them. They would perceive that in some countries events which they dreaded, and in others those they desired had indeed occurred, yet without either fulfilling their hopes, or justifying their apprehensions. There probably never was a time when unanimity in religious belief was so far from making progress, as at present. The influences of education, of political authority, and of international intercourse in this respect lose all power. The domain of religious thought alone remains thoroughly independent of every worldly change that lies in the power of man. It is a subject indeed about which the wisest have always differed despite all educational enlightenment. The present time of unprecedented social knowledge and national intercourse leaves this most sublime of subjects as much a matter of opinion as ever throughout the educated world.

Such is the religious spectacle presented at the close of this extraordinary century. New habits, inventions, and discoveries are seen in every direction of human enterprise, while amid them are actually reviving in the belief of educated men some of the oldest religions the world has ever known. The intellectual paganism of Greece has, indeed, vanished from human credibility while surviving in works of art and in poetry, transmitting its wonders to posterity. The old faiths of northern Europe and of Arabia have likewise vanished, apparently never to return. But two religions of equal, if not greater antiquity, Judaism and Parseeism, each protected by British rule, still enjoy the belief of some men whose means of knowing all that this world can teach have never been surpassed from its earliest history.

WORKS by the Hon. ALBERT S. G. CANNING.

RELIGIOUS STRIFE IN BRITISH HISTORY.

SMITH, ELDER, & Co., Waterloo Place, London.

'Mr. Canning's account of these religious conflicts and proscriptions does equal and impartial justice.'—DAILY NEWS.

'A very temperate exposition of the evils of religious persecution.'—THE TABLET.

'Mr. Canning has displayed much fairness and ability.'—ROCK.

'We have in "Religious Strife in British History" one of the most lucid expositions of religious life and thought in our own country that has seen the light for some time past.'—CHRISTIAN UNION.

PHILOSOPHY OF THE WAVERLEY NOVELS.

SMITH, ELDER, & Co.

'This volume estimates very truly and fairly the moral and intellectual qualities of the great novelist.'—SCOTSMAN.

'There are few who will rise from its perusal without feeling that they understand Scott better than they did before.'—THE QUEEN

'Mr. Canning dissects the several novels, sketching the plots, examining the characters, pointing out defects and excellences, and we can endorse most of his conclusions as opportune and judicious.'
LITERARY CHURCHMAN.

WORKS BY THE HON. ALBERT S. G. CANNING

PHILOSOPHY OF CHARLES DICKENS.

SMITH, ELDER, & Co.

'Mr. Canning has produced a pleasing book. He has shed much light on Dickens' genius and methods, and we heartily thank him for his volume.'—BRITISH QUARTERLY REVIEW.

'We have to thank Mr. Canning for a very agreeable book.'
THE GLOBE.

'The book is admirably suited for lectures at an institute; it will recall the plots to those who have forgotten them; it will incite others to read Dickens in preference to trash.'—THE GRAPHIC.

'A book full to overflowing with true criticism and sound common sense.'—THE ENGLISH CHURCHMAN.

MACAULAY, ESSAYIST AND HISTORIAN.

SMITH, ELDER, & Co.

'Mr. Canning describes the purpose and scope of each of the Essays, traces the outlines, and sums up the general conclusions of the history with praiseworthy fidelity.'—SCOTSMAN.

'Mr. Canning's little book is admirable.'—MORNING POST.

'This is a book of rare merit, clear, concise, and instructive.'
WHITEHALL REVIEW.

'Probably no single volume, lately published, will do more, few so much, towards placing the character of Lord Macaulay as a *littérateur* fairly before the English reader.'—YORKSHIRE POST.

WORKS BY THE HON. ALBERT S. G. CANNING

THOUGHTS ON SHAKSPERE'S HISTORICAL PLAYS.

W. H. ALLEN & Co., Waterloo Place, London.

'It is in fact a painstaking and intelligent interpretation of the plays in modern English prose.'—SCOTSMAN, *March 22nd*, 1884.

'Mr. Canning has brought much scholarship and research, as well as thoughtful study, to his work. A sketch of each play is given. The analyses are all so good that it is almost invidious to select.'—LITERARY WORLD, *May 9th*, 1884.

'Discrimination, erudition, and refined discernment have been given to the production of this excellent work.'—WHITEHALL REVIEW.

'Mr. Canning possesses claims to consideration that justly belong to but few of his predecessors in the field.'—MORNING POST, *June 23rd*, 1884.

REVOLTED IRELAND, 1798 AND 1803.

W. H. ALLEN & Co.

From Mr. Lecky, Author of 'History of England in the Eighteenth Century,' &c., &c.

'Athenæum Club:—Mr. Lecky begs to thank Mr. Albert Canning very sincerely for his kind present, and he has been reading it with great pleasure and admiration.'

'Among recent books and pamphlets relating to Ireland one of the most useful is the Hon. A. S. G. Canning's "Revolted Ireland." Mr. Canning's clear and dispassionate enquiry is of great value just

WORKS BY THE HON. ALBERT S. G. CANNING

now. The application of the historical lesson to the present political situation is plain and legible on every page.'—SATURDAY REVIEW, *June 19th,* 1887.

'It is refreshing to turn to the instructive and impartial pages of Mr. Canning. His little book "Revolted Ireland" is that rare but almost unique thing in literature—a sketch in Irish history uncoloured by religious or political partisanship. It will be read with profit.'—SCOTSMAN, *September 11th,* 1886.

LITERARY INFLUENCE IN BRITISH HISTORY.

W. H. ALLEN & Co.

'This is a useful compendium on an interesting subject. Mr. Canning's brief summary will be found exceedingly convenient.'—PUBLISHERS' CIRCULAR, *November 15th,* 1889.

'The soundness of Mr. Canning's judgment, his nice sense of historical perspective, and his neat literary style make his work enjoyable in no common degree.'—SCOTSMAN, *August 9th,* 1889.

'The writer's modest hope that his book may be useful to readers not familiar with larger works on the subject is not perhaps unreasonable. There are passages in it which such a reader may read with profit.'—THE SPECTATOR, *November 11th,* 1889.

'No page of this book is open to anything but praise.'—GLASGOW HERALD, *August 12th,* 1889.

'This volume will be found eminently useful, and it is certainly written in a pleasant and lucid style.'—PUBLIC OPINION, *January 10th,* 1890.

WORKS BY THE HON. ALBERT S. G. CANNING

'The tone of the book is very impartial, and the literary judgments seem to us remarkably sound.'—THE TABLET, *August 31st*, 1889.

'We find page after page of suggestive remarks and biographical touches, which stimulate thought and contribute to genuine literary enjoyment.'—BELFAST NORTHERN WHIG, *October 7th*, 1889.

'The author reviews in bright, entertaining style representative literature of every period of English history.'—LIVERPOOL COURIER, *February 8th*, 1890.

THOUGHTS ON RELIGIOUS HISTORY.

EDEN, REMINGTON, & Co., King Street, Covent Garden, London.

'Mr. Canning is always a thoughtful and instructive writer. The passages that he collects from the works of great writers on the position of the Jews in history are full of interest.'—THE OBSERVER, *August 2nd*, 1891.

'Mr. Canning is evidently a fair-minded man and writes in a spirit of charity. He strives to deal even-handed justice to each party as it passes under review.'—THE SCOTSMAN, *August 3rd*, 1891.

'Mr. Canning's workmanship is eminently scholarly and thoughtful.'—THE PEOPLE, *August 2nd*, 1891.

'The work is characterised by a rare impartiality and an obvious desire to take wide views, and paint both the sunshine and shadow of religious history.'—THE JEWISH CHRONICLE, *October 2nd*, 1891.

'The picturesque and entertaining style of this scholarly work is the more striking because of the dispassionate comparison of conflicting authorities, and the painstaking research, the actual hard

WORKS BY THE HON. ALBERT S. G. CANNING

study and reflection that have necessarily been bestowed on its production.'—WHITEHALL REVIEW, *September 26th*, 1891.

'A sensible and evenly-balanced summary of the world's religions. It shows with much clearness and judgment the relations in which Paganism, Christianity, and Mohammedanism stood to each other in the past, and the place of Judaism in the march of religious progress. Mr. Canning is certainly sincere, honest, and thoughtful in his appreciations of the faiths of the past and present.'—THE GRAPHIC, *October* 1891.

'There is really a good deal of information to be derived from this little book.'—THE WORLD, *August* 1891.

'The evils of intolerant dogmatism are dispassionately criticised, while the writer is singularly free from the extravagance and captiousness so commonly associated with the criticism of religion.' MANCHESTER GUARDIAN, *July 28th*, 1891.

WORDS ON EXISTING RELIGIONS: A HISTORICAL SKETCH.

W. H. ALLEN & Co., LIMITED.

'Full of sincere appreciation of the many elements of truth in various ancient and modern religious systems.'—THE GUARDIAN, *May 24th*, 1893.

'Mr. Canning, a most fair-minded and impartial writer, has evidently read widely and has collected in his pages many important and useful facts.'—RECORD, *July 28th*, 1893.

'The book is evidently the result of much labour and wide reading, and the author shows considerable skill and discrimination in drawing from his somewhat numerous authorities. Though

WORKS BY THE HON. ALBERT S. G. CANNING

writing from a professedly Christian standpoint, he deals fairly and sympathetically with the other religions that he touches upon. The attention which has latterly been devoted to the comparative study of religion is one of the most remarkable features of the thought of the century, and those who are curious to know what the results of that study of them are, will find them admirably summarised in Mr. Canning's book.'—SCOTSMAN, *March 20th*, 1893.

'Gives a very just and sympathetic survey of the world's religions.' DAILY CHRONICLE, *April 8th*, 1893.

'These thoughtful and instructive essays will do something to popularise this wider and nobler view.'—BRADFORD OBSERVER, *May 5th*, 1893.

'An interesting and instructive volume, characterised by profound thought and great research.'—BELFAST NEWS LETTER, *April 12th*, 1893.

THE DIVIDED IRISH.

W. H. ALLEN & Co.

'One cannot but admire the tone of charity and justice which pervades this work from beginning to end.'—THE NATIONAL OBSERVER, *September* 1894.

'One of the most valuable books which the present year has produced.'—IRISH TIMES, *November 23rd*, 1894.

'We can heartily recommend a perusal of this work, for Mr. Canning shows that he has a great grasp on his subject by his lucidity, his shrewdness, and his fairness.'—PUBLIC OPINION, *July* 1894.

WORKS BY THE HON. ALBERT S. G. CANNING

'This book is one which everyone should read who wants to understand Irish political movements, and the part played in history by Irish political factions.'—THE SCOTSMAN, *July* 1894.

' Mr. Canning's book may be commended to all Englishmen who want to understand Irish history, and to all Irishmen who care for the amelioration of their country.'
MANCHESTER GUARDIAN, *August* 1894.

'Mr. Canning treats of " Divided Ireland " up to date and from all points of view ; in doing so he has consulted a large number of authorities of most diverse opinions, so that this re-issue of his book will be found really helpful by all interested in the relations of England and its sister island.'
PUBLISHERS' CIRCULAR, *July* 28*th*, 1894.

RELIGIOUS DEVELOPMENT:

A HISTORICAL SKETCH.

W. H. ALLEN & Co.

' The political aspects of the question are considered from an impartial Christian standpoint, and we recognise the general value of Mr. Canning's mode of treatment.'—THE GUARDIAN.

' We heartily commend the work to all thoughtful and discriminative readers.'—PUBLIC OPINION.

'Distinguished throughout by the impartiality of a sincere enquiry, and it will be read with profit by everyone interested in its subject.'—SCOTSMAN.

WORKS BY THE HON. ALBERT S. G. CANNING

'This thoughtful and dispassionate survey of the growth and influence of religious thought may be read with interest and profit by all students of history.'—LIBERTY REVIEW.

'A studious, comprehensive, conscientious, Christian-spirited book.'—WHITEHALL REVIEW.

HISTORY IN FACT AND FICTION:

A LITERARY SKETCH.

SMITH, ELDER, & CO.

'The work will be read with interest and profit.'
SCOTSMAN, *Jan.* 1897.

'I do not think I ever saw the difficulties of the Eastern Question in so clear a light as I did after reading the short chapter which Mr. Canning devotes to it.'—PALL MALL GAZETTE, *Jan.* 1897.

'We recommend "History in Fact and Fiction" as a valuable work.'—PUBLIC OPINION, *Feb.* 1897.

'Excellent reading for all sorts and conditions of men is liberally provided.'—THE PEOPLE, *Feb.* 1897.

'The title gives but a faint idea of the main theme of a most interesting work.'—LIVERPOOL COURIER, *June* 1897.

'Mr. Canning's knowledge of modern literature is so wide that he is able to criticise almost every well-known name for purposes of llustration.'—SCHOOL GUARDIAN, *August* 1897.

WORKS BY THE HON. ALBERT S. G. CANNING

'People who have no time to plod through the great histories, if they take up this book will gain much historical knowledge.'
LLOYD'S WEEKLY NEWSPAPER, *Feb.* 1897.

'A delightful contribution to the historical literature of the day.
MORNING ADVERTISER, *June* 1897.

'The Hon. Albert Canning deals with conspicuous fairness and in an interesting way with the conflicts between the historic religions of the world.'—JEWISH CHRONICLE, *Feb. 5th*, 1897.

'Whatever Mr. Canning discusses he is distinguished by dispassionate candour.'—RECORD, *August 20th*, 1897.

'A valuable contribution to historical philosophy.'
PARENTS' REVIEW, *April* 1897.

'This is a very readable work. The author exhibits in a lively, instructive manner the respective positions of Paganism in ancient Rome, Hinduism, Buddhism, Mahometanism in Asia and Africa, the Jewish system throughout the various nations of the world, and the Christian system in Europe and America. The work merits a very careful perusal.'—ASIATIC QUARTERLY REVIEW, *Jan.* 1898.

www.ingramcontent.com/pod-product-compliance
Lightning Source LLC
Chambersburg PA
CBHW020226240426
43672CB00006B/427